DEAF LIBERATION

Writings from

DEAF LIBERATION

A Selection of NUD Papers

1976 - 1986

Edited and Compiled by Raymond Lee

NATIONAL UNION OF THE DEAF

Published by National Union of the Deaf
288 Bedfont Lane, Feltham,
Middlesex, TW14 9NU

British Library Cataloguing in Publication Data

A catalogue record for this book is available from the British Library

ISBN 0-9519312-0-2

10.5pt on 11pt Times Roman
Typesetting & LaserJet printed by Clearprint, Southbourne, Emsworth.

This book is dedicated to two of NUD's members whose inspired contributions and support have helped to change the course of history for every member of the British Deaf community.

STANLEY WOODHOUSE
(1920-1983)

EMIL STRYKER
(1917-1990)

“Towards Deaf Liberation

..... it is vital that those interested in the furtherance of the Deaf community review the past in order to prepare for the future. We need to look where we came from before we can determine where we are going."

National Conference on Deafness:
Fort Monroe, U.S.A. September 1987.

CONTENTS

EDITOR'S NOTES

Between the years 1976 and 1986, papers written and presented by members of the National Union of the Deaf were numerous and my task in selecting and compiling a few papers from the mass was not an easy one. I had to set a theme for this publication and select the papers in accordance with the chosen theme. "Deaf Liberation" was used as the theme and amazingly a large number of papers were selected under this heading. One might query, "Deaf Liberation?" It must be said here that the Deaf had for many years suffered under the suppression of a system that was mainly dominated by the hearing. The education of the Deaf and the strict enforcement of the oralist system had been run in accordance with the hearing people's veiws and without consultation with, or thought for, the Deaf people themselves. This system had taken away every Deaf person's self-respect and dignity. It had imposed on every Deaf person a feeling of inferiority. The Deaf person in turn became encapsulated in their own world - a world which limited oneself to their home, Deaf clubs, a few friends and lowly paid jobs. It had come to the stage that the only way a Deaf person could liberate oneself from their world was to rebel and speak out. A number of Deaf people took this action in 1976 - hence this selection of papers and Deaf Liberation.

At the outset, there was an idea of placing papers in this book in chronological order. After careful consideration it was decided to group papers in the respective and relevant areas of topic. These topics range from debates on social status of the Deaf to education, employment, the battle against oralism, Deaf history and others. I have included prefaces which precede each paper, or a group of papers, to give the reader an idea to the background in which given paper or papers were connected. It must be pointed out here that not all the best NUD papers were included here; some have sadly gone missing and others needed a separate category or theme.

During the recent years there was a growing tendency among the Deaf to identify themselves with a capital "D" so that they can be distinguished from others with a hearing loss. The people who stand out as users of a language outside the conventional mode, namely sign language, have stated a desire to be regarded as a linguistic minority. The move is an attempt to dispel the stereotype that was commonly attached to them for centuries. Their particular language caused them to congregate and they became known as the Deaf community. To recognise these people writers, ingrained in their relevant way of life, use the capital "D" when referring to them. Others with a hearing loss like the hard of hearing, and others not yet integrated into the Deaf community have "deaf" in the lower case.

Such a capital label is not unusual in fact we have Jewish and Moslem people and ethnics like Red Indians, Aborigines and Blacks. Deaf people's claim to ethnic status surely qualifies them to such specific classification. Hence the capitalised

“Deaf” in this book to distinguish them apart from other segments of hearing impaired people.

The reader will find that some of the papers in the book may appear to be similar or repetitous. It is the NUD’s hope that the reader would look at each paper as a paper in its own right and given under its relevant background or circumstances, rather than be compared with other papers in the book. Another important factor must be mentioned here, English. It is usual and normal for English to be checked, corrected, edited and improvised. I have done very little of this here. In fact, I have left the original structure in each paper intact and unedited, for the NUD wanted every one of you to read in Deaf people’s English.

It is hoped that the reader will get a picture of the history of Deaf people’s struggle between the years 1976 and 1986 by reading through the papers. Another experience of history can be felt in one of Harlan Lane’s two papers in this book, “Why the Deaf Are Angry”. History is not like a statue; it is an ever changing pattern of lives and events and such changes must be recorded. It must therefore be noted here that references to other organisations or likewise in the papers stand true at the times such papers were given. Great improvements may have been made by various organisations for the benefit of the Deaf and this occured from around 1981 onwards when new faces took over the running of such organisations and establishments.

Finally, the reader will notice that most of the papers were given by a small group of Deaf people. It must be noted that behind each paper lies the true voice of the Deaf in general. The authors were merely fortunate to be able to read and write, and so able to put pen to paper. This was not so with many Deaf people who were deprived of this ability through the horrendous oralist education system. It is the NUD’s expressed wish that every reader regard every paper as not being the authors’, but Deaf people’s papers.

Raymond Lee
February 1992.
Feltham, Middlesex.

FOREWORD
Feeling Good and Feeling Bad about Deafness

Harlan Lane. Northeastern University, Boston. USA.

Deaf people in America and Great Britain, and their hearing friends, are living in an unique era in Deaf history; a time that will be noted and discussed for decades to come; an era that will be recognised, I believe, as the renaissance of Deaf culture.

There is a Deaf university president in Washington, a Deaf MP in Parliament and a Deaf Under-secretary of Education in the US. In the US, Deaf businesses are booming. A Deaf lawyer has pleaded before the US Supreme Court. Deaf people are playwrights and authors, administrators and teachers, engineers and missionaries - Deaf people can do anything! There are those who measure deafness only in terms of loss, not in terms of gain. I say to them: Enough audiograms, look at the art. Enough laryngology, learn the language. There are those who say, "It's a hearing world." I have news for them: It's a Deaf world, too.

Of what is this renaissance, this rebirth made? There are the Deaf arts - painting, sculpture, and design, dance, film, television and theatre; Deaf literature - poetry, narrative, humour and rhetoric, plays and folklore - and written works by and about Deaf people. There are studies of Deaf history, contemporary and past; government, law and Deaf people; examinations of Deaf education - its conduct and its consequences. The study of sign languages - their analysis, instruction and interpretation; systematic reflections on Deaf culture - from church to sports, from family studies to the workplace. All this investigation, dissemination and application constitutes the present renaissance of Deaf culture, all this and much more.

We have been witnessing the flourishing of Deaf arts - to take one good example, the huge success of the play, 'Children of a Lesser God'. The field of Deaf history is thriving; I'll cite the first major work of this era and the most recent, both by Deaf scholar, Jack Gannon: *'Deaf Heritage'* and *'The Week the World Heard from Gallaudet'*. The study of sign languages is burgeoning: ASL is taught in over 750 post-secondary programs in the US and a plethora of scholarly works and instructional texts and videotapes have appeared of late. Interpreters are more plentiful, more trained and more rigorously tested than ever before. We are witnessing an increase in Deaf leadership of programs for Deaf children and adults; for example, the number of Deaf superintendents of schools for the Deaf have tripled here in the US in the last year. There has been a surge in the activism of organisations of Deaf people. There is a growing awareness of Deaf culture: there are courses around the nation and several recent books including Padden and Humphries' *'Deaf in America'*. All America took notice of the courage of our young Deaf leaders at the time of the Gallaudet Revolution in 1988. Many states have established commissions on deafness to act with and for Deaf people. And according to state law a student may offer ASL in satisfaction of the high school foreign language requirement in Alaska, California, Connecticut, Maine, Michigan, Texas and Washington - with several more states soon to join the list. No question, there is mounting hearing acceptance of the Deaf difference.

From this distant shore, it appears that a similar renaissance of Deaf culture and language is taking place in Great Britain. My 'in basket' contains the first issue of 'Signpost', the newsletter of the newly formed International Sign Linguistics Association based at the University of Durham. There too I find a flyer from the RNID describing the May conference on "Deaf Worlds: Together Towards 2000"; a notice concerning the BDA Centenary appeal, and a request from the Anastasia Trust to support the founding of a Deaf Cultural Centre in London. The pioneering television programs, See-Hear and Listening Eye are in full swing, as are the BSL Tutors Training Course. Of course, I was moved by the Channel 4 production, "Pictures in the Mind" based on my history of the Deaf; and the BBC is scheduled to broadcast in 1992 a major production based on the same book. There are many important books on Deaf culture coming from Britain these days; I think at once of the work of the BSL Research Group in Bristol; Dorothy Miles' guide to BSL *(British Sign Language: A Beginner's Guide)*; Lorraine Fletcher's account of her struggle to secure her Deaf son's right to sign *(Language for Ben)*; and Brian Grant's survey of deafness in literature *(The Quiet Ear)* - to mention just three. And now this important collection of papers assembled on the tenth anniversary of the National Union of the Deaf joins the swelling ranks of the Deaf cultural renaissance.

An anniversary is an occasion for rejoicing in solidarity and for looking back and ahead. As the NUD looks back, it must do so with satisfaction and pride. History has largely vindicated its stand. From its inception, NUD has affirmed, more stridently perhaps and more lucidly than any other organisation in the world, the richness of the Deaf language and culture and the inalienable right of Deaf people to that language and culture. The cultural renaissance that is taking place is a proof of their foresight and a product in part of their labours. Moreover, the National Union of the Deaf, more than any other organisation in the world, issued a clarion call to Deaf people to affirm their rights and demand reform, to employ the methods that other minorities have employed - reason, media, force; to never give up; to never accept what is unacceptable. It is remarkable, then, that it was not in Great Britain but in the United States that this strategy was followed most dramatically and proven right. Four young Deaf leaders at Gallaudet University, strengthened in their resolve by the cultural renaissance, took an immovable stand against prejudices and ignorance - and won the acclaim of the entire nation. Each week brings new fruits of their courage.

All of these developments give us hope as the NUD looks to the future. But there are also reasons for deep concern. The forces that have historically resisted the cultural model of deafness have not been idle as the acceptance of Deaf language, Deaf history, Deaf arts, Deaf culture has grown. *Through educational integration programs, Deaf children are being deprived in larger numbers and for more years than ever before of the opportunity to learn a language and to discover their heritage.* Through the extension of cochlea implant programs to early deafened children, their medicalisation and enforced oral rehabilitation is being pursued as implacably as never before. *Recent achievement-testing confirms that the failure of Deaf education has not changed* but the demands on the workforce are changing. Whereas many Deaf people could until recently turn their backs on that failure and become skilled tradesmen and women, those trades are for the most part dying out. In the year 2000, the average American worker will require 13.5 years of education - not to be the boss mind you, but just to bring home the paycheck. *The gap between current educational practices with Deaf children and the needs of Britain's Deaf community has never been wider.*

Times change. We cannot blame educators and administrators for not having known all along that ASL and BSL are full-fledged languages, before the fact was discovered and confirmed in recent years. But we can blame anyone who rigidly adhere to old and unsuccessful practices now that the evidence is in and scholars, educators and community leaders alike, in Britain as in America, are calling for changes. The United States Congressional Commission on the Education of the Deaf states: We urge that outmoded educational policy be brought into line with recent scientific discoveries in linguistics and psychology. It has been shown repeatedly that children whose primary language is ASL; like those who speak minority languages such as Spanish or Navaho, are at severe educational disadvantage in a system that disbars, denigrates and denies their primary language. It is reasonable to believe that the same educational remedies provided by the Congress and the courts for the speakers of all minority languages will benefit ASL-speaking children. In any case, it is the law. Some years earlier, a UNESCO commission on Deaf education had reached the same conclusion: "Now that the importance of the national sign languages for Deaf education is better understood, it is no longer admissible to overlook them or to fail to encourage their integration into Deaf education". The endorsement of the national sign languages by the European Community is now well known. A few years ago, the Ontario Commission on the Education of the Deaf added its voice to the clamour for radical reform of Deaf education through the involvement of Deaf adults, Deaf language and Deaf culture

Great challenges await us, then in the next ten years to come. Thanks to the renaissance there will be no shortage of intellectual tools nor of hearing allies. What will determine the outcome is Deaf determination. The forces of darkness are the paternalism of the hearing experts, the inertia of the universities and the apathy of the Deaf community. The forces of light are organisations of the Deaf like the NUD that dare to dream of equality and struggle to make that dream a reality.

INTRODUCTION

Dr G. W. G. Montgomery

"Verschlossen het Gekommel" (Liberation is here), sang the Afrikaners at the beginning of this century, jubilantly throwing off the yoke of Victorian colonialism and fixing it firmly on the necks of their fellow citizens. Slaves usually do not want freedom but rather wish to own other slaves. Now another wave of liberation flows over their beloved country and the subjection of apartheid is ending. It remains to be seen whether or not the majority in South Africa institute a truly liberal democracy or simply become the dominant race sustaining the racist divisions of apartheid in the way that the Afrikaners changed roles from colonial underdogs, to colonial masters. This classical 'palace revolution' is unlikely because the ending of our century has seen a massive swing to genuine liberation subsequent to the breaking of information barriers due to modern information technology. The virtually unpredicted swing to genuine democracy in the Soviet Union and the many bloodless, civilised revolutions in East Europe give greater cause for optimism than anything since the ending of global strife during the Second World War.

We have always seen Deaf Liberation as a similar struggle against isolation, undemocratic barriers and conspiracies of silence working oppressively against deaf individuals and the Deaf community. Rarely has a prediction hit the nail on the head so neatly as when Murray Holmes, John Hay and myself opined on behalf of the Scottish Workshop with the Deaf in totalitarian Bulgaria in 1980 that "Sign languages thrive on repression, subject peoples burst free from decades of enslavement". Our further comments about the genocide of Deaf minorities were received with cold hostility by almost all Deaf organisations with the honourable exception of the National Union of the Deaf. "Sensationalist", "Couldn't happen here" they shouted, jostling each other in their haste to get their heads comfortably buried in the sand. One professional 'guardian' of the Deaf even wrote a whole-heartedly denigratory letter to the 'Scotsman' newspaper condemning us on the basis of a short and rather cool report of it by Sally Magnusson, WITHOUT ever reading the original conference paper. But our suspicions were more than justified: "Genetic counsellors may easily overstep ethical boundaries" we wrote, "and where a national medical complex has a monopoly of services in a given area then the stage is set for the 'final solution'". Only in 1990 has it been revealed how devastatingly accurate was our intuition as the revolution which opened up Romanians showed that large scale secret genocide by the state medical monopoly was well under way in the neighbouring dictatorship at the very time we were delivering our 'Bulgarian Thesis'. In institution after liberated institution for the Romanian handicapped, the marked absence of females implies medical action along Nazi eugenicist lines as does the herding of HIV children to die in barbaric, uncaring isolation.

The decade since the founding of N.U.D. has seen a similar beginning of Deaf liberation also to a large extent aided by increasingly effective information technology, especially the TV programmes for the Deaf which were piloted by the pioneer work of the NUD on 'Open Door'. This volume details the story of this civilised bloodless revolution which, like that in Romania, still has some way to go. It would be nice if this Deaf Liberation could avoid the role-flip trap which lumbered the Afrikaners with a century of apartheid and resist the folly of replacing repressive oralism for Deaf children with repressive manualism. Deaf schools are strongholds of Deaf culture and language but if they adopt 'pure' Sign without permitting speech or lipreading, as some extremists now advocate, then they will be forced to close down for lack of children. Only some of the ten percent of parents of Deaf children who are themselves Deaf would be likely to send their children for an exclusively manual education and in most areas of UK that is not enough children to keep the school open. Thus the paradox: too exclusive a zeal for Sign Language could well destroy the main centres for the development of Sign Language - just as an exclusive concentration on the oralist skills of speaking and lipreading produced generations of kids who could do neither. In our newly-found pride in the legalised status of European Sign Languages for which we all have worked and fought for so long, let us not celebrate our admiration of these treasured Golden Eggs by cooking the goose that lays them. In that way we can take Deaf Liberation along the civilised, disciplined path of democratic revolution like the sensible nations of East Europe today and escape the bloody stupidity of the French Revolution and those who model themselves on it by replacing one stupid tyrant with another in the manner so vividly described by Anatole France so long ago in Les Dieux ont Soif.

As the following papers show, our advance has always accorded language and communication a key part in the struggle. Sooner or later all Deaf discussions come back to the need for freedom of communication and linguistic preference. In this we are little different from the global revolutions growing from the breakdown of the information barriers set up by the dictators. As a radio operator I may regularly communicate with anyone in Europe by courtesy of the Russian satellite which zooms rapidly over my home in Scotland at 19.00 hrs each evening. I treasure the Christmas card sent by Igor of Siberia to confirm our contact. In 1987 at the World Federation of the Deaf Congress in Finland, we demonstrated with Eddie Montague's BBC TV Team how Sign Language visual transmissions could link Deaf people across the wires, walls and iron curtains of the world's frontiers. Little then did we know how much closer the world was to the future we predicted where the adjective 'inter-continental' will call to mind images of friendly international communication and not, as it so often does today, images of mutual military destruction.

Doubtless, there will continue to be many setbacks in the future course of world liberation but today in 1990 the lessons seem clear. The logic of freedom is eventually irresistible and Europe and Africa today are full of self-styled hard-nosed realists whose acceptance of tyranny has beeen shown to be unimaginative pessimism based on an untenable denigratory view of their fellow citizens. Let us never be persuaded by the 'guardians' to give up the ideal of liberation. With quiet tenacity and civilised insistence on the rationality of Deaf Liberation, NUD will continue to remove the barriers and eventually break down the last dividing wall between us and full freedom to develop in our own way. Thus it is with mixed feelings of hope and nostalgia that we hang up the old combat jacket, put away the gelignite, and move forward to a more positive dialogue of the Deaf in a new Age of Reason. But if it is only gold medals you want, then you are in the wrong army: on mij met een kus te beloon.

PART ONE

Spreading the Word

National Union of the Deaf

Paper for insertion in Gallaudet Encyclopedia. 1982.
Paddy Ladd.

The National Union of the Deaf (NUD) was founded in Wimbledon, London, on March 13th 1976 when Deaf people assembled to form an organisation exclusively run by themselves. Its aims were "To Restore the Rights of the Deaf" and since that time it has become a pressure group, initiating and involving other Deaf people in campaigns, usually focused on the issues of sign language and Deaf involvement in decisions that affect Deaf persons. Operating with several hundred members and a small, entirely self-financed budget, it consists mainly of grass-roots Deaf members and hearing associate members. It has several branches and publishes a newsletter and occasional papers.

The NUD began a total communication campaign in the summer of 1976, a time when re-evaluation of Deaf education was beginning. By publishing direct appeals to teachers, written in the personal language of Deaf experience, the campaign forced a previously academic issue onto a level of humanism and basic human rights. Some teachers and schools responded and the NUD became involved in helping them create total communication programs. This, together with the British Deaf Association's (BDA) more academic approach and the publication of momentous research, meant that by 1982 more than half the Deaf schools in the country and a few Deaf units had embarked on total communication programs. There was less success with the campaign for Deaf teachers, whose numbers are still minute, although more Deaf people became classroom assistants and governors. But the involvement of Deaf people in campaigning and reaching hearing people was equally important in raising the self-esteem of the Deaf community. The NUD believes, however, that major improvements in the education of Deaf children will not occur until the oralist peripatetic service legislation is abolished and Deaf people's beliefs control the education system.

In employment, the NUD was able to prevent Deaf car and HGV drivers from having their licences removed by linking enlightened employers, haulage associations and American statistical evidence. The NUD also worked to awaken the conscience of labour unions, where it is believed the ultimate change lay.

In 1977, the NUD initiated links with other disabled groups to campaign for a government allowance, Although the Thatcher administration ended the campaign, the historical importance of the links remains. NUD also has campaigned on behalf of establishing guiding principles for registered interpreters and in support of better telecommunication devices for Deaf people.

In 1978, the NUD began to promote British Sign Language (BSL) and Deaf culture as a source of pride and outlined a national program of language planning. Part one was based on dialect sign books, leading to agreement on a national vocabulary that would preserve United Kingdom's rich dialects. Part two, a BSL/Total Communication National Liaison Centre, was essential in linking parents, teachers, social workers and other hearing people to the Deaf community. Resources to carry out the plan were not available, but the strategy remains crucial to the concept of building a national Deaf community.

In addition to launching campaigns directed at specific problems faced by Deaf people, the NUD provides help for individuals (members and non-members) and encourages others to fulfil their potential in Deaf work. The NUD believes that it is crucial to have grass-roots Deaf people involved in activities rather than creating a Deaf elite to replace a hearing one.

Perhaps the most successful area of work has been in television. In 1976 proposals for a regular national programme were outlined, and by 1979 a pilot programme, SIGNS OF LIFE, was aired on a BBC access slot. Following the success of the programme (which was placed in the BBC archives), liaison with the BDA saw the inauguration of the Deaf Broadcasting Campaign (DBC). Pressure was maintained and in 1981 a nationally networked, twice-weekly, BBC programme was started. The campaign's success opened the floodgates; several regions started to use news interpreters; three regions started regular Deaf programming; and a disabled programme started to include Deaf items.

The NUD next turned to establish a charter of rights of Deaf people in the world and focused on what it perceived to be an emerging threat to the Deaf community - the mainstreaming of Deaf students into hearing schools. The 1981 Education Act gave legal force to the idea of integration of Deaf and hearing pupils, and this law provided the means for education authorities to cut spending on Deaf education, as well as enabling oralists to work towards the closure of schools converted to total communication.

The NUD proceeded from the logic that Deaf people were a linguistic (BSL-using) minority to see if the United Nation's Rights of Disabled People protected them. Finding that the Rights did not, the NUD turned to the UN's International Convention on Political and Civil Rights and found protection there for linguistic minorities under Article 27. The NUD then detailed the ways that this article and the UN's Charter of Rights of the Child were infringed by oralism. The NUD also discovered three clauses relating to the destruction of linguistic minorities in the UN's Convention on the Prevention and Punishment of the Crime of Genocide that might be applicable to the situation faced by Deaf people in the United Kingdom.

The evidence was sent to the UN's Human Rights Commission in 1982. The significance of this document is as yet unmeasured, but the NUD has suggested that oralist practices throughout the world could be brought to a halt through legal means. Swedish Sign Language legislation seems to reinforce this conclusion, but world-wide co-operation of Deaf organisations will be necessary to counter the arguments of oralist educators and their supporters in government.

Whatever its ultimate success, the achievements of the NUD in its short history have made it impossible for organisations in Deaf work to maintain credibility without major Deaf involvement and have transformed the possibilities for Deaf people in the United Kingdom.

Preface

The following paper is a full reproduction of NUD's first ever pamphlet which was distributed in November 1975 in preparation for NUD's anticipated launch as an organisation in the following year.

The root of the angry tone of the contents was both of anger and frustration at the major organisations' failure to date to make the right and true noises on behalf of the Deaf. These organisations tended to be more concerned in projecting a clean and goodygoody image rather than to face up to the truth about the situation concerning the Deaf and thus engage in dirty work to fight for the rights of the Deaf.

When 'NUD 1976' was distributed, it made a few friends in Deaf people who felt the same way as those in the NUD but many enemies were made. These enemies were those in the then current major organisations and Deaf people who had been raised all their lives to love and accept the paternalistic attitudes imposed on them. However, 'NUD 1976' caused an erosion of feelings within many Deaf people and the Deaf community was never the same again .....

NUD 1976

London. November 1975.

Deaf people have had enough! We are tired of having hearing people trying to tell us what is best for us. So long as they remain our mouthpiece, the rest of the world will continue to regard us as puppets. They will still think we are not capable of contributing, of teaching them anything. We know this is not true. But it is up to us to prove them mistaken. We say, "Help to form and join the NUD. Let the public hear what we have to say. Let them see us marching, helping others and being willing to go out into the hearing world to make friends and contacts." So long as we hide in clubs, we will never prove anything. We do not want sympathy. We seek only respect. But until we can be seen to do things and make changes, we will get neither. We must come out into the open .... Too many of us have sat around for too long, just moaning. We only get what we deserve. If other oppressed groups in society get more than us, we have only ourselves to blame. Blind people, working men, gay people, women, black people, wheelchair people; all have had to fight for themselves. We must do the same .... The public is not aware of us. But we are aware of what is wrong. Then we must do something. An aware mind means an active mind, doesn't it? Let's take for our inspiration the story of the Tolpuddle Martyrs. If you do not know the story, please go and find out.

Now we know most of you who read this will agree. But you will say, "Why do we need another group, a NUD?" We say: "Because all the organisations for the Deaf have had long enough time to change things and prove themselves. We do not want a lot of little groups for the Deaf. We are our own best spokesmen; we want an organisation that is of us. We want to hear the Deaf's own voice - our own union of unity. Not another fragmented organisation. Let us look at these other organisations and see why they cannot make the progress we need".

ROYAL NATIONAL INSTITUTE FOR THE DEAF. (RNID).

The original idea behind the RNID was to provide a service for Deaf people and to inform the public and those in authority of the needs of the Deaf. The RNID provides homes and hostels; it offers a good hearing aid service. But, somewhere it has lost its way. As an example, let us quote the editor of 'Hearing' .... "There are 34 full-time staff in this Institute and if you ask them all what the object of the RNID is, you will get 34 different answers." At the meetings from Tooting to Timbuctoo, the same old faces are seen. And because there are only a few Deaf people involved, the government get the idea that Deaf people cannot do anything for themselves. This is very dangerous. We feel that the RNID has its place but we know that the majority of Deaf people have no confidence in it. We feel that they know too much of the dark side of deafness and very little about its potential. Our potential. We do not want this bad impression to continue.

NATIONAL DEAF CHILDREN'S SOCIETY. (NDCS).

This group work for children and parents. They try to get the parents together to work to help their children. And they are powerful in the education and medical fields. But there are many disadvantages. Most of their members are very middle class and this really puts ordinary people off. Their biggest fault is their paternalistic way of life - hearing parents know what is best for you, so shut up and don't argue. More than anyone else, they got oralism going. And they help to cut Deaf people off from Deaf children (because of signing). So the children suffer because they cannot find people who they will grow up to be like; so they think they should be ashamed of themselves. And we grown ups suffer because we can help the children a lot, because we know what it really means to be Deaf. And the world suffers because it is the old 'help the poor Deaf children' bit all over again. A prominent member of this group still cannot even fingerspell after nearly 30 years in office .... THIS WILL NOT DO.

THE BRITISH DEAF ASSOCIATION. (BDA).

This is perhaps the most dedicated and best of the organisations. It has done wonderful work to provide Deaf clubs and many social activities. But more than the others, it has become FOSSILISED. Deaf clubs are on the decline. On the whole, the young Deaf do not go to them anymore because of the strong orthodox religious base which controls their thinking. Look at the BDA Congresses. A sight of fantastic potential...... Thousands of Deaf people gathering to discuss their problems and views. And what happens? We pass resolutions and go home again .... Deaf people have their vote. It passes through regional councils and up to that celestial body at the top .... The views of thousands of Deaf people waited to be acted on. And what do we find? A small bunch of hearing people who have run out of steam and energy, making noises and trying vaguely to influence people ....

No-one who has read the Lewis Report, that chance in a lifetime for Deaf people, will ever forget paragraphs 162-163. Through an unprofessional approach, the views of the Deaf were ignored. Now, we have a great respect for the BDA. Their vital place in the history of Deaf people will never be forgotten by us. But today their work should be on the SOCIAL side and leave the POLITICS to a more dynamic and go-ahead group. That is what we want the NUD to be. If you are a young and able Deaf person, what is your future? Many of you are stuck with being social secretary of your club for the rest of your days on earth.

BRITISH ASSOCIATION OF THE HARD OF HEARING. (BAHOH).

Really, this group is for Deaf people with speech. We tend to forget this but partially Deaf people often have more problems than the born Deaf. They can be more isolated and overlooked by hearing people because they can speak and the welfare services for them are terrible. But BAHOH are stuck with their 'bunch of old ladies' image and many go-ahead partially Deaf people get frustrated with them. Part of their problem is this name of 'hard of hearing'. We are all Deaf and we all are in the same boat. Many of these people would be really useful. We would love to have you. Join up and we will work together.

BREAKTHROUGH TRUST.

Lastly, we come to the newest group. Their aims are to build a Deaf person into a first class Deaf person, not a second class hearing person. They also want to bring the Deaf and hearing together on an equal level to show each what they can offer the other. Up to now because of the domination of the hearing in our own affairs, we have built up a resentment to them. But hearing people built this world and we must always be trying to learn from them. This is the Breakthrough thinking, and they have done wonders in only a short time.

But there are disadvantages and Breakthrough is only half the answer. There are many Deaf people who are hostile to the Trust because they feel they are elitist. Many members of Breakthrough are good lipreaders and use very little signing and fingerspelling. This tends to put up a communication barrier with those of us who have always signed. Also their work is concerned with taking Deaf people into the hearing world, and not with the clubs.

The NUD recognises their ideas; they alone of all the groups have a majority of Deaf workers, and Deaf people who have fought their way into teaching or social work often are found to be members. But much of their work is aimed towards the next generation and they prefer to work on small informal levels. They do not want to be contaminated by 'vulgar' political fighting. But we of the NUD see the need to get on with the fighting. We see the power of the media just waiting to be used by the Deaf people. We must come out into the open ....

Breakthrough does not wish to end up fossilised. So they never write pamphlets saying 'This is what we are'. They feel that if they stay this way, people will always have to think about what Breakthrough really is. This is fine for them. But we, the NUD, want to unite Deaf people; we want to bring out our care and concern for each other in fellowship. And to make this easier, we must have simple and basic aims. We may become fossilised ourselves in the future but by then we will have served our purpose and die fighting on the job, aiming for self-respect for Deaf people.

So now you have an idea of where we stand and why we need a NUD.

Now. What are we fighting for? We are fighting to run our own affairs.

And where are we fighting for them?

1. EDUCATION

We will not attempt to express our anger at the treatment of Deaf children in schools. We are sure that you have heard it all before. If not, do not worry. We will be publishing some pamphlets on the subject and you can write to us for them. Recently a Deaf man was made a governor of a Deaf school - only the second Deaf person in history. The other thousands have been hearing. Deaf people have said they want total communication in schools. Not a system. We want a flexible scheme to fit the child. Not trying to flatten children into a theory. The sheer prejudice which has kept Deaf people out of their schools for so long is fighting a losing battle. The NUD will be there to help justice to be done.

2. MEDICAL FIELD

Our 'distinguished' professors and doctors have kept Deaf people apart from each other for too long. Parents who need help are fobbed off with isolation and oralism. To these highly paid witch doctors, we ask: "How much time do you spend with adult Deaf people. How many Deaf people are your friends?" The NUD seeks to work together, shoulder to shoulder, with those who are really interested and we will expose these people for what they are.

3. EMPLOYMENT

We all know the disgusting ways that we Deaf people suffer with work. We are capable of much better jobs than the ones we get. We are capable of more responsibility. But we can fight much better as a body than on our own. And this is what the NUD will try to do. We seek affiliation to the TUC which has always worked for a better deal for the working person. More of this later.

4. FURTHER EDUCATION

In the USA, there is a Deaf university. In Great(?) Britain, we can boast of only a few Deaf graduates. It is unbelievably difficult for us to get into further education. Most of us give up in despair. The NUD wants to work to change this sad and unnecessary picture.

5. SOCIAL WORK

Deaf people can educate social workers in their job. Many of them have a low expectation level of Deaf people and we must work to put this right. The social workers' views are not really heeded. Their union is too weak. We must try to work with those who really believe in us.

6. IN THE WORLD

There are many Deaf people with the talent to become interesting figures in the public eye. We must use our own talents to become known. We have Deaf people who are capable of making plays and acting. We must get together to make plays, films and books to give the public an idea of what it is like in our world. All that holds us back is self-confidence. The NUD wants to help give Deaf people this confidence. Think of the potential of comedy. This is the best way to communicate and to help break down the barriers of fear and resentment.

So now you know what we are fighting for. And now you know where we are going to fight for them. But all battles need allies. And this next chapter is written for them ......

TEACHERS. You may or may not know that the majority of Deaf people in Britain are not happy with the educational systems used on Deaf children in your schools. We also know that there are a number of you who are not happy. That is why there is a shortage of teachers. We know that you are stuck; that you are tied to the autocracy of your head and the system of the school. The NUD offers you a way out of your dilemma. We welcome you to join us and we will offer you the support of Deaf people. We welcome you if you are happy to stand shoulder to shoulder with us and be seen in our company as equals. We need your support and your informed opinion. Please step forward .... NOW.

MEDICAL PROFESSION. We know that only a very few of you will heed this appeal. If you believe in us and agree with our potential, then let us hear your voice. We need those of you who are committed to put over our views in the quaint jargon so favoured by your unseeing colleagues.

SOCIAL WORKERS. You, more than the others, are aware of the needs and desires of Deaf people. Yet because you work in little isolated areas and because you want to get on quietly with your work, you are losing the chance to make important changes for Deaf people on a national level. If you join with us, you will have less need to fear for your employer's dissension. You will be able to organise good grass-roots co-ordination and a chance to have your views on employment, etc., backed up by a show of strength. Now, there are two classes of you and you both have your faults. You, the missionaries, often think of yourselves as superior to Deaf people and often do not allow Deaf people to feel confident about the chances of changing their own lives. You, in local authority, are often less committed, more career minded or just plain wishy-washy. But there are many of you who care sincerely and would like the chance to show this more. Please write to us now ....

POLITICIANS AND DECISION-MAKERS. Some of you in the second category will already have a stake in the carcass of Deaf people's welfare. Some of you will be fresh to all this discussion. What we need from you is a declaration of your support. We realise that you all have other commitments. But we need your influence and let's be open about this. If you are brave or farseeing enough to give us public support, recognition of your generosity and honest thinking will not be long in coming. For those of you who have made the right noises in the past, we would ask a little more. We request your direct help. We make no bones about reporting your commitment or otherwise among our members .... Presumptuous words, indeed! But we are not aiming low. Thank you in advance.

AND TO THE REST OF THE HEARING POPULATION, we say: "We know that many of you are familiar with Deaf people, friends of Deaf people and related to Deaf people. We need your support just as much. We need your determination and numbers for a start ... We want you to join local groups, to help endorse the good working ability of Deaf people and to help get this message through to trade councils, schools and the government". So Associate Membership is waiting for you. The addresses are at the end of this booklet.

So far, so good. Now you see how many of us there are .... And here's some of our plans for action.

1. We want to start local groups. We must never lose touch with the grass roots. Many of you will have more ideas and plans for action. We will not suggest them. This is for you to think out for yourselves, although we will be pleased to chip in with you.
2. We can then build up national campaigns. The tactics for this include marches, demonstrations, get together to show our fellowship and goodwill to each other as fellow human beings.
3. We want to bring out Deaf people to start our own projects. Many of us run our own small businesses. Why don't we get together to start larger concerns, or to offer advice to those who would like to start. If you are a good photographer, film-maker, writer, actor, electrician, why not chew over some of the ideas underneath?

Right? Here are some ideas that we can put into practice.

1. DEAF PEOPLE'S CHARTER OF RIGHTS

We must have some idea of what we are aiming for. It makes it easier for us. And it makes it easier for the public to see what we are trying to do. We must finish working this out soon.

2. DEAF PEOPLE'S NEWSPAPER

We need this because we need to show the world that Deaf people are capable of writing and editing an interesting newspaper. This as opposed to the static, technical and often irrelevant magazine stuff which is all we have now. We will show that a Deaf person has something to say and can show by example, by humour, by humility and by insight. It should be a learning experience for all.

We need a paper to keep us in touch and to make us a stronger body. We need to see what other Deaf people are doing to spur us onwards. We need to believe in ourselves and respect ourselves and our paper can do this. We can hold it up and say, "This is what we can do." We can get onto the bookstalls of the nation. We need to educate ourselves more, to find out what really happens behind the scenes with those who are supposed to work for us. Unless you are offered a wider responsibility to other human beings, how the hell can the public fairly criticise you for being apathetic or narrow-minded? If there was no unity, no England, we would all still be a handful of biased little castles ....

Teachers, professionals and other hearing folks - we offer you the chance to point out the wrongs in our system and promise you the anonymity to speak the truth without fear of reprisal. This is the chance to take the mystery and superstition out of your work to make it easier for those who want to work with us ..... WE NEED TO BE SEEN.

We must reach television (Nationwide, Open Door, etc.) and put Deaf people in places they have never been seen before. We need posters, badges, T-shirts and pamphlets on every aspect of deafness. Any way of showing where we stand to the public ....

3. CAMPAIGNS

We must start campaigns. Here are a couple of ideas.

a) Total Communication in schools.

b) Tax allowances.

c) Rented teleprinters from the GPO.

d) More TV programmes for Deaf people.

e) Better further education. More interpreters.

f) Houses to be made available to Deaf youths who want to leave home like their hearing counterparts.

g) Better employment. More chances of promotion. Deaf Teachers.

h) Proper acceptance of sign language. National book of signs. Compulsory fingerspelling in hearing schools. Compulsory lessons for all professionals and workers. University courses in sign language and a Deaf university.

j) More lipreading classes and facilities. There are many more obviously. It is now up to you.

OTHER AIMS OF THE NUD

1. EDUCATION

The NUD seeks to fight for the Deaf to be accepted in the training to be teachers of Deaf children. The NUD wishes to secure representation for Deaf people in this field. Deaf people should have a major say in education.

2. EMPLOYMENT

To fight for regional training centres for technical and vocational training. To fight for more reasonable employment prospects, including posts charged with executive responsibility.

To secure a good weekly wage for the disabled and blind Deaf people in the sheltered workshops.

3. GENERAL

To secure direct NUD representation on all bodies charged with the administration of education, employment and welfare of the Deaf people.

To offer compensation to members who are victimised and involved in lock-out or strike action.

To offer legal assistance to eligible members.

We have now given you hope. You may come forward slowly at first. But now you have no excuse to moan. Your future now rests in your hands, in the shape of the most exciting publication in the history of Deaf people. Your future may be changed with your participation in the NUD. Write and let us have your support now.

Pens and paper out .... It is up to you now!!!

An Address to NUD Members

London. March 1977. A. F. Dimmock.

I look back over the 55 years in which I have existed as a Deaf mute, with the daily ordeal of struggling in an alien world. My early life was not too bad; all my acquaintances at home, school and later on at work spoke my lingo which was entirely manual. The cinema showed silent films and there was fun and games from which I was not barred. Almost imperceptibly as the years passed, former joys and facilities slipped away till conditions are what they are today. Everything appears to be geared up for the benefit of people with hearing. Almost all forms of entertainment make no provision for the Deaf. The television set is just a talking box. On the jobs front, positions of importance and responsibility are not for the Deaf. What they get are the menial jobs that no one wants. Should there be a mess, it is old muggins, the Deaf one, who is called upon to clear it. The dice is loaded, fully and totally, against all who have the misfortune to be Deaf or hard of hearing.

Now I am going to talk about something that happened in India nearly 200 years ago. The country was ruled by the wealthy Rajahs and the British Army. The common people were treated like dirt and they accepted their fate without complaint. Except for one man, Umai Tinnesvilley, who burned with suppressed rage. He was Deaf, dumb and illiterate, but he discovered he could gesture to people and be understood. He started the Poligar Rebellion by the power of sign language. It did not succeed however. In fact many people died and Umai himself was put to death. But it awakened the people of India and today they are free.

To us, it should be a lesson. All of us, whether Deaf and dumb, Deaf speaking, hard of hearing or those euphemistically known as 'hearing impaired', should stop our squabbles over trifling matters and be united, body and soul, and shout with one voice for the many things denied to us for so long. Our long overdue rights will only come if we work and strive as one.

Preface

The National Campaigns Team (1976-79) was set up to spread the word of the NUD and create an awareness of the need for a new organisation of the Deaf. The team visited Deaf clubs and gave talks in places such as Southampton, Liverpool, Luton, Bath, Leeds, Glasgow, Manchester, London, Newcastle and Belfast - other places would take up too much space here. The talks were mainly given without prepared papers as NUD members on the team knew exactly what they had to say.

However, the following two papers are typical of those given at the talks, the Newcastle Paper being an extension of the original talk as the meeting at Newcastle was called specially for the purpose of the NUD to justify its existence.

A word on the National Campaigns Team (NCT) here may be of interest to readers. The NUD formed the NCT basically to inform Deaf people of the NUD and thus win support and members. Not only that, this was also a campaign to arouse Deaf people into taking positive steps to run their own affairs.

In spite of the fact that the NUD had very little money and little time as Deaf people were giving up their spare time to join the campaigning, the NCT managed to give talks in some 22 clubs about the NUD.

However, there were many other clubs whose welfare officers refused to allow NUD to give talks thus preventing word to be spread to such clubs. These welfare officers even went on to warn their clubs about the NUD and told the club members to shun the organisation. Partly as a consequence of that, the NUD was unable to grow any further than it hoped for.

The problem of living in council flats which are governed by entryphone systems as mentioned in the Newcastle Paper is an ongoing fact. In September 1988, the NUD was assisting three Deaf families in two London Boroughs to force the council to fit flashing light bells and the like. The present situation is no different from that of ten years ago. In spite of the much publicised present trend towards greater enlightenment and understanding of the needs of the Deaf people, local councils have a tendency to ignore Deaf people in preference to dealing with various hearing minority groups. The word, "Ignorance", is inseparable from the words, "Hearing People". This is a tragedy that Deaf people may have to live with, but this battle against ignorance shall continue.

National Union of the Deaf

National Campaigns Team 1976 – 1979 Raymond Lee.

Most of you will say, "What is NUD?" and even more of you will ask, "Why do we need another organisation?" I would like to take the opportunity to explain the background first before coming to answer these two questions.

For nearly one hundred years we, Deaf people, have been living at the lower depths of society and have been continually ignored by the hearing members of society. Deaf people are not even considered for well paid jobs; we are treated worse than second class citizens. Let us look at some of the facts:

1. Blind people are more respected than the Deaf. They have their own union, the National League of the Blind, which is affiliated to the TUC, and their members fight for their own rights and needs. Their general secretary, Tom Parker, is also blind. What about the Deaf - they do not have an organisation of the Deaf run by the Deaf.

2. Other oppressed groups like the black people are winning public respect. They have had to fight for it themselves. What about the Deaf - they do not fight for anything themselves and always rely on hearing people to run their affairs.

3. Working men have had to fight for better working conditions decent pay packets and promotional opportunities within their companies. What about the Deaf - they always humbly settle themselves with lower paid jobs and never complained.

Deaf people cannot expect to get anywhere or gain respect if they do nothing and leave everything, even their own destinies, in the good hands of hearing paternalistic charitable organisations. Deaf people have lived for far too long in the shadow of hearing people trying to tell them what is best for them. These hearing people are our mouthpieces and the world listens to them, not us Deaf people. In that way, the world will continue to regard us as nobodies and they will think we are not capable of contributing to society. The public are not aware of us. We are nobodies.

We now have a number of organisations who are supposed to be there for our benefit - but they are not. Let us take a look at three of them:

1. Royal National Institute for the Deaf (RNID). All of us know that the RNID is run by upper middle class hearing people who look down on us merely as "those we are supposed to serve." The RNID does not do any campaigning, fighting, or the like for us. It is more concerned with its image and prefer to present other hearing people's works and views on the Deaf, and the organisation as a whole has no appeal to us.

2. National Deaf Children's Society (NDCS). This is a very paternalistic, oralist and middle-class organisation which work for children and parents. They

support the ban of signing in schools - so the Deaf do not wish to be linked with such an organisation. A prominent member of this group still cannot even fingerspell after nearly 30 years in office. This will not do.

3. British Deaf Association (BDA). The BDA is the best organisation in Britain. It does wonderful work to provide Deaf clubs and social and sporting events and activities. That is just about all. Look at the thousands of Deaf people who flock to the BDA Congresses - a sight of fantastic potential. They gather to discuss their problem and needs, pass resolutions and go home. Those resolutions are put on the shelves to gather dust. Who by? A bunch of hearing people at the top who tell the Deaf members of the organisation what to do and how to do things their way. They inhibit young and able Deaf persons from trying to improve the organisation. What is our future with the BDA for as long as it remains what it is now?

The only solution is to do something about the situation OURSELVES. We do mean what we say. Everyone of you is your own best spokesman. Lets give the hearing people a bit of a shock for a change. Let them see us coming out into the open, see us fighting for our rights and hearing the voice of the Deaf - directly from Deaf people themselves, not via the mouths of other hearing people who represent and work for us. To hell with them; they have had their chances for far too long to prove themselves and have done nothing for us in real terms. A group of Deaf people who are dissatisfied with the current organisations have decided that enough is enough and got together to form the NUD.

The NUD is not just another organisation. It is the first and only organisation formed to be run by the Deaf for the Deaf. Although it has membership and constitutional structure, the NUD is essentially an open organisation for every Deaf person to take advantage of and use for his or her benefit. Its two main aims are:

1. To restore the rights of the Deaf.
2. To make the voice of the Deaf heard.

In the first aim, you may be puzzled by the word "restore". Let me tell you that in the past Deaf people were in occupations which they are banned from working at present. Take an example; in the past there were many Deaf teachers but they cannot get teaching jobs now. There are many different jobs which Deaf people cannot get because changing and improving technological advancements have rendered Deaf people unsuitable for such jobs, even though Deaf people did these very jobs in the past. We want to bring back - restore - the rights of the Deaf to work and be employed in such jobs.

The second aim is very important. As I said before, Deaf people will gain nothing if they let hearing people speak on their behalf. Deaf people must come out into the open and make the hearing world aware of them. We must show the world what we are capable of doing. We must show them we can be useful and contributing members of society. We will have to tell them our needs and views ourselves, not via our missioners, social workers and representatives from our organisations. We will have to demand our rightful place and status in society; we will demand politely but firmly - never again shall the Deaf have to grovel and beg. If we do all these things ourselves we shall win back our pride and self-respect. At first this may sound difficult. It may be because you do not have the confidence to face up to this new change. Do not worry. You can do it in groups and this is the best way to start building your confidence.

The NUD is an organisation OF the Deaf, not FOR the Deaf. It means Deaf people working together for each other and other Deaf people all over the country. Hearing people can become associate members and give advice, but they have no right to voting and decision-making which is left to the Deaf themselves. You may ask "What is the NUD going to fight for? And where will they be fighting?"

We are fighting to run our own affairs. We will be fighting them in different fields of life and at all levels of society. There are the fields of Education, Employment, Social Work and so on. There are also the Medical and Political fields. If the views of the Deaf need to be known in every field, then we shall get into each one. We are not afraid of the great wide world in front of us; we look forward to the battle ahead and see what we can achieve, or rather what changes can be achieved.

One area in which the NUD intends to work is that of politics. We know that the word, "politics", is a dirty one to most of you. Most Deaf people avoid any involvement in political activities. Why? Can you give us one good reason why no Deaf person or group should meddle about or become involved in politics? Please understand this: the NUD is a politically motivated organisation and we have no shame in saying this. Politics does not mean the Government and the different parties. No. Politics is the means by which our society is run or governed. Everyone of us - every Deaf person in fact - has a right of say in how our country, and thus our affairs, is run. Take the example of discrimination in employment. We know there is discrimination against the Deaf in employment. How can we get rid of this discrimination? There are politicians who can help if we present them a well prepared document, outlining firm evidence of cases of discrimination and detailing all the facts. Politicians can raise the matter in Parliament and who knows this could lead to new laws banning discrimination in any form against the Deaf and other disabled people. To you, this may sound far-fetched but for such a thing to occur is not impossible.

This is but one example of the benefits that can be expected by working in the political arena. Deaf people should become politically motivated and involved if they are to make life a better place for them to live in.

Another important function of the NUD is working together with Deaf people. The NUD was created for you all. It is there for you and your friends. You can join in and work with other Deaf people, learn from one another, fight side by side with your friends and help to share the work. The NUD has a democratic structure and is very open to every Deaf individual wishing to join in. The NUD has sub-committees. The NUD is very young and needs your help to guide its growth and make it strong. In exchange, the NUD will make you strong and confident; the NUD will make you regain your pride and self-respect.

You can, if you want, form local branches of NUD and work in your own area. That way you can work to promote the needs of local Deaf community and fight for the rights of its members. You can get in touch with local trade union movement and political parties for help and support. You can also get in touch with other underprivileged minority groups, work together and plan action. There is practically no limit to what the Deaf can do and achieve but this will depend on all of you - whether you are willing to work for it or not.

If I am to talk about the NUD down to the very last detail, we will probably still be here tomorrow morning! I think I have spoken enough on my part. If you want to know more about the NUD, it is better if we do it on a question and answer basis. Please feel free to ask questions and my colleagues and myself will be more than happy to answer.

Newcastle Paper

Newcastle. June 1978. Raymond Lee.

Old friends! How pleasing it is to see you all here today. I would like to thank you for the opportunity you have given to myself and my colleagues, Christopher Marsh and Robert Anderson, to talk about the NUD and to answer your question, "Do we really need another organisation for the Deaf?" As many of you here today know, I have regularly come back home and met all of you. I am sure you all know enough about the NUD itself and I trust you all will agree with me when I say we shall look at your question and beyond for the afternoon, leaving out the NUD bit as you know so much about it.

The answer to your question, "Do we need another organisation for the Deaf?", is clearly no! We do not need another one! But we do need an organisation of the Deaf! There is a vast difference in the words "of" and "for". When you use the word, "for", it means the organisation is being run by hearing people for the Deaf. But "of" implies that Deaf people are running their own organisation. That is the big difference. And again, some of you asked the NUD to justify the need for its existence. I will explain again that there is a vital need for the NUD. Deaf people need to be seen. They need to be seen working for themselves. They need to be seen as a dynamic group, fighting for the rights of their own people. We do not need hearing people from the BDA and the RNID speaking and doing things on our behalf. They are not capable of doing anything for us - you all need to look back to their past to remind you of that. If ever there were any achievements by these two hearing run organisations, we all will need a microscope to find them! If we all stick to the past and current organisations, we will never make any change for the better. You have to change yourselves in order to change these organisations. A group of Deaf people decided to make changes. One of these changes was to form the NUD. The NUD is only two years old and please remember - Rome was not built in a day. I do see the NUD playing a very important role in changing and influencing the course of history for all Deaf people in Britain and time will prove me right.

The NUD is only as good as the people who participate in its activities. What that means is the more Deaf people break away from the shackles of the past and change their attitudes, the more they can change their world for the better. You all can do it.

We all need to change hearing people's attitude towards us and rid them of their ignorance. The BDA and RNID both have had years to do that and what did they do? You know and I know that they are phlegmatic and are only interested in their image and reputation. The RNID is contained and run by upper class hearing people. These people are more interested in the medical aspects of deafness, as well as hearing and speech aids and you all can see that in their journals and literature.

The best we can do is to show that organisation that it is completely out of touch and out of tune with the Deaf world. Let them see our campaigns, our works and what we are fighting for. This will make hearing people see the vast difference in what Deaf people actually need and what they thought the RNID says Deaf people need. Once hearing people realise that the RNID is not actually catering for the true needs of Deaf people, they will start asking questions and this may lead to the RNID to change its attitude. Who knows it could happen? It is up to us all to make this happen.

The BDA is a huge dinosaur with a very tiny brain. The body is that of the Deaf membership but the brain is that of the hearing people who run it. It has become fossilised. What the BDA needs is an input of dynamic and intelligent young Deaf people to turn it into a very active organisation, fighting well for its members. Its executive council very often contain Deaf people (as well as hearing people) who are basically "Yes" people. The BDA's electoral structure is terrible and many able and intelligent young Deaf people find it hard to get elected onto the executive council - and this is not only the BDA's tragedy, but ours too. If only Deaf members wake up and make noises to make changes, then things could have got better.

One of the biggest faults of these two organisations is their lack of both vigilance and giving 100% effort whilst working for the Deaf people. Let me give you two examples. From the mid-fifties when hearing aids were becoming compulsory in most Deaf schools, staff of the RNID gave hearing aid use great publicity and promotion. Its magazine contained articles giving both technical information about hearing aids and articles on success stories about "Deaf" people who can hear, when in fact these children were not Deaf but hard of hearing. For many Deaf children to whom hearing aids were worthless burdens, the RNID did not bother to campaign against its use.

On the other hand, the BDA is naive and blind. Lets talk about buildings. Architects and councils are building new blocks of flats and more and more are having entryphone systems fitted. What use is an entryphone to a Deaf family in such a flat. When entryphones were built in, no provisions were made for flashing lights. Again, how can a Deaf couple tell who is ringing the doorbell on the ground floor when they are standing on the 7th floor? And looking at the same situation in a different aspect, I know of a number of Deaf couples who could not get into their relatives' flats because they could not answer the entryphone after ringing it. On the other hand, it takes them ages to discover that the relatives were out after trying to speak through the entryphone. One Deaf man literally spoke through the entryphone, "It is me, Bob" a few times over and when he looked round he saw a group of kids laughing at him. One of them told him it was not working. Things like that could have been overcome with foresight if people were aware of the needs of the Deaf. That was a job for both the BDA and the RNID. But they were ignorant - which means they did not work hard enough for the Deaf.

Another thing you all must bear in mind is that the NUD is providing competition to these two organisations. They both have existed for a long time and gained a grip, or monopoly, on the affairs of the Deaf. Once they have this monopoly, they tend to relax and get the feeling that they are the know-all and end-all of what people need to know about the Deaf. And also because of this absolute control and lack of opposition, these two organisations tend to overlook the developing events which put increasing pressure on Deaf people's survival to exist. Hence the NUD. Can you all see it that way? A BDA general secretary or a RNID director is useless if they don't keep in touch with the grass-roots Deaf people regularly from time to time in order to keep their organisations up to date or well informed.

I could spend the next twenty four hours trying to list all the faults of these two organisations, but we do not have much time on our hands. We all of course accept that nobody is perfect and mistakes or faults can be made. But the faults of these two organisations are beyond belief and it is about time they put their houses in order. What better to do that by creating a new organisation of the Deaf, run by the Deaf? In this way, the works and achievements of Deaf people will put these two organisations to shame and this will make their members feel embarrassed enough to make drastic changes. That is one of the reasons why the NUD was formed in 1976.

Another important aspect of NUD's work is to persuade Deaf people to form pressure groups and do their own work themselves, instead of relying on others to do it for them. Deaf people do not need people from the territory of the others to make a living out of their deafness and it is high time hearing people give way to Deaf people to run their own affairs. I remember clearly you all suggested this to me some four years ago. I have put your suggestion into practice. Now will you take it up?

We shall go into a discussion based on what I have said today and I hope we shall build up something from this dicussion.

President's Message to NUD 1st Convention

London. June 1978. Stan Woodhouse, MBE.

The hour has arrived for me to welcome everyone taking part in the first Convention of the newly-formed National Union of the Deaf, and to thank you one and all for whatever you are about to do in a good cause.

I hope you will join with me in giving our congratulations and grateful thanks to the band of people who have made the NUD possible, and who have proved so far that the Deaf can do it. They have had to blaze a trail, armed only with their efforts and true grit in the face of many difficulties and problems, including the financial side that bedevils us all. The honour is now upon you to take the helm in a more active capacity. Whatever you do, may it be done with the same enthusiasm and support as it has been in these initial stages.

Needless to say, the task ahead is a formidable one, for you have yet to set sail on the stormy seas and oceans of the hearing population which does not notice its clumsy and oppressive power that acts upon the tiny pools and droplets of the Deaf people. This can be seen, for instance, in the fact that Deaf people do not get any tax relief to offset their hardships and loss of status - being as fully taxed as the hearing population. Another example was the television authority that took a young Deaf person to court for non-payment of television licence, and the magistrate who fined him remorselessly without heeding his case. (In the name of Justice, as in the statue atop the Old Bailey, it is my personal opinion that this beak should have resigned).

All in all, it is a minor miracle that the image of the NUD has emerged. The more Deaf people who come together as an united body in the NUD, the better chance we have of making our voice heard. We are truly pleased that we can count on the support of the Disability Alliance and the National Council for Civil Liberties who have already helped us in several ways.

In conclusion, here you are at this Convention to do something positive for the future well-being of Deaf people. Whatever you do, and whoever you are, you help to form a vanguard. Be valiant, and then the cause of Deaf people in this country should in the end be a victorious one.

PART TWO

The Education Battles

Preface

After delegates to the RNID Harrogate Conference received the NUD's "First Epistle to the Teacher of the Deaf", they went inside to hear this following speech by Dr Reuben Conrad. It is impossible to describe the momentousness of this paper - at last after 100 years of oralism, someone had actually bothered to do comprehensive research into its results. By attempting to test **every single** Deaf school-leaver in the United Kingdom, there seemed to be no way the oralists could wriggle out of Conrad's findings and conclusions.

How they did do so is another fascinating story. But what Conrad explained in this paper cut away vital arteries and limbs from the monster's body; for many younger teachers at the meeting were changed forever that day. NUD fondly recalls handing leaflets to two such teachers who are now heads of residential schools, and one who was very prominent in a national Deaf children's organisation thereafter.

This is the appropriate point to focus on hearing people. NUD has included papers like Conrad's, Montgomery's and Lane's because they were inescapably part of NUD's history. Each one was given in tandem with historically significant NUD activity at that time, and the support we got from each of them was immensely heartening.

Rarely in Deaf history had so few of us made so many enemies in so short a time! We also learnt much from their approaches - they were less defensive than we were in what they said. We were all too aware that the slightest strong remark we made would be taken as a sign that we had chips on both shoulders and a bomb under our cloaks!

The debate which followed the Conrad paper was truly heated. It was perhaps the first time that Deaf people angrily confronted oralists in public. It was all the more gratifying, therefore, to gain hearing Associate members of the NUD as allies from that day forward. Some were teachers, some parents of Deaf children, some social workers, some relatives; a full spectrum. We will never forget or cease to value their support in the difficult days of the late 1970s and the early 1980s.

Dr Conrad's paper here is a little cautious and defensive; hardly surprising really! This is therefore a good moment to point out that all the authors in this book know that there are terms, phrases, expressions and so on that they would not use now. But we have tried here in this book to be faithful to history as it occured. Merely a year later, for example, Conrad was to give a beautiful and emotional paper at the BDA Congress at Eastbourne that deserves to be read. But here at Harrogate, the barricades have at first to be scaled .... or squeezed between ....

Towards a Definition of Oral Success

Dr R. Conrad. RNID Conference. Harrogate. 1976.

The recent excitement at the William Tyndale School in London presented in sharp focus the question of objectives in education. Why do we insist that children spend at least ten years at school? Apart from the natural development that will occur in ten years of a child's life, what changes should we try to make by deliberate intervention? The 'we' in this case is our society, and we entrust specialists - called teachers - with the task of achieving the desired goals. Overall, there is a vague concept that education should enable children to adapt, to a large extent vocationally, to the needs of society. From time to time both aims and methods are questioned - sometimes, as at William Tynedale, sharply. But we do live in a complex and flexible society and without question most children find that their education permits them to achieve an acceptable degree of integration into the world outside the school gates.

This attitude of relatively unaggressive interest is quite inappropriate when our concern is with the education of handicapped children. Without special intervention, that is special education, these children never could become integrated into our society. The question of objectives therefore hardly arises for the education of handicapped children. Furthermore, because of the handicap, in ten available years teachers will not have the luxury of being able to utilise a flexible and rich curriculum. Inescapably the handicap itself will define the curriculum and the handicap will circumscribe the means available for pursuing the curriculum.

In the education of Deaf children there is effectively total agreement that all other aims must be subordinated to that of ensuring that the child leaves school with effective means of communication. If we persist with an aim of integration into out society, then the primary objective of educating Deaf children must be to achieve workable levels of attainment in speaking, in understanding speech and in reading, at least. At that level, educators have little freedom of manoeuvre - the handicap has pre-empted it. We are here to discuss how to achieve this objective. Indeed we may have to discuss whether it can be achieved, or who can achieve it; and, then what of the others?

Having said that, I see my role here (since I am not a professional educator) as little more than to describe what is currently being achieved. But it is quite pointless simply to present quantities, which in themselves are literally meaningless. So I also want to suggest ways of assessing the significance of the quantities. I will discuss criteria. And because the quantities I am concerned with relate to those skills of communication I mentioned, high values imply oral successes. So in this paper I want to suggest some of the issues involved in deciding what is a high value. You must decide which criteria you find more useful than others; you will then be able to consider more realistically how much oral success is being achieved in our schools, and you will be more able to decide whether or not there is a need to examine alternative educational treatments.

We have just completed a study, supported by the Medical Research Council, of the levels of attainment of children at the very end of their ten years of special education. We achieved almost 100% coverage of children aged 15-16.5 in schools for the Deaf or partially hearing. The results I am going to talk about do not come from a partial or selected sample, but from practically the entire population of Deaf and partially hearing school-leavers. We also have had comparable results from partially hearing units. These are not yet fully analysed and I am not going to use them here. But I can say we do not find massive differences in attainment as between school children and unit children of the same degree of hearing loss and intelligence.

We have tested about 450 children in schools in England and Wales, but I have excluded from the results those children who became deaf after their third birthday (about 10% of the total), children from homes where English is not the mother tongue, a few untestable children and a group of children (about two dozen) for whom we could not get adequate historical and medical information. I should also say that we did not test at Larchmoor School or at Rayners. These exclusions left us with some 360 children.

I do not want to waste time going into details of procedure and tests and so on. For anyone interested, I have the information and I promise that I can justify every procedure we used. But of some importance, I would like to mention that the tests were administered by two experienced qualified teachers of the Deaf.

Let me talk about reading first. It raises the issues of standards and criteria very clearly but also in a fairly manageable way and therefore makes an easy way in. We used Brimer's Wide-Span reading test. This is a new test of reading comprehension and it covers a reading age range of 7-16. Summarising very briefly, we found the following. Of the children with average hearing loss of less than 65db, half had a reading age below 10.8; of the children with hearing loss greater than 85db (let's call these profoundly Deaf), half had a reading age below 7.6. Now taking the entire population of school-leavers, of all levels of hearing loss, we found six out of 360 who had a reading age which correspond to their chronological age, and almost a half had not reached a reading level of nine years.

So there are bare facts. How are we to assess them? In other words, what criteria ought we use to decide whether our reaction is to be: how awful! or well, that's pretty good! It seems to me that there are at least four possible standards against which this reading performance can be placed. The popular one of course is the standard of hearing children. This is what a reading age implies. When I said that half of the profoundly Deaf children do not reach a reading age of 7.6, this is an average reading age of hearing children aged 7.6. The principal value of this criterion is in its simplicity. It is easy to understand. But because we have no means of determining how many years of deficit of reading age a given degree of deafness is theoretically worth, the criterion really has little value. If a fifteen year old profoundly Deaf child has a reading age of 15, we can certainly applaud but we have no basis for assessing the level of retardation which is unacceptable. If we use hearing children as the standard, we are not comparing like with like.

So here is a second possible criterion: we can compare like with like. We can ask the question whether British Deaf children read better or worse than some other population of Deaf children. In a sense this becomes a limited but direct comparision of educational methods. In the event, the only useful comparative data I can find comes from the USA - which at least has the advantage that both populations are learning to read English. We then find that, taking degree of deafness into account, reading achievement is very similar in the two countries. But once again we cannot say whether this is a matter for sorrow or for rejoicing. British children are the equal of American children. But equally good or equally bad? So this criterion is not of great value either.

A third criterion is one which relates reading ability to some qualitative standard of literacy. We ask what level of reading ability does any child need? Deafness itself is irrelevant. If society feels that by school leaving age a child ought to be able to read *'Winnie the Pooh'*, or the *'Daily Mirror'* or *'War and Peace'*, or the regulations governing old age pensions, these provide objective standards which have an intrinsic meaning which is not inherent in a simple value of reading age based on a synthetic reading test. It would obviously be convenient to relate various literacy levels to neat reading ages, for then we would be discussing real performance rather than a point on an arbitrary scale.

Well, numerous guesses have been made at what is a socially acceptable level of literacy. An old Ministry of Education report considers a reading age of nine to be the very lowest limit of functional literacy. But values of 11 and 13 have been quoted. At present these are little better than guesses. But as a criterion, literacy is quite valid and only effort stands in the way of determining acceptable levels. Translated into the terms of this discussion, one might ask what kind of reading material can be 'bought' with a reading age of, say nine, which is about the 50% point of our Deaf school-leavers.

Finally there is the criterion determined by theoretical limits. Fifty percent of profoundly Deaf children do not reach a reading age of 7.6 years. It may well be that a reading age of 7.6 is socially unacceptable in terms of the literacy criterion. But it may also be true that that value represents a theoretical limit determined by the very nature of prelingual deafness. At present we have effectively so little scientific understanding of the nature of the cognitive problems facing a Deaf child learning to read, that it is pointless to try to put a reading age value to this theoretical limit. But limit there will be; true, constrained by many individual factors, and perhaps some situational ones as well. But in effect, this criterion requires us to know whether a Deaf child's capacity is a pint pot or a half-pint pot - because more will not go in.

So much for reading. I have told you what level of reading ability Deaf school-leavers have. I cannot tell you whether it is good or bad, but I have suggested some ways in which the assessment might be approached.

Now consider lipreading. An absolutely vital oral skill for the Deaf child. It is quite easy to 'measure' lipreading ability in a relative way. That is to say, whether or not one child lipreads better than another. We used a modified version of the Donaldson Lipreading Test. This employs a face to face live situation with the questions becoming increasingly difficult in terms of vocabulary and language involved. Just like a reading test, a child ends up with a score. But because there is no other standard - such as the reading norms for hearing children - the score does not answer the important question: how well will this child cope in the world beyond school? Again we are forced to seek criteria for assessing the qualitative value of the quantity represented by the test score.

This presents problems of great methodological difficulty. Certainly some of the criteria used for reading are applicable. We must indeed consider theoretical limits; in theory we certainly could use a criterion analogous to literacy. But there is at the moment hardly the faintest glimmer of the body of knowledge which would permit us to do this. We could compare with other populations. But again we would not know whether our children were equally good or equally bad. As a result of a great deal of testing, I was left with a statement which said that profoundly Deaf children have an average score of so much percent. We could have made the test easier and the score would have been higher. Similarly we could have made the test harder and got a lower score. But what we want to know is: how well can profoundly Deaf children lipread? We need not only a score, but a criterion: is X% good or bad?

I cannot pretend to have solved this. But let me tell you briefly my search for a solution. I argued something like this. After ten years of education, a Deaf child ought to be able to lipread better than someone with no training at all. So we took a large group of 15 year old hearing children of average intelligence and gave them the same test. But we completely masked speech sounds - they wore headphones which pumped white noise into their ears. Suddenly hearing children were forced to lipread, without training and without experience. We could then ask the question: are there any deaf children who, at the end of their school life, cannot lipread better than the noise-masked hearing children? It turned out that on average there was no difference at all between the two groups.... Again, I leave it to you to decide whether this criterion is harsh or lenient, and then whether you think that the Deaf children's lipreading performance is acceptable or not.

The last so called fact that I want to pull out of our research data concerns speech quality; how well can people understand the speech of Deaf children at the end of their school years? Conventionally, as you know, there are several ways of going about this - it rather depends on exactly what it is you want to know. We used two methods. In one we had the children speak prepared statements which were taped recorded and later played back to groups of ordinary people unfamiliar with Deaf speech. This is a reliable and objective procedure if you merely want to compare one child with another, or if you want to examine the relationship between hearing loss and speech quality, for instance. But we also wanted to know in absolute terms how easily can this or that child be understood? So we asked head teachers to make an assessment of their own pupils on a five-point scale, and we provided a verbal guide to each rating point. I'd better tell you how the five points were described: (1) The child's speech is wholly intelligible. (2) Fairly easy to understand. (3) About half can be understood. (4) Very hard to understand. (5) Effectively unintelligible.

This procedure also has weaknesses. Not least the fact that different people are rating different children, and subjective biases are inevitably present. But it is well established that on the whole, teachers are reliable raters of their own pupils, and furthermore the ratings were very closely related to the objective scores we obtained from ordinary listeners listening to taped prepared statements, and I think the ratings are of real value. For present purposes the rating scores are particularly appropriate, because a rating is in itself the application of a criterion. A rating of (2) simply as a number is a score which in itself - like others - is meaningless, but useful for comparative purposes. But in this case it is attached to an absolute judgement. It tells us that most of the child's speech is fairly easy to understand. And on this basis we can assess the speech quality of Deaf school-leavers using this socially meaningful criterion. But I think we ought to recognise that this criterion is probably on the lenient side. The rater is very used to deaf speech, he is familiar with the speech of the particular child and he also knows the child's repertoire of vocabulary and syntactic forms. But let's accept that.

The outcome produces these results. Considering all children in special schools, and regardless of hearing loss, school heads report that almost 50% of school-leavers' have speech which is either very hard to understand or effectively unintelligible. If we take those children with hearing loss greater than 85db, the figure rises to 70%.

Now instead of looking at bad speech, let's count the number of children who might be regarded as oral success with respect to speech quality. There are about 200 children in the survey with hearing loss greater than 85db. How many of them do their own teachers consider to have speech which is fairly easy to understand or better? Well, in the entire country, for this age group, there are 21 - just 10%. Should we be pleased with these results or despondent? Once again we have to ask ourselves whether the way we are educating our Deaf children is leading to acceptable performance or not, and you must choose the criterion for judging.

Let me very quickly summarise the levels of oral skill reached by profoundly Deaf children in our schools. When these children leave school, half of them have a reading age of less than 7.6; half of them lipread worse than the average hearing child, untrained and inexperienced; 70% of them have speech which on the whole is too difficult to be understood, and only 10% have speech which is easy.

I have already said that these bare figures are in themselves meaningless. But in a way no quantity is wholly meaningless. Every one of us here has developed a concept which, without having clarity and difficult to justify - our hunch if you like - nevertheless lights up a warning lamp when a quantity approaches what this hunch reaction tells us is an unacceptable value. I do not know whether these values are unacceptable; I just have a lot of warning lights flashing in my intuition box.

These results worry me, and I would be inhuman not to want to be involved in discussion beyond observable evidence.

So often, it seems to me, we lose sight of very simple concepts. One of the most fundamental concepts of linguistic development - and this of course underlies all the oral performance I have been discussing - is naming. This is really too trite to expand. Until children have names for objects and activities and characteristics, they will have no language. When I say 'have' names, I mean a lot more than simple recognition or crude vocal mimicry. By 'having' names I mean having consistent and consolidated internal representation which the child can internally manipulate.

We have good evidence now that the majority of Deaf children never achieve this. In effect, they are without an adequate internal linguistic facility. These children, after ten years of education, appear positively to be without a formed and usable internal language. If these children have a mother tongue at all, and most seem not to, it is quite unrelated to the language of classroom instruction.

The need, at a very early age, to achieve fluency in a mother tongue, which would then be available to be used internally, is so crucial for the developing child that I believe the nature of that tongue to be of secondary importance. There seems to be no great difficulty in learning English as a secondary language, but I begin to find it hard to evade the evidence that oral English is not an effective mother tongue for profoundly Deaf children. We seem, without difficulty, to have achieved a sizeable population of non-lingual Deaf children. I suspect it would be just as easy, and infinitely more rewarding, to achieve a population of bi-lingual children.

Preface

Education was the main issue on which the NUD expended its time and efforts. Indeed, whenever we gave talks in Deaf clubs up and down the land, we found that education was by and far the most hotly expressed topic for discussion by the club members. Many had stories to tell of their experiences which we have longed to film and set down in a book, to make people aware of the sheer extent of the damage done. This task, as part of Deaf history, is still urgently required.

Education reform started at the BDA's 1974 Conference, urged on its way by a powerful paper from McCay Vernon and throughout the next ten years, the BDA published academic papers and tried to persuade the professionals, from one hearing person to another, of the need for change.

By 1975, there was a feeling in the air nationally that change was coming. The RNID put on a seminar to discuss Deaf education. NDCS had a conference entitled "What went wrong?" But as yet, there was little Deaf input to the discussion.

In the summer of 1976, the NUD took a delegation to a similar conference at Harrogate. We gave out a paper, included here, lobbied and picketed the teachers directly. Many still remember this event as the first of the many since, where Deaf people addressed teachers directly for almost the first time in a century. This emotional impact complemented the BDA's intellectual impact, (to simplify the issue a little) and change had gradually come.

The papers included here represent some of these direct approaches. The latter ones, part of the struggle against mainstreaming, are perhaps the only ones here which still contain useful thinking for the 1990s, largely because this issue is still being hotly fought whereas arguments in favour of signing are now well established.

The NUD Charter of Rights, a 70-page book aimed at the United Nations in 1982, made little headway there. Yet one of the most encouraging spin-offs has been the BDA-led campaign to have the EEC national sign languages recognised. Arguments for banning oralism and mainstreaming for their breach of rulings protecting linguistic minorities have not been taken up, partly because the correct U.N. legal term for this is "genocide", which is misinterpreted by people to mean only "murder". Until oralism is banned in this way, however, Deaf communities will never be sure that some political or philosophical tide won't come along in the future and sweep us all back to the bad old days again. Already the talk about cochlea implant developments shows all the worst features of oralism.

The culmination of 11 years of education campaigning was in April 1987 when NUD members picketed the Department of Education and Science (DES) to get reforms in teacher training provision. In the year that followed, discussions were held with the DES across the whole range of Deaf education; the first time these people had even met Deaf consumers directly. The full report of these meetings is available, but to sum them up, nothing was achieved. Little was conceded by the DES who used arguments the oralists were using (and had lost!) ten years ago.

Those, then, who read the following papers may feel that things have changed altogether for the better since they were first written. The truth, the sobering reality, is that most of what they contain has in 1988 been rejected by Her Majesty's highest level of government officers responsible for the future of Deaf children's lives. If we are talking about achieving a fully comprehensive and professional bi-lingual education for Deaf children, we have, all of us, barely started to scratch the surface of real change.

Meanwhile, more and more Deaf schools close, more children are placed uncomprehendingly into hearing schools, and less and less money is spent on Deaf education. As fast as bi-lingual education grows, so does the essential care and heart of the Deaf community decline.

The most shocking thing is that there is still no special national campaign group in Deaf education - words cannot express how urgent is the need for it. YOU are needed, parent, teacher, Deaf person or ally!

1st. Epistle to the Teacher of the Deaf

RNID Conference Handout: Harrogate June 1976. Paddy Ladd.

Re: **Total Communication.**

Dear Teacher of the Deaf,

First of all, a few words on the subject of NUD. This long overdue organisation shows the determination of Deaf people that their voices, their views and their policies should be heard at national level wherever decision making is carried out on behalf of the Deaf. It is time the voice of the consumers was heard, as it can be convincingly argued that 'the customer knows best'. This is not to say that other views are not valid. Far from it. What we say is that communication is the crucial factor that delineates deafness so that this communication must be two-way.

Most of the points that need to be said regarding total communication have been raised already. We want to highlight the important ones here so that you see the issue as we, the Deaf, see it.

1. THE DEAF VIEWPOINT

Few of you seem to understand the strains of lipreading used on its own. Over a long period it is boring, as if you yourselves had to listen to a monotonous mumble all the time. It is tiring and thus when used on Deaf children, their reception ability drops markedly after a while. Also you have got to have a language to lipread and to guess, as lipreading is at least 75% guesswork. So Deaf children lose vital years chasing round in this vicious circle. Don't forget also that many teachers are difficult to lipread.

By the use of the oral-only system, you are killing and impoverishing the Deaf world. This does not mean that the younger Deaf are joining the hearing world. No; it means that they come to us emotionally and socially retarded, offering the older Deaf no new ideas nor even the ability to accept responsibility. The greatest disadvantage of the oral system is that it creates, in our language, the "Dummification Process". The result of such a system, producing Deaf pupils who can neither lipread nor speak clearly during their schooldays, results in turning out dummies of living human beings. There are many living proofs to testify to this side effect of the oral-only system, though some do shake it off when they find true communication in the Deaf world.

You are keeping us out of the schools quite deliberately, leaving the children no adult model who can set them an example in life. Even though systems of experiment like Cued speech and Paget system go part of the way, removing the stigma from signing, they do not allow Deaf adults or professionals to have a natural relationship with the children.

If you remember the example of Louis Braille and the system he developed now named after him, you will see our point. The sighted said that it would cut off the blind from the seeing. The blind found it marvellous because it was easy to learn with. This gave them more confidence to go out and integrate into the world, and history has proved the blind were right. So with total communication.

You must realise how important your job is to the Deaf. Hearing children can learn from society and from each other. We cannot. We are in your hands. You have the responsibility, not only academically but in life's patterns and social behaviour codes. So please let us into this to help you and to work with you. As the Deaf poet, David Wright, put it - "Only the Deaf can teach the Deaf to live without trading on their deafness".

2. LITERACY

The illiteracy of the Deaf school-leaver is a fact. Please stop hiding from it and reconsider your methods. Children's speech is not affected in the long run through total communication. It is, if anything, better. At present any deviance from the oral-only path makes the child and his parents feel failures; repeated 'failure' means that a child loses his curiosity. He loses his confidence and self-respect. And he and his parents give up. They bluff you through school with the minimum understanding, and you don't see this simply because you do not want to see this. So given current literacy standards, we are born to fail. You take away our one basic right - means to communicate - and condemn us to second class citizenship because when we leave school illiterate, our chance and confidence have gone. Total Communication cannot but aid literacy, as it gives us an equal chance to participate in the classroom discussion situations which gives us the motivation to learn. If you are honest, you will admit that discussion in the classroom is at present impossible. Deaf children have enough difficulty lipreading a hearing person. How on earth can they lipread each other?

3. LEARNING

We may, you feel, be using harsh words. But we are not against you, unless you reject this out of hand. We want you to enjoy yourself in teaching. We want you to find teaching and learning interesting and easy for you to develop a confident and true rapport with the children. Those of you who say they have it at the moment have truly only the tip of the iceberg at the moment. You can bring colour and life into the classroom if total communication is used, for you can explain more and thus keep things interesting. Learning is a natural process. Why make it as hard as possible for us? You would soon have truanted from school if you had only understood 25% maximum of what you were taught.

Please remember this point. Comprehension precedes expression. The Deaf child's very late start in comprehension leaves him hopelessly behind hearing children who can hold sensible discussions with adults at the ages of five, six and seven. And when one can express oneself, one has far more motivation for learning. If you don't allow 100% communication, comprehension and expression, you will never get anywhere.

Put yourself in our shoes. We, as children, want to tell you something or ask a question. We were excited but you could not understand our voices. We tried to use our hands but you stopped us. Then you smiled and nodded and changed the subject or walked off. It was obvious that you had not understood us but you, trained in the system, could not break into a true communicative relationship. Now please think..... what did we as children think to ourselves as you walked away, leaving us with our trapped requests and secrets that we wanted to tell you because we relied on you? We cursed. We cried. We became hardened inside. And we lost our trust, our confidence, our self-respect and our curiosity about the world. Please think on that.

It may or may not be true to say that it is the majority of Deaf children, the not-so-bright ones, who are handicapped by the oral-only system. But, because of the ensuing low standard of education, the bright ones suffer too. Their level of progress is held back to the level of the school, whereas they could have made O-levels and CSEs if their IQs are to be believed, and their school level is often only equivalent to the 11 years old level of the hearing schools. If you are honest with yourselves, you can see that all this is not due to communication difficulties on the child's part, but on your part. And this, we feel, is caused by not being able to understand the psychology of a Deaf person. If you had listened to us on this point, it would have been properly incorporated into training colleges, or you would have accepted the role of Deaf adults in Deaf schools.

4. SOCIAL DEVELOPMENT

In the haste to condemn total communication, one thing is overlooked. If you want to integrate, don't you think it might be easier for a hearing person or child to learn to fingerspell and sign? Fingerspelling takes five minutes to learn. And we have seen in our work real interest and desire from hearing people to learn it - children too. They are especially fascinated by a code of language that they can use. Knowing this, our language releases the fears of a hearing person who cannot understand us when we try to say something, however basic, in the voice of a sealion or a coyote. That is not the way to integration. We at the NUD are in fact pushing for fingerspelling and signing to be learnt at all hearing schools in an effort to try and restore the kind of integration that took place at Donaldson's Hospital, Edinburgh, before the war.

Trapped in our vacuum of inexperience with our school years lying fallow behind us, what kind of social development do you think we attained? Listen to Dr John Denmark when he tells you of mental health problems of the young Deaf people caused entirely by communication problems of oralism in schools and in family relationship. Rigid social behaviour, emotional immaturity, lack of understanding people or society, lack of religious or moral guidance and egoism could have been ameliorated or averted with total communication. Join the two years waiting list for psychiatric help for our young Deaf people and see for yourself.

How do we get on at work? Poorly in many cases. We cannot lipread our workmates with the exception of one or two, and they certainly cannot understand our speech. THEY CANNOT? But we were told by teachers and parents that they could understand us when we spoke. The penny drops! Meanwhile the keen workman writes down things. "Oops - can't read it. What now?" What indeed? Ask yourself that one. We have many workmates who have learnt total communication and are astonished that we never used that method in school. Please face up to it. This is true of the majority of school-leavers.

Our social development has been so limited by our intake that we could spend pages describing the problem. But suffice to say that if we widened the use of total communication at home and at school, at the dinner table for teachers and at decision-making time for parents, then we would understand so much more of what goes on in the world and why it happens. Until we can do this, it will be impossible to produce Deaf people who are capable of holding their heads up in the world and of being responsible for the destiny of their lives and of others around them. And this is what you should be training us for, is it not?

5. PARENTS

The parents of a Deaf child want to rid themselves of their guilty feelings, naturally. But while the oral-only method is the only option given to them, they will never be able to develop their relationship with the child. Tantrums are very rare among Deaf children of Deaf parents, simply because they have natural communication. They are able to explain. They can deal with that oh-so vital question, "Why?"

All parents of a Deaf child should have the right to use total communication so that they can enjoy their child as an equally contributing being. So that they can learn together. At present this rarely happens. You see parents give up and fall into a pattern before the child is seven, and never have the hope of a stimulating relationship. In despair we see them cover up and pretend that their child is progressing well. They don't realise that other parents are also covering up when they say how good their child is. And they feel even worse because of this false comparison. They feel branded as failures. Oral failures, for instance. Parents of a Deaf child have little knowledge of the problems of deafness when they first had their child. Not so surprisingly, they go along with the line that the professionals know best. By giving them an oral-only package, you, with the help of peripatetic teachers and doctors, are depriving these parents of the right to choose. This is a very serious matter.

With total communication, a child can be part of the family. The atmosphere can be relaxing as total communication releases the family's emotional pressure simply by lessening the strain on the mechanics of understanding. As a result of this, you at the schools would have a far better relationship with everybody then.

6. BE A SUCCESS..... BE 'NORMAL'.....

If you have read so far with an open mind, you may ask as do lay people; "Why on earth did we take the path we did?" Quite apart from hearing aids, there are other factors waiting in the wings. "To be oral is to be normal. To be normal is to deny deafness. To deny deafness is to relieve our own guilt and discomfort at having to face up to deafness." "But to understand and comprehend things? Ah, that is a different matter. That goes on (or rather fails to go on) inside a person's head and is not visible to the eye, unlike the nasty sign language."

This is the crux of thinking behind the oral-only approach, if only one would face up to it. The 'normal' syndrome and its brother, the 'success' syndrome, are very closely related, and the path of despair is the one marked out for those who deviate from those two illusory routes. The tension involved in this leads to nothing short of subtle brainwashing, as every parent wants to believe their child is normal. And those who are guardian of Deaf children's lives give the parents enough rope to hang their hopes by reinforcing this.

To make this clear, the NUD is conducting a survey of parents of Deaf children now grown up. Statistical evidence will then be shown that the sorry tale of 'if only we had known' to be far more widespread than ever before. Then, armed with this knowledge and together with the knowledge of Deaf people, those professionals who truly understand the repression and authoritarianism of the last 50 years will be encircled by what we see as the dawning of a new age for Deaf children.

This is purple prose, you may say. But up to now all the arguments of the oral-only factions have been similarly rhetorical. For example, the teachers and the headmasters who talk only of their successes or professionals like Edgar Lowell who say, 'if oralism can work for some, then why not everybody?'

There has been enough overwhelming statistical evidence to prove the case of total communication. Let us see the research from the oral-only side. Let us see them also use thinking that does not ignore psychology, social conditioning and basic living patterns (because with a relaxed and happier relationship through total communication the family is less likely to break up, and deprived families can cope better with their Deaf children).

At present, they are dictated to by the 'Bootstraps' theorists who, because they have a middle class upbringing, can adjust their lives to cope with the oral-only training and use their children as examples of success to boost their egos. When will they, and some of you too, realise that publication of success stories does more harm than good to parents who are struggling with oral-onlyism?

Anyone who has noticed the number of intelligent Deaf people who are lost in the hearing world and do not want anything to do with the Deaf world because they were taught that they were better than the other Deaf or not even Deaf at all, will understand why the Deaf world lacks drive and initiative. The unhappiness caused by being brainwashed into living in no man's land derives from the greatest oral fallacy of them all. That is the concept of the oral environment.

"The world is oral. Everywhere. All the time. So the Deaf child must be oral only because he will not fit any other way." So goes the line of thought. And yet it is exactly the opposite to the truth because a Deaf person understands virtually nothing that takes place in the oral environment, in spite of all his training to speak and to rely totally on lipreading at the expense, as it is generally said, of comprehension.

7. THE NEXT STEP

This is a historical pamphlet. It is the first time that we, the Deaf people, have addressed you directly with a point of view. PLEASE do not think we are against you. To use that pitiful point of reference of many hearing professionals, we welcome you as equals. We welcome your friendship and your willingness to work side by side with us. We should be allies, and in many cases we are. But to those who are not, please remember why we write so strongly. You are not the villains of the piece. You are the victims of subtle brainwashing and a vast subconscious deception that has been deep-rooted in our society ever since the first Deaf man was put into an asylum. Please be brave enough like some of your colleagues to change your views. It does not cost much pride because it is us, the Deaf people, who are telling you this and you can truly say that it is our voice - the voice of the consumer - that has inspired you to understand more fully. You can gain in self-respect by demonstrating that the greatest quality in a human being is having an open mind.

This is, as we have said before, emotional. But this is deliberate because we want you to see not the letter of the law, but the spirit of it. Not the letter of the system, but the spirit that lies therein. Who is better than our humble selves to tell you about the spirit which lies trapped in a system that does not understand because it has not sought the feelings of its recipients? We end here. The rest is in your minds.

Yours Sincerely,

National Union of the Deaf

2nd. Epistle to the Teacher of the Deaf

NDCS Conference: London February 1977. Paddy Ladd.

WHAT WENT WRONG?

We Deaf people see four basic answers to this question. The first is mirrored in the subject of this conference. We hear the over-emphasis on speech at the expense of all other vital ingredients of education. This includes language, psychological development, internal motivation, and real self-knowledge, confidence and identity.

To devote so much concern to speech above the factors above is pandering to the 'White Nigger' syndrome, which tries to pretend that Deaf children are not really Deaf and that, if they learn to speak, they will be able to integrate and live happily ever after. This is pure fallacy. There is little ground for believing that Deaf speech aids integration and, as the result of withholding manual visual cuing, all you have achieved is unintelligible speech for the vast majority of profoundly Deaf children. On these grounds alone, your philosophies are clearly misguided. If you do not believe us mere Deaf people, go to Dr Conrad's research studies as reported at Harrogate 1976. And so, if you give speech training its rightful place in a total communication system, you won't need another conference like this - that's for sure.

We want to put total communication aside for the present. Our case clearly stands in our first Letter to the Teachers, which is still available to you. Let us look at the second cause of our children's dismal failure. Deafness is a handicap of communication like no other handicap. But communication is a two-way process and you have never attempted a two-way remedy for this problem at hand. You have never listened to the voice of the consumer. You have never tried to see the education of Deaf children as a process in which you too can be educated, both by Deaf adults and Deaf children. You prefer to treat them as guinea pigs; imposing your theories on them and making them conform to the strait-jacket of your own narrow idea of what a Deaf adult is. Why not seek help in understanding the child from those who do know, in seeing things through the eyes of a Deaf child who is now old enough to tell you 'what went wrong'?

Why not indeed? But instead you prefer to give profoundly Deaf kids a method of education that makes it impossible to discuss things in the classroom, to ask questions, to contribute their half-formed ideas and to learn from each other. You give them a method that cannot meet their needs when visiting places of interest, going on holiday projects or discussing complex subjects like sex education or even most secondary school subjects. Come to that, you cannot give them language that involves sport or hobbies where they would have been keen to acquire more vocabulary. You separate them from Deaf adults, deny any connexion between them and are actually afraid of meeting Deaf adults on non-authoritarian terms. You therefore deny the kids the kind of self-image or identity, leaving them without any place to stand in the world they have to understand and live in for the rest of their lives. Small wonder that self-respect is a rare quality in the Deaf world.

What is the response of your kids? They either are cut off from all adult models of advice and band together more strongly in the identity hacked out from within their peer group, or they do, numbly and blindly, all that you impose on them, with the result that, when they leave school, they have no positive thoughts or feelings of their own. In the case of the first response they will say, "I can't do it. I am Deaf. You can. Alright for you. You're hearing." And what can you say to that? You are caught in the same trap as any well-meaning white teacher in an immigrant area. But their reaction is not only to you but to all hearing adults who speak without using their hands. So follows a period of extreme reaction at a crucial age for listening to what the world is doing. In short, you do not only put them off the very thought of further education but you leave in them the seeds of a resentment that other people will have to deal with. In the case of the second response, we end up with the dummification process where you have produced a passive human being, capable only of parroting whatever his elders say with question. There's another name for this kind of thing but we'll leave it to you to work it out for yourselves.

There is no way these insecure kids are going to integrate without the basic confidence of a self-identity. So instead they band together in hostility against the hearing world. Thus your oral method achieves the very thing it seeks to prevent. How can you have missed this? The answer is you are no longer interested in them after school.

Time and again we have seen a complete lack of understanding of basic psychology like this in Deaf schools and units. Motivation for learning and growing in a way apart from exam-thinking is unheard of. This is simply because you see these kids as in a vacuum. For example, imagine you were a blue kid who never saw a blue adult. You would soon conclude you would either die or turn white when you were sixteen. And as long as Manchester, Malet Street and Oxford continue to brainwash you into keeping these Deaf kids in a vacuum, we will always be born to fail. We Deaf people cannot but be angry about this, because we know what is wrong but our opinions are ignored - a truly silent minority. Of course, deafness is not the only subculture with this problem. But we have been dependent on hearing people to speak and act for us, with the result that we have not fought to be heard as have all the major subcultures over the last ten years - for examples consider women, black people, homosexuals. Thus the changes in the world are passing us by and our lives are lived in pre-war mentality of 'haves' and 'have-nots'.

Deaf children need the motivation of example that can only come from having Deaf adults working and helping in their schools and homes. This applies to partials as well as the profoundly Deaf kids. They need their heroes - their Kevin Keegans, their Gary Glitters, their John Cravens at least as much as hearing kids, if not more.

This brings us to integration, that basis of oral-onlyism. Like the officers of the Light Brigade, you blithely base your theories on a path you have never reconnoitred yourselves. The equation that 'speech = integration' is only partly true for the partials and a fallacy for profoundly Deaf children. Integration means saying as I do now, "I am not normal. I am Deaf. I am different from you in the way that a Cockney is different from a Geordie. And I can mix with you as these two groups mix with each other - if you meet me halfway." Halfway is not through speech alone as any hearing child or adult knows when they meet a Deaf child or adult for the first time. They are nervous. They need a straw to grasp in order to relax, for you cannot communicate unless you are relaxed. And that straw must be the tangible one of manual cues supplementing the oral and aural approach. Between all our members we have run many integration projects. And we achieve lasting friendship from just that base.

Now Deaf people are keen to develop their voices as much as possible. Ask any in the audience today. They know that speech, like all learning, can develop best through the catalyst of motivation. And that can only come from the maximum communication and from models to identify with. Research alone shows you that it is time to put your 'flat earth' theory to rest. Signing and the presence of Deaf people do not affect speech. If anything, they improve it.

Do you want me to tell you what lipreading on its own is really like? I am only partially Deaf; i.e. I have a decibel loss of 80-120db. I have been to college studying English Language, and now a higher degree, and have integrated in varying degrees of pleasures and pain on a very wide scale. And I have no faith in lipreading on its own. One of the most important days of my life came when I realised I had been brainwashed into denying my own deafness, and that I needed visual clues of sign language. You also have been brainwashed. You are not to blame. But now that you have heard Deaf people telling you how you can improve the lives of Deaf kids, and get more out of teaching as well, you will certainly be culpable if you do not follow up what we have been saying. Think of all the damage that have been wreaked on innocent parents, as well as Deaf people. I have an almost impossible task in trying to join in with society. Cinema, television, theatre, pubs, groups - you name it and we can't relax in it. Except one thing, and that is books. I am lucky enough to be able to read and seek no pity. But just think how angry I feel when I see that so many of my friends are unable to even enjoy that only recourse.....

Let me give you some information from this second area of failure. Why not look more closely at lipreading? Dr Conrad's survey shows that hearing school-leavers can lipread just as well/badly as any Deaf school-leaver who spent his last twelve years at school supposedly relying on just that. As Harold Wilson would have said, that makes thirteen wasted years. What do you think? Another example I'd like you to consider very carefully is this business of hearing aids. As you can see, I am wearing mine like a good little boy. In the left ear that is. I do not wear one in my right ear, though it has the same decibel loss. Would you like to know why? The sound in the left ear is bassy and mellow but the sound in the right ear is like a telephone conversation across the Atlantic with Gale Force Ten blowing. It is harsh; it snaps and crackles, it is unable to pick up the spoken voice and it gives me a bloody headache after five minutes.

Yet on your audiograms this does not show up. Both ears are the same, quantity-wise. The difference lies in sound quality. If one hears reasonably melodic sound it is understandable that it will be used. As you know, that is where the private aids score over the Medresco. But if one ear is simply translating what goes into it like a cheap Woolworth's transistor radio type of sound magnified to 100 decibels, do you wonder that I don't wear it? The doctors would not believe me as a kid. Fair enough. But when they don't believe me now, what am I to surmise? That I am mad, or stupid? That I imagine all this? And so I bring to your attention the fact that many of your Deaf kids complain about hearing aids to us. They use two words from a limited vocabulary. "Hurts" and "Too loud". And I put it to you that if you listen to Deaf adults on this, you might actually find out more about how to use hearing aids better on your Deaf kids. You might also find that few Deaf kids pick up meaningful sound below 100db, and possibly this figure could be moved up as far as 85db.

Let us leave this subject of what Deaf people can teach you and get onto the third answer to the question of what has gone wrong. It is the question of class interests. Deafness is no respecter of people's income brackets. It strikes right across society. After a few years of Deaf education, a pattern begins to emerge. Middle-class interests begin to take over. Perhaps the best example of this is what Weber called the "Protestant Ethic"; namely that a puritanical belief in hard graft and success, together with an unquestioning acceptance of authority, is seen to be the only way of working. This happened in the hearing system too. But there emerged a liberal and humanist pattern of thought that was concerned about the number of failures being produced. In the Deaf education system, this has never happened simply because the only terms of reference have been those of the 'experts', to whom you give your unquestioning allegiance. Parents of Deaf kids do the same. They surrender their kids to you and do not question any lack of progress because you, the experts, say you know best. This could not happen in a hearing school. People are all the time comparing notes on different schools, deciding which are good and which are bad; this is easy since they all had a hearing education and they all live close enough together to compare notes automatically. You are almost free of this responsibility to produce results. Peripatetic teachers, for example, are allowed to work without any form of supervision as to how well they are working. That system does not produce progress because progress only comes through honest criticism.

Three examples come to mind. The first is the unceasing admonition, "Talk, talk, talk to your child and he will respond one day." Those ordinary parents whose child does not progress through this Protestant Ethic are made to feel guilty. That is their fault. They have not worked hard enough. So full of remorse, they give up trying to make an impression on you on your official sherry-sipping occasions and sink into apathy. Which you then blame them for.....

Another example is the existence of Mary Hare Grammar School. This conforms to the middle class success pattern, being the equivalent of Oxbridge for certain types of parents. There the best partials are creamed off for certificate training. Many of these should not be at a Deaf school at all. They should be in local units. The number of profoundly Deaf kids at this school is very small compared with the number who are intelligent enough but whose speech is deemed not good enough. While such a school exists, other schools will be content to play second fiddle instead of raising their sights higher to offer decent secondary programmes. Another result of having such a school is that it drives a wedge through the Deaf world. Instead of coming back and offering their talents to the Deaf world, many ex-pupils from Mary Hare become conceited and decide that they should have nothing to do with the Deaf. Contrast this with Gallaudet College which is the major factor in creating a genuinely progressive American Deaf society and you'll see what I mean.

The third example concerns the fee-paying schools, a middle class tradition that is far stronger in Deaf education than elsewhere. Work it out on a percentage basis if you're not sure. What happens here is that the creaming-off process continues to impose a conformist strait-jacket by saying, "Our method works. See....." This way, you carefully ignore the large numbers of Deaf children who are not progressing in other non fee-paying schools. And the success-ethic being what it is, the educationalists prefer to look at the success rather than to study the percentage of failures. There will always be successes is what we say. You should concern yourselves not with showing off kids who fit your theories but with finding different solutions for those who don't fit them.

If you want to put all this right, listen to Deaf adults and to parents of Deaf children, especially those who don't progress. We will give you one more example of middle class thinking. Reliance on lipreading alone has more chance of limited success if the speaker has a nice clear voice and is easy to follow. Now, what is the prime example of this? Yes, that's right. BBC English. But what happens if the parents of the Deaf child are Geordies, Scottish, Irish, immigrant or just ordinary folks who don't speak proper? The fact that you have never considered this shows you now the danger of your bias. I am not slamming the middle class. I am asking you simply to balance one class of teaching and thinking with the rest of the picture.

Here is the fourth answer to the title question. You may have gathered by now that total communication, plus class-free thinking, plus giving a role to Deaf adults and more attention to parents, adds up to nothing so much as a change of heart rather than a change of method. You may also now remember how well Deaf kids with Deaf parents usually fare. And we hope by now you realise that part of the problem is that you work in isolation from each other. Teachers versus social workers versus Deaf people versus parents. We must all be on the same side for once if progress is to be made. That way you get the extra manpower that you need to undertake a more ambitious educational system, as well as the tremendous psychological shot in the arm that co-operation does bring. Ask any Deaf school that has changed over about the complete transformation in their teaching experience. They will tell you that for the first time they welcomed in Deaf people as human beings, let them work with them, learnt from them, understood the true concept of deafness and began to enjoy, yes enjoy, their work as never before. (The Protestant Ethic, incidentally, has no place for enjoyment .....)

Imagine teachers, parents, Deaf adults, social workers, hearing brothers and sisters, Deaf children, hearing children of Deaf adults, even aunts, uncles and grandparents, all under the same roof, learning to work together, understanding what this thing called deafness is all about and learning the language of Deaf people. To which you add your teaching skills, linguists add their language teaching skills, speech therapists and their speech training skills form a basis of total communication. This is the spirit of education - not the dead letter of the law that rubs off on children and teachers alike.

This is the spirit that at present lies trapped in the vacuum of a system that 'goes wrong' because it has never sought the views of those people that it processes. This is the spirit that we Deaf people will teach you about. It is available to you now ...... unless it is you who are really Deaf to this plea......

3rd. Epistle to the Teacher of the Deaf

BATOD Conference, Southern Region: London October 1978.
Paddy Ladd.

Good afternoon! Since I have been given a free hand this afternoon, I must leave out two particular areas of family problems which are covered by other speakers; namely immigrant families and Deaf families. There is enough to cover as it is!

First of all, I must pick up on the whole concept of problem families. I feel that this kind of labelling is already used to the extent of being unable to see the people involved as people. We Deaf people get enough of that ourselves. We all use labelling in life but over the last few years we have realised that some kind of labelling seriously restricts human potential. I heard an example the other day when a child, who had been at school for only one day, was already being labelled as a troublemaker. But the way this term is used actually provides me with a good way into the subject of how we must improve our services to families with Deaf children. For our particular sphere of work is one that is so closeted from the real world that we persist in thinking habits which were discarded as illiberal by mainstream society several years ago. And a good example of this is our philosophy of stereotyping and labelling. In persisting with these habits we deny the possibilities for reform that will bring about genuinely qualitative improvements in the lives of families with Deaf children.

Several examples come to mind. The 'Protestant Ethic', as Weber called it, is one of these and works thus:- we approach these families and say that 'You must work very hard with your child, pushing him all the time to achieve and if you don't, the failure of your child will be your fault'. Now, how many Deaf children grow up to be what society considers 'normal'? And how many parents does that make, who feel thus guilty without cause? In my time as a social worker, for example, several parents approached me about behavioural problems of their child - too loud, too aggressive, too withdrawn, too silent. In nearly every case there was an underlying feeling of being a failure because their child was not behaving and speaking 'normally'. This feeling has paralysed them from action, rather like that of religious guilt, in that they could not do anything to improve the situation because they feel their failure was too severe. No matter how hard I tried, it was too late in the day to remove this 'blame fixation'. This is of course the natural outcome of the 'Protestant Ethic', the pull-yourself-up-by-your-own- bootlaces method.

The role of happiness or of being able to enjoy your child are out of place here as in any Wesleyan chapel. This is a middle class method for social workers, teachers and parents with a lot of confidence. It should not be unthinkingly forced onto working class or petty-bourgeois families whose self-confidence level is low. Come to that, it should not be forced onto any parent whose confidence is low after the trauma of giving birth to a Deaf child.

Parents know nothing about deafness; they entrust their child to the professionals' advice and rarely question it until it is too late to solve the problem as it arises. This is acerbated by the 'Normality Neurosis' where parents are encouraged to see normality in terms of speech. Whenever family behavioural problems arise whether at home or at school, the solutions are sought through these kind of lens. One girl I knew, whose speech had been force-fed to a good level and who is very bright, posed great problems for her mother - including violent tantrums even at the age of 14 years. The solutions were sought through Valium, Mogadon, faith-healing of her deafness and, on the school's side, the problem was seen as wilfulness, spoilt behaviour, need for discipline, etc. None of the solutions attempted to examine the subject from the child's or the parents' point of view to locate reasons for this behaviour pattern. One doctor went as far as to attribute it to the full moon - not very comforting advice when we were standing in a youth hostel in mid-Wales, with the nearest psychiatric hospital in Wrexham!

All of these solutions are the results of stereotyped attitudes and of placing client motivation factors well down the list in importance. I could multiply this example endless times, but one more will suffice.

Parents of a teenage Deaf child whose speech was very poor and whose behaviour was immature even by Deaf children's standards, met me one evening at the youth club and exclaimed with a mixture of excitement and despair that they had just heard of a new method for improving the child's speech through the 'handkerchief rhythm' method, known to you as used by what we call the Manchester Hit Squad. They were convinced this would solve the behaviour problems which they linked with the need for speech improvement. This example shows the lengths to which families go to clutch at straws equating the normality of behaviour and normality of speech. It is to our shame that we not only allow these illusions to grow, but actually encourage this way of thinking. When the child leaves school, the family are left with no supportive value system to tide them through what often becomes the most difficult period of Deaf family life, because no one will take responsibility for examining, stating and providing solutions for the family problems of Deaf adolescents. You leave school and that's it; you're on your own.

At this stage a social worker may be assigned to the family or, rather, to the child. For all of you who feel I am being too critical of teachers of the Deaf, let me say a few words about social work services. After all, one would expect from such people a client-centred response. As a social worker and Deaf person myself, I was appalled at the low standard of work aimed for and achieved by my colleagues. If it was not (a) the patronising and authoritarian attitude of the missioner/welfare officer or (b) inexperienced local authority social worker, unable to communicate with the child and without an understanding of basic behavioural problems of deafness, it was (c) the inability to understand or to relate to the problems of the family of the Deaf child - though in the last three years there has been some improvements.

Add to all this the usual refusal of education departments to allow the social worker to have any contact with the Deaf child of school age and you have virtually the absence of any kind of supportive system for the family and child. It is true that some teachers feel that they can solve family problems themselves with some degree of success. But it is not something that should be left for the teacher to shoulder alone - a comprehensive net must be laid with the right kind of supportive skills. A teacher is not a social worker any more than a social worker is a teacher. (We are not through the Dark Ages yet; I was banned from my local Deaf school on unsubstantiated and unspecified charges of subversion, and never regained that confidence until I was made a governor of one Deaf school and given a free hand to help in another.)

Let us carry this critique one stage further. Audiologists and otologists are among those who reject social work help and influence the parents against it. Yet their knowledge of behaviour in the field is very limited indeed. Educational psychologists are often ignorant of the special characteristics of Deaf child behaviour and how they should be handled.

One example concerns a child who was desperately lonely and unhappy at her school and at home, and the only solution left to us was a transfer to a residential school where she had more peer group contact and was allowed to use signs as a means of expression. This child had exceptional gifts in visual expression which were clamped down on. At our meeting, the educational psychologist refused to countenance this transfer. Her reasons were that she would not want any child of hers to go away to school. Explaining that this was not the point, I gave background information that this cause of action was the last hope and not our normal practice. Still refusal. Later we pushed hard and long for this transfer and won it. The child is now much more socially mature and happier and her school work has consequently shot up. But I was reported by the educational psychologist for 'pressuring parents to take their Deaf children out of the local Deaf school' and in general, interfering. The result was a top level meeting which was more like a court and in which I needed the support of my Assistant Director to see the matter cleared up with no blame attached to anyone bar the head of the school. I was never clear how he ended up the scapegoat; I suppose not being at the meeting was as good a reason as any! But how many professional workers should have to go through all this just to make sure a family's problems do not slip through the net? I can think of a couple of brave social workers but not many.

The other problem area is with the allocation of the family from the child's age of 0 - 4 years solely to the peripatetic teacher. Now the most basic of child psychology stresses the importance of these years of development. And another equally basic psychology stresses the importance of considering the effect of the birth of this child on the family. We virtually ignore these maxims and I'd like to give you an example of how those early days can affect parents. My father's first visit to the Nuffield Centre with me is completely forgotten on my side. But the other day my father described the room I was first shown into with exact detail; the toys here, the books there, the equipment in that corner and the hammer and pegs just so. Knowing that his memory is not usually good, we were able to conclude that what he had seen had stayed with him as if he were a man on a gallows having his last sight of the world before the hood went on. Is it any wonder then that the family reaches out to the first firm voice that turns up with an ideology? In comes the peripatetic teacher, untrained in those areas and often unaware of their importance. She is there to 'teach speech', full stop. But in the absence of other help, the parents pin their hopes on all the things mapped out by teacher and hospital, which are based around speech - not child development.

The peripatetic teacher who sees this is in a most unenviable position of being unable to help, which may be why so many don't see those needs - a subconscious blind eye? After all, the tools of their trade are inflexible compared with the range of children they will meet, from the partial who will survive in a hearing school to the additionally handicapped profoundly Deaf child with behavioural problems.

In the face of all this, the few social workers who do work with school-age kids are in a dilemma. Should they advise on school placement matters? Should they tell parents what is really wrong in a home where the child behaves badly out of frustration at being unable to lipread home conversations, and being lonely and cut off? Should they point out that the parents and child may need to sign, running the risks of disillusioning the parents who have avoided thinking about what will happen if their child's speech and writing ability don't improve by the method they have pledged their faith to? It is a difficult decision and one that I usually back out of, I am ashamed to say, using the rationale that the parents would see it for themselves sooner or later. I found on the whole that once parents did realise that the kid would leave school with little improvement on the model they currently had, then they began to question all the assumptions they made. But this was usually in the last year or penultimate year and by then too late to provide workable solutions. So when we talk of using social workers, we must think how we are going to face up to these questions at the same time.

Grim, eh? Worse to come though! We tend to think of the family with problems as the one where the child's behaviour is disruptive or aggressive. But personally I find this a much smaller problem - it usually means that the child is intelligent enough to want a better deal, a response more appropriate to his needs, however naively he or she acts this out in their subconscious. There is for example the syndrome of the bright profoundly Deaf child who gets kicked out of Mary Hare!!

No, the real problem kids are those where the kids are docile and sit in the corner, eat when told, go to bed when told and are astonished and apathetic when you ask their opinions on things or when you try to discover if they have any interests. These kids are often 'good' at school for reason similar - they don't play up. But if you want to bring them out to be human beings, taking part in the world, you have a stiff task ahead, for they have no go in them - or else it is deeply suppressed that you have to virtually excite them to rebellion before they will even ask permission to come to the youth club, or take the dog for a walk on their own, even at age 15 or so. One such kid - no problem to his school or parents - was required to stay in all day every day during the holidays, including the seven week holiday break. What chance does he have of becoming a participating adult taking responsibilities? In these kind of cases, it is harder to solve the problem because the parents are usually severely authoritarian and occasionally neurotically so, and they freeze the social worker out if his view will not totally adapt to theirs. I feel it could have been a different story if counselling had been adopted earlier - I was often greeted with remarks like - "Where were you five, ten or fifteen years ago when I needed you?" or "If I knew then what I know now", etc.

My conclusion from this is that all Deaf kids and their families have problems of some kind, usually in inverse order to the degree to which they are recognised to have one. So.... there's nothing wrong with having problems. Everyone is handicapped in one way or another. It's a question of facing and tackling them and especially getting rid of the guilt syndrome.

Having talked about stereotyping and the two-tier syndrome, there are a couple of other things before I attempt to suggest some solutions. The absence of debate, publications, discussions, seminars, papers and professional training on almost all of the really important issues in Families with Problems. Nothing can be found in "Teacher of the Deaf". Nothing comes from the National Council of Social Workers with the Deaf. The subjects are beneath mentioning at the National Deaf Children's Society's meetings, in "Talk" and in PTA meetings, except for desperate outbursts. I remember one such meeting where the parents of a child poured out their worries to the panel. They were derided, and chided, scorned and rebuked by the audience for having caused these problems. No one suggested solutions or owned up to the commonness of such problems amongst their own kids. Who among those 70 people would dare to be honest again?

So here, in an attempt to get these other subjects into the light of debating day, may I present you another half dozen themes:-

(1) TEMPER TANTRUMS.

What a cruelly pejorative label for the child demanding to make sense of his environment! This one caused more problems from ages 0 - 20 years than any other, and yet no one investigates why they come about despite the fact that they involve window smashing, pushing people downstairs and hurling oneself bodily around rooms, etc. I won't say what I think is an answer but will give you a clue. Why do Deaf children of Deaf parents not have this problem to anywhere near the same degree?

(2) SEX/PUBERTY.

Dirty words in Deaf schools still, despite the introduction of these areas to the curriculum of hearing schools. Not only is there no debate on this, but the problems it causes in a child's school life are often ignored.

(3) MARRIAGE BREAKUPS.

Has anyone done a survey of the implications of the high incidence of this in Deaf children's families? Or attempted solutions? We found that over half the kids on our club and camp came into this category.

(4) ADOLESCENT MISBEHAVIOUR.

Aggression/obsession/withdrawal/crime, etc. How much thought has gone into the factors involved in the teenage years of the Deaf child, and the needs that are being expressed in a misguided way? This includes social and personal maturity. Could it just be connected with the way we treat the Deaf child as a permanent baby, that we are afraid to realise that they have views of their own about their lives and may be strong enough to express their disapproval of the things that happen to them? Consider the people who are behind the oral-only thinking. Do we not find that most of them specialise in working with primary and junior children who cannot answer back against their authoritarian methods? Would most of them dare to implement their views in a Deaf secondary school?

(5) HOME COMMUNICATION.

This was the second most common problem that I found - that the lives of the family with a Deaf child are related on such a primitive level that it was more like having a pet in the house, an enfant sauvage, than having a human being who took part in what happened around him. This seemed to be the base for a whole load of offshoot problems.

(6) HEARING AID USE.

How many parents and children know how to use them beyond the coercion level? How can we know ourselves if we do not ask those who wear them to explain problems of pain threshold, sound quality that is poor but does not show up on the audiogram as such, etc., etc.? How many parents have ever heard a tape of what speech sounds like to their child to help them understand?

Well, enough of this. I hope the point is taken that we do not know enough about the clients' needs as distinguished from what we think he or she or they need. And now for solutions?

(1) All schools should have a counsellor whose job it is to draw out from the kids the problems they are facing and give them means by which to solve them. This person, I feel, should be a Deaf person because the kids will respond to one like themselves more readily. There are many examples of the Deaf parents who visit schools being surrounded by kids firing away questions at them. No matter how many times they visit the school, this situation continues. I have frequently heard Deaf kids express envy of the Deaf child with Deaf parents; and it is rather moving. This new angle into education should be welcomed, not feared by teachers. After all, can we deny that the black teacher has a much better chance of relating to the black kids than we whites do? This person will be in a good position to give that vital neglected area of Deaf education of moral guidance, motivation

to do well, social maturity, etc., that many of us consider one of the most basic educational functions of all. They will be able to give the rest of the staff much more help and information about the kids, and insights into the way they think and live Deaf lives. They will be able to help break in the new teacher to the school. In fact, the role of such a counsellor offers scope for re-thinking the whole concept of a teacher of the Deaf, and could thus be the pivotal point of changing for the future.

If there are doubts as to whether as to such a person would be needed full time, rest assured. He or she could take up the idea of a youth club and youth and teenage activities outside the school involving all the other Deaf children in that authority's responsibility.

Now, when we say that this person must be Deaf, I mean fairly severely or profoundly, at least able to fully understand the kid's communications between themselves. Such a person can cross over to work with partials much more easily than a partial or oral-only Deaf person who tries to counsel the Deaf kids who are suspicious of you if you can even talk somewhere near normally. They won't buy it because they know that such a person has spiritually disowned them by not being able to speak their language. They know who is on whose side.

Here I must add a parenthesis on this aspect. I don't know if you are aware that resolutions 3 and 6 of the Association Policy will, if passed, in your half-hour national AGM, close the door to the former class of Deaf person and let in only the latter. If passed, they would close the doors to me becoming a teacher of the Deaf, for example, or Clive here. This would be fatal because you would end up claiming you have Deaf teachers of the Deaf when all of you have are a few Uncle Toms eating out of your hands and failing to get through to the kids in the way expected of the counsellor. Don't let these motions get through!

(2) The need for well trained social workers to be used by schools and education departments as family social workers to approach and tackle all the problems that I mentioned earlier, to name but a few. There should be an overlap with youth and children's club running in order to take attention away from your visit as being connected with a family problem - light relief to gain trust.

Deaf social workers are useful in answering questions relating to what the child is doing or experiencing, giving the parents first hand stuff. But there is a disadvantage in that it prevents the parents from letting out their anger and frustration at having a Deaf child to the Deaf social worker. The easy solution is to have two social workers under a SSW, one Deaf and one hearing who are juggled by the SSW to fit the families' needs in each case. This numerical statistic I would base on areas of 250,000 hearing people. As I said earlier, it is absolutely vital that the social worker be much more informal than the teacher and have lived in the world a bit. I think it would be a great mistake if the social worker is based at the school, for parents then see the social worker as the long arm of the school, like a probation officer; they should be based instead at Social Services Departments.

(3) A greater involvement of Deaf people and parents in the child's education. Remember that the partially Deaf child also need adult models and counselling, especially if they are alone in a hearing school.

(4) An awareness of teachers and teacher training courses that all these ideas and principles should be understood as part of the training qualifications.

(5) What you haven't guessed about the importance of total communication in all this is not worth pointing out!!

PART THREE

Persuading the World

Preface

After the publication of *'NUD 1976'* which explained why a new organisation had to be set up by examining critically each organisation for the Deaf, the NUD was deluged with vitriolic opposition. As a fledgling that had not yet learned to fly, it was very heartened by the support it found among courageous individuals and organisations. Chief among these was the Scottish Workshop with the Deaf; in particular George Montogomery, John Hay and Murray Holmes. The two organisations exchanged publications, letters of support and invitations to speak at each other's meetings. The following paper is one example of this. Reading it now, we are surprised to find how far-seeing some of the proposals and comments were. History is a funny business. Often we feel that one idea or another is new and burning in our veins. Yet when we look back, we find we have had the idea for longer than we were aware of. It almost seems that we are not totally aware of the full implications of what we suggesting, even when we think we are!

Occasional Paper No.1.

Scottish Workshop with the Deaf, Glasgow. September 1977.
Paddy Ladd.

So here we are in 1977, with the BDA Congress at Eastbourne and the Deaf World Games now in the past. For minority groups, it has been a year of setbacks. Mary Whitehouse and Sir James Goldsmith won court cases against "Gay News" and "Private Eye". The black community suffered a loss in credibility at Notting Hill. Women have seen the Equal Pay Act openly flaunted and the trade union movement is failing to make headway against George Ward. Here, perhaps, you feel that the SNP is not making the progress you hoped for, though you will be going to Argentina for the World Cup......

But the Deaf world still stands, as always, with both feet stuck in concrete, looking over the fence of recognition. True, with the coming of the SWD (Scottish Workshop with the Deaf) and the NUD, plus the advances in total communication and teletext, the future looks rosier. But all we really are doing is to loosen the concrete around our feet so that we stomp around with blocks of cement around our ankles like a ball and chain - still unable to climb the fence.

For the average Deaf person, 1977 has been just another year, with a BDA Congress blowing fanfares to its hierarchy and showering praises on daring initiatives taken in countries safely far from here. Though the "Soundbarrier" conference with the Prime Minister's presence brought deafness briefly to the public eye, it did not bring Deaf people to the public eye. No, indeed. The same cliches of paternalism came forth while the average Deaf person continued to bemoan his lot. We all know, I hope, that this is so. Maybe we even know why this is so. But what people may not be clear about is why the blind and the disabled have broken free from paternalism enough to form their own organisations when Deaf people have not.

It seems to me that the weight of paternalism must be thrown off or ignored and allowed to wither. It clearly will not get off the backs of the Deaf unless it has another to ride on. This is where the blind and the disabled go in first. They could hear and thus be aware of the changes in the world, even if they could do no more than observe them. They could speak, thus making their dissent known loud and clear. We Deaf people, unable to do either and often unable to read through this same authoritarianism, are easy prey for those who want to have a comfortable ride through life. So are the mentally handicapped. But there is one important difference there which we'll come to later.

Paternalism may be on the wane but it is still doing pretty well for itself. We live in a supposed democracy in the UK hearing world. But in the Deaf world? In the world of BATOD, RNID, BDA, NDCS, NCSWD? If you try to make constructive across the board criticisms, you bring down the wrath of the great god Paranoia himself. It is virtually impossible to get a word in any of the Deaf periodicals that is really controversial or relevant in order to initiate a rational public debate without emotional invective that shatters light bulbs in its shrillness, leaving all of us in the dark. It can even be said that this Deaf world, including professionals and organisations, subscribes to the "Mushroom Theory" which is that we're all kept in the dark and fed a load of bullshit. If this is democracy, give me an honest dictatorship any day......

The only alternative is a kind of separatism; to break away and start afresh. But there are immense problems in doing this and we in the NUD have run into these as we knew we would. If we want to consider the status of Deaf people and really come up with an answer, let us examine these. There are at least eight of them.

1. FAMILY LIFE

The oral system prevents Deaf children from understanding or participating in any family decision-making. This leaves a Deaf person often socially immature in the context of doing things for themselves and in expecting that they have any role to play in life's affairs.

2. SCHOOL LIFE

The same problem again. No attempt is made to teach about life, about decision-making individually and collectively. This fosters the expectation of receiving things from heaven without the self-respect necessary to resist this negative philosophy. The kind of work Peter Llewelyn Jones was attempting at the BDA with school-leaving groups in terms of collective decision making for kids is a marvellous exception.

3. ORAL STIGMA

The oral system produces a vast area of waste product but none more frustrating than its 'successes'. These people, who could have been of a great use to the Deaf community, are often obsessed with the oralist attitude to integration to the extent that they deny they are Deaf and pretend that they don't sign in public - or even in private. Clinging to the coat-tails of the hearing world is a sad way to go for aspiring middle class Deaf. There's not much happiness in being false to yourself and I contend that many of these people are really unhappy in their lives. Some of the better ones can be found in Breakthrough but they are still lost to the Deaf club community because Breakthrough Trust, for all its great pioneering work, is not aimed at the public issues concerning the present generations of adult Deaf. Much of this, of course, is tied up with the class system. But we Deaf cannot afford the same number of snobs as the hearing world has. Our numbers are too small for this to leave us unscarred.

4. AGE PROBLEM

Age is very relevant because the few Deaf people in England in positions of influence are older and much more conservative than the young and are happier to accept paternalism. The Deaf young are severely handicapped by oralism and cannot give organised vent to their spleen, whereas over the last 15 years the hearing young have changed the whole western world as we know it!

5. SOCIAL PROBLEM

Any Deaf person who survives 1 - 4 above and wishes to lead the way for his fellows has to face the problem of living in such a tight knit community. It is easy to backbite and cut him down to size by recalling things from his schooldays and youth that can be used to embarrass him publicly. Many potential Deaf leaders are thus frightened off......

6. CONFIDENCE AND SELF-RESPECT

This, the biggest problem of all caused by 1 - 3 above, involves a task of overwhelming enormity. Without self-respect a Deaf person cannot break out of the helplessness caused by feeling inferior and stupid, a process reinforced every day quite unintentionally by the world. Perhaps the psychologists here would like to consider this point.

7. THE BRAINS GONE WRONG....

1 - 6 covers a sadly large percentage of the UK Deaf population. One particular remaining group is left. These are the individualists. They are highly talented Deaf, even brilliant. But they function largely as self educated, self-made people who think that success lies in following their individual recipes, right down to the last quirk of their character. They have so much to offer. But it is offered in such an individualistic way that it makes them hell to work with because they have little faith in collective education through action. Perhaps this is because they have a low estimation of human nature. Lonely in their intellectual superiority within both the Deaf and hearing worlds, they find it easy to see others as foolish, heartless and ignorant. To ask them to take the leap of faith into the philosophy that people are basically good and not intrinsically stupid is to wish for the moon. They are usually right-wing independents who can dazzle Deaf fellows, but not inspire them with emotional warmth for real action.

8. HEARING PEOPLE

Hearing people, as allies who generally believe that Deaf people should stand on their own feet, are not as common as we should wish for. This can only be cause for regret since we need their help to start off with. It is partly because deafness is an unfashionable handicap which thereby does not attract the dynamic young people of the last ten years, who can be seen in droves applying to work in mental hospitals and so forth. They are also few because they see the appalling reactionary nature of the Deaf world and its organisations. How many do you know with the talent who have got out through sheer frustration at having their ideas stamped on? We cannot afford to lose them for the only ones who gain from this are the 'Old Guard'.

So what solutions can we offer today? I will list eight and hope you can throw in some more.

1. THE NUD

I am obviously biased here but I believe that the NUD, or any political organisation run by Deaf people, will be the biggest shot in the arm. Whether this happens depends on the quality of Deaf people that come forward to help. Our feet are still in concrete, remember!

2. DEAF SCHOOL

A complete sweeping change of approach here is the only answer so that the whole issue becomes consumer-based. Total communication will never be enough, though it will get rid of the feeling of being Snoopy and having to chase after the stick of decent education when all the time it is there in Charlie Brown's hand. Good Deaf professionals, music therapy, real drama work, collective decision-making, the giving of responsibility to Deaf children and integration on the Deaf kids' base of security are the other changes that must come too.

3. THE MEDIA

Regular television programmes for the Deaf by the Deaf are crucial. So are sub-titles. And so is a national Deaf newspaper which covers the professionals as well and which is not afraid to be controversial.

4. TELETYPEWRITERS (TTYs)

Deaf people cannot organise themselves without Deaf telephones as you can see if you imagine a hearing world without the phone. The callousness of a Government that sits back and lets Finedon* go bust, making vague promises of something in ten years' time, would not be tolerated in a more enlightened world.

5. INTERPRETERS

Until we have a large number of full-time paid interpreters, we will still be like the blind man without his white stick. The dignity of an interpreter is something that would put oralism in its place quickly and would allow Deaf people to join in public affairs as well as being able to give 'talks' to the outside world through reverse interpreters. We in the NUD have found the strain in having government meetings without interpreters as well as having few Deaf phones to link us nationally.

6. DEAF CULTURE

1 - 5 are fairly obvious. But this is not; for the need to build up one's culture is quite crucial for the self-respect and the respect gained from others. Sign language, for example, needs to be properly publicised. Far more hearing people need to learn it and indeed want to. Books, research and articles on sign language are vital. We need more new signs. We need sign books, nationally and locally, preserving the dialects. We need books on the history of Deaf people and those who work for them, with open discussion on what really happened this year, last year and forty years ago. We need more drama, sponsored sign-ins, T-shirts,

* Finedon Communications Ltd.

badges, etc. Anything that is Deaf needs to be written, published, filmed and preserved. Think Deaf. Become first class Deaf citizens, not second class hearing citizens.

7. THE LEAP OF FAITH.

Hearing people in the Deaf world should face up to their real role too. Think in terms of a Deaf millenium and how you can best help Deaf people onto the path of self-help. This means you must have a real belief in the Deaf and be able to see the Deaf world as a culture that is moving towards a series of goals, all of which you can encourage Deaf people to attain for themselves collectively. At present you tend to see it as a static little village in which you do your little bit and then go home to the hearing world to watch and participate in real cultural changes and exchanges. No one is blaming you for this and, of course, it is not up to you to change the Deaf world. But aiding and abetting can be fun! And it will be more fun after half-time when we change ends and find the wind blowing at our backs instead of in our faces as at present.

8. POLITICS.

Finally I come to the crunch word for these solutions - Politics. It is a dirty word in the Deaf world which just shows how backward we are. I have even heard Deaf people say that if such and such an organisation become 'political' they would leave it! We define politics as the mean by which a community is run. So we should have no fear or shame in saying we are 'politically motivated' or that we are members of a political organisation. It simply means that we are dedicated to progress; keen to change the position of our people for the better. It does not mean sending the tumbrils round to the RNID or posting poisonous spiders to the members of the 'Gang of Four'. It does mean finding ways to achieve all the remedies I have mentioned here.

In the NUD, our first basic step has been to insist on 'home rule', if you like. McCay Vernon has shown how a subculture is healthy or sick depending on whether successful leaders emerge from the subculture itself, or imposed from outside. By the light of this criteria, the Jews and Mormons flourish. The red Indians and negroes live at the bottom of society, governed by a white administrator in a nice big house.

The next step forward is to identify the millenium. Next year, we hope our "Charter of Rights" will be published. Once we have thus mapped out the field, then Deaf and hearing can join in to achieve them.

That leaves one major point. Those who have seen "One Flew Over The Cuckoo's Nest" will recall Chief Bromden, an American Indian as a voluntary patient in a mental institution. He seems to be Deaf and dumb. But this is a psychosis brought on by the American society which will neither talk to him nor listen to his views. He lives in a stupor, ruled over by the 'Big Nurse' with a sweet heart and iron fist. He has not even the self-respect or confidence to realise that he is a voluntary patient and is free to go when he wants. Until one day along comes

Ken Kesey, himself in the guise of Randall McMurphy, a brawling convict who bucks the hospital system to the point where he stirs up the patients and gives them hope.

Eventually the hospital puts him down. They lobotomise him and thus think that by killing him they have quashed the signs of revolt in the patients. Far from it. Once Chief Bromden sees that his crude, swashbuckling friend was really committed to their own cause, he gains a tremendous amount of confidence to realise how deeply someone believes in his essential worth and is able to pull himself back together again and leave the hospital, taking with him half the ward who were sunk in helplessness till they saw this commitment. The final inspiration for them was McMurphy wanted them to help him and each other. Till that time no one had ever considered them worthy of helping either themselves or anyone else.

If this inspires us all half as much, the dawning of a new era for Deaf people can be reached with ease......

The Road to Hell is Paved with Good Intentions

Cumbrian Association for the Deaf AGM at Carlisle. October 1977.
Paddy Ladd.

In this paper this afternoon, I hope I can make the dust fly a little bit so that we can all have a fruitful discussion that really does jump over the barriers that the Deaf world puts up. Before I start, I'd like to make it clear that when I refer to the Deaf world, I am including all who work with the Deaf as well as the Deaf themselves. This world fears controversy as only an authoritarian system can. If those of you listening this afternoon have the courage of your convictions, we may be able to think out steps that will drag the Deaf world into the more liberal atmosphere of British society at large.

Let us paint a quick historical picture. Any time up to the 19th century counts as the Dark Ages for Deaf people. We are classed as sub-humans. Then over the last 100 years, Deaf people have been brought out of the closet into the status of third class citizenship. This can be called 'Stage Two', and was undertaken by churches who, for a time, had a role in Deaf education as they did in hearing education. Stage Three has come about over the last thirty years, where those at the helm have built more of a secular base, particularly in local authorities,where they have taken direct responsibility for dealing with Deaf people's lives. Stage Two is still with us in many areas and there is a standing controversy still about the relative advantages of each kind of service.

Over the last ten years other sections of British society have moved on to another stage. They have got up and demanded that they themselves should play a role in society, in particular over matters concerning their own welfare. These include the obvious ones like the trade unions, black people, the women's movement, but it also includes teenage cultures, schoolchildren and other handicapped groups - notably the blind and the disabled. In all this the Deaf have been left behind and we show at present little sign of catching up.

In view of this, when we talk of associations for the Deaf, we are faced with a time for crucial decisions of which the first is the nature of the goals that must be set. In particular, we have been concerned with only helping the Deaf and this, though necessary, has left us with a people lacking in self-respect, self-belief and self-confidence, whose consciousness has not risen to the level of self-help or helping their fellows of any kind on a national scale. This leads us to question the kind of help that is being given and I suggest here a re-definition of goals that should become a part of an association's contributions.

1. That the ultimate goal is to see Deaf people standing on their own feet and being independent as far as can be established.

2. That Deaf people should take responsibility for their own affairs, those concerning them and the responsibility of helping their fellows.

3. That Deaf people should be working with the community to get their share of local and national facilities.

4. That the Deaf should participate as far as possible in community affairs at all levels.

5. That a genuine wish to remove the inferiority complex that haunts Deaf people be established in professionals and voluntary agencies (and this means removing the things which cause it).

A voluntary organisation could place these goals before them and adjust their works accordingly. I will not go into the implications of this; suffice to say that if No 5 is followed, then there will be a concerted attempt to involve potential Deaf leaders and to inform and educate the others. This would ultimately result in a Deaf community that knows what it has to do, how to achieve it and why it has to be achieved. I do not see an end to hearing people's work with the Deaf in this respect. What I do see is a modifying of the tasks and responsibilities of those workers. There are some extra goals arising from this which are more specific.

6. To take on the responsibility for adult Deaf education. This to include not only literacy, but courses and lectures about this world we live in. Relevant lectures, that is. Topics like social studies, the role of women, sex and men, the work of different people in society, trade unions, politics, elections, local affairs, etc. It has been often said that this would not work but it could be done, depending on the quality of the speakers and interpreters in making the subjects interesting and amusing. This would also include the vital area of training Deaf people for positions of responsibility. For example, leadership as opposed to personality politics, how to work collectively, how to discuss and compromise, etc.

If an association sells all this to a further education department, you can do it. But it is not only a question of facilities. It is a question of the all-too-often neglected other half of the problem. That is, educating and persuading Deaf people to want these facilities. The real time-consuming factor is here, because a lot of thinking is needed into how this can be achieved by the association's workers. You want to get Deaf people themselves to make the running, doing the pushing for these facilities, consulting all the membership at every level and stage so that things are supported through understanding. That way they will not collapse. You can find a good parallel for this in something like an adventure playground. If one starts from humble beginnings, involving the kids in the fight to get better facilities, you can be sure they will not smash it up because they will feel it is theirs; because they have fought for it. If on the other hand you look at a desolate area and decide to build a super duper playground there, you can bet your sweet life that the kids will wreck it. To them it will mean nothing because they have not been emotionally involved into it.

7. The following goals are tangibly vital to Deaf independence. Without their existence you can safely say that the Deaf world is backward and that the roads to self-fulfilment are blocked. The first is interpreters. There is a crying need for a much larger number of these people. There is no way that the social workers can

find time to interpret in all situations a Deaf person might wish to explore in order to feel a part of society. So a registry of interpreters is vital. It should be one from which the association can easily draw and they should be able to budget for this with more local and central government funding. The time is not ripe yet, so the associations have the task of finding hearing people in their area and actively assisting them to become good interpreters. In this context Deaf people are vital. They can teach these people by social mixing which is the stage on from classroom learning of sign language.

8. Inextricably linked with 7 above is the need to promote sign language. It is Deaf people's chief claim to fame in the eyes of society, and is also the greatest hurdle. An association should seriously think of teaching and promoting sign language in as many imaginative forms as possible. The best of these would be local schoolchildren and an association could get together with the local education department to work this into the curriculum. Again, the right Deaf people could be encouraged and trained to carry out this work since it is a task well beyond the social worker's timetable.

9. The Deaf telephone is another essential tool but, as remarked in 6, it is no use having these things if Deaf people are not actively encouraged to use them. All over the country the same picture emerges; the machines are installed and then hidden in someone's office rather than a corner of the clubroom where they can be brought into use more quickly. Much more needs to be done in the way of showing Deaf people how they can be used to their benefit for inter-club arrangements, social and committee meetings, etc. Once this starts to happen, the next need is for more of the machines in relevant places; i.e. committee members' houses, the houses of Deaf people and their relatives who want to keep in touch, police stations, town halls, and so on. None of this will work unless the groundwork of educating Deaf people is done first.

10. The next vital step is for the association to have a regular newsletter, preferably a newspaper or magazine, and preferably put together by Deaf people. This will serve as a focal point for all issues of local concern and could be self-sufficient through advertising. In such an idea, the hard of hearing could be included to make the project financially viable. Perhaps the most important result would be that regular sessions would occur at the local clubs where those who could read would translate into sign language for those who cannot. This would result in more group interest and mental activity. Progress has never been made until man sat round in such groups; indeed this was the way that hearing people taught their communities before they became literate.

11. I now return to the subject of Deaf clubs. It should be self-evident that Deaf people should run their own clubs, yet this does not happen in many parts of the country. In Hillingdon, where I come from, it works well. Deaf people should be their own representatives to the management committee and should be given every encouragement to take on more responsibility on that committee. As you know, it is always easier to cook yourself than to teach others how to cook and this is often the basic reason why social workers do not let Deaf people into the kitchen of

responsibility. It is tedious and initially far more time-consuming to have to explain time and again how things should be done but in the long run it repays everything put into this. The social worker should be proud to be able to prove that Deaf people in their area are capable of such independence and should be pleased not to be wanted in the club, unless as a friend or a caseworker with a surgery.

12. I now suggest that Deaf education should be within the scope of the association. We all complain about the state of it; we suffer from the results of it and we have children and parents who are members of both a school and voluntary association. So an association has all the rights to act on behalf of its members and should get together to bring pressure to bear on the local Deaf schools which can be incorporated into your goals. At present residential schools put up a 'Berlin Wall' to keep you from seeing how bad things really are. If it was a hearing school, this barrier would not be there. Parents would act locally using the media and their collective conscience. So can you. So sit down and work it out, and for God's sake bring in the Deaf people who are ex-pupils there to give you real clues as to what goes on there.

13. I have talked in 12 of a pressure group. There seems to me no reason why an association should not incorporate this into its function. After all, if it is concerned for its members it will surely take steps to help them. Indeed I would interpret this as an actual responsibility to act, and that if it does not do so, then it is failing its Deaf members. Similarly, if it does not involve its Deaf members in both the action and in understanding the reasons for acting, it is failing the Deaf people even more severely because the failure is more subtle.

So these are some of the ways in which Deaf people can move onto Stage Four of their evolution with the help of their association. One thing is clear; if we persist any longer with stages 1, 2 and 3, it is the road to hell that lies ahead. Good intentions might have been thought to be enough in the past - now we need tangible goals and roads.

THE MILAN
CONFERENCE
1880
ORALISTS
ORALISTS
TWO-HANDED ALPHABET
ONE-HANDED ALPHABET
A. HOLCROFT 1992

Preface

In the early days of the NUD, some members were much taken with the fact that the National League of the Blind had been affiliated to the TUC since 1899, even before several of the major unions of the 20th century. It seemed clear that this had led to a higher profile for blind people in the labour movement.

NUD officers were regularly being approached by members for help with employment problems. The piecemeal system of having to have social workers plead with employers for jobs was humiliating for Deaf people and not good for social workers.

Since it was clear that all employees had improved their working lives via the trade unions, it also became clear that there was a way forward for a national solution for Deaf workers. Provided that the unions could be persuaded, that is.

Unfortunately the NUD's attempts to persuade both the TUC and individual unions were unsuccessful. In the succeeding decade, there has been the odd burst of support inside some unions, notably the USDAW resolution of 1986.

But much, so much, remains to be done. In fact, with the mass unemployment of the 1980s, the work situation has worsened for large numbers of young Deaf people, and the areas of YTS, TOPS, MSC and the like have become a twilight zone of neglect. The Greater London Council's (GLC) model policy of equal opportunities, which has been copied by many councils, is an encouraging sign. This policy emerged out of a 1960s philosophy of civil rights and actually had opposition from the trade unions in some workplaces. But the British Constitution takes no account of civil rights; they have always had to be fought for both within and by the labour movement.

Although these equal opportunity policies will undoubtedly improve Deaf employment prospects in some areas, perhaps the more urgent need is to take on Deaf young people from that twilight zone and train them, since they have been left to rot both in education and in subsequent Government schemes.

Although trade union power has declined, NUD still believes that proper exploration of this field can solve many Deaf people's employment problems. The American Union of Post Office Workers is a model we would all do well to study closely.

Letter to the Trade Unions

London. February 1977. Paddy Ladd.

The NUD was formed in 1976 because Deaf people felt that it was time that they had some say in running their own lives. Deaf people were literally a silent minority whose views were never listened to because people could not communicate with them, and who have had to put up with the stigma of being treated often as half-wits though no less intelligent than the rest of the population. If there was any dirty work to be done, it was given to 'old muggins', the Deaf one, to do because he could not answer back. His position in society now is still parallel to that of the worker before the TUC was formed - he had no organisation of his own to fight on his behalf and was left to the tender mercies of the charitable organisations and patronage to help him out. Consequently, like the worker, he had no belief in himself or his fellows and left everything to those 'kind' enough to run his affairs for him.

This is where the NUD came in. A group of able Deaf people got together to raise the image of the Deaf in society and to start doing work for themselves. The NUD looked round for a source of funds for their urgent need to have full time workers and agreed that the trade union movement was the exact ideological parallel for their work. The NUD then began negotiations with the TUC with regard to affiliation along the same lines as the National League of the Blind who were affiliated to the TUC in 1899.

The TUC rejected NUD's application for affiliation on grounds that existing unions covered the needs of the Deaf on the shopfloor. The NUD did not agree with this, since it was manifestly obvious that Deaf people could not take an active role in union work because of the difficulty of lipreading at meetings, and it was also true that the Deaf were never informed of what was going on. The NUD decided, however, to pursue another line by applying to all the individual unions, stating the need for Deaf union members to be represented by a Deaf union. The NUD does not want to interfere with the closed shop policy, but seeks an amicable relationship with existing unions so that the Deaf working man's voice can be represented by other Deaf people to the higher level. The NUD also have high hopes that the individual unions will be closer to grass-roots union socialism and be more willing therefore to support their Deaf brothers.

There is urgent need for improving the Deaf man's position at work. Discrimination is rife and those Deaf people fortunate enough to get jobs often find themselves working well below their ability level. Because of the telephone, promotion is denied them, as well as the problems which occur when promotion involves talking to a lot of other people. Opportunities for vocational training, rehabilitation and any kind of educational training are almost nil, and consequently the Deaf worker lives a life of little hope or understanding.

So, what is the solution? We of the NUD feel that it is essential to have Deaf workers fulfilling the same kind of role as union officials - negotiating, persuading, spreading the word to the employer that Deaf does not mean 'stupid', and working hard to create the kind of opportunities so far denied to the Deaf. By having Deaf workers, this automatically raises the credibility of the Deaf man's position, both with the rest of the working fraternity and with the Deaf, giving them almost a structure of hope. The work of such officers would be very much one of full-time workers in order to achieve adequate national coverage, and even their work in industry would be the tip of the iceberg as far as Deaf affairs are concerned.

What aid the NUD is therefore asking for? The target is for each union to sponsor one Deaf official, which is not much if one considers the amount of subscriptions paid by Deaf people over the years.

Your response to this letter will probably involve a request for a meeting or for further information. We will be happy to provide both. We do not know how each union administers its financial situation, but assume that you have some kind of trust fund which would cater for this kind of request. We are only too aware that such a request from such people as ourselves is unusual. The point that is unusual is that it has taken Deaf people as long as this to evolve to the stage where they come to you in this way. We hope you will see our ideological parallels and come to meet us half-way in the brotherhood of second-class citizens.

Deaf History

The Darkest Day in Deaf History: Sept. 7, 1880

by Eugene Bergman

On that day a congress held in Milan voted in favor of the oral method of instruction. The vote was held by the "International Congress on the Education of the Deaf," held in Milan, Italy, from September 6 till September 11, 1880.

I place the name of that Congress in inverted commas because, as E. M. Gallaudet argued, it was neither international nor representative. It was, "entirely in the hands of a party inflamed with a spirit of conquest, seeking for the present victory of a vote rather than for the tardier triumph that might follow unimpassioned discussion and the simple presentation of facts and results." Of the 164 delegates 87 were Italian while 56 came from France, 8 from England and 5 from the United States. The five American delegates led by Gallaudet [illegible]

had already been determined [illegible] previously in Paris by its Organizing Committee. That committee was controlled by the Pereire Society, a foundation established by a wealthy banking family who contributed large sums of money to promoting oralism, and which paid for the trip of the French delegates to Milan. Wealthy doctrinaire philanthropists apparently are not an American monopoly.

Once in Milan, as part of pre-Congress schedule the mass of the participants attended special examinations for pupils in the two Milan schools for the deaf. Incidentally, 46 of the Italian delegates to the Congress were teachers from these two schools alone. That also was a stage-managed farce, since the pupils so tested were what the deaf writer Albert Ballin calls "decoys" – deaf children that lost their hearing at age 7 and afterward, so that their voice did not yet become the typical deaf voice, and whose lipreading ability was particularly good.

The farce continued. During the Congress the delegates politely ignored the protests of Gallaudet, Peet and other American delegates, but applauded the speeches of the promoters of oralism, sometimes giving standing ovations and growing positively rhapsodic over the supposed total superiority of the oral method. No opposition would be tolerated and, in fact, the chairman of the Congress, Abbé Tarra, highhandedly decided not to print the speeches of Gallaudet and other [illegible]

Chatterboxes Paul Dodson and Hong Hong Tran communicate in the sign language which many schools have banned

Deaf children get a helping hand to break their silence

by Bruce Kemble
Education Correspondent

SIX months after arriving in Britain from Vietnam, 14-year-old Hong Hong Tran watches expectantly as her schoolteacher tells her what will be happening at Easter.

She is excited because she has just discovered that all her teachers will visit her at her foster home during the holiday. She can understand what she is told, despite the fact that she is totally deaf.

But Eileen Samuelson, her teacher at Oak Lodge school in Wandsworth, southwest London, is doing something which would be frowned on at many schools for pupils with impaired hearing – using sign language.

By using signs, Samuelson is breaking an [illegible] [illegible] year-olds and their speech is unintelligible.

In an attempt to improve the prospects of deaf children, the union is calling on the government to launch a new course training teachers to use signs. At present, teachers concentrate on teaching pupils to speak, but pupils who have never heard speech find this difficult.

At a meeting organised by the union in London yesterday, Harlan Lane, of North-Eastern University in Boston, Massachusetts, and an expert on the education of the deaf, said the attempt to educate deaf children with teaching methods appropriate for hearing children had proved a failure, decade after decade. He said: "In a classroom where spoken and written English are the basic means of communication, deaf pupils are baffled and withdrawn."

Dr James Kyle, chairman of Bristol University's centre for deaf studies, supports the campaign to restore the use of sign language.

According to Kyle, prejudice against sign language is so strong that until recently deaf pupils were told to sit on their hands, had their hands tied behind their backs or were warned that if they waved their hands they would go blind.

But while the campaign to revive sign language gathers momentum, its opponents insist that its use would place the deaf in ghettos where English is a foreign language. They advocate the use of lip-reading and concentrating on pupils learning to speak.

Kyle admits that only about 50% of the English language can be lip-read. For instance, words like but, rat, mat, cat or cushion are impossible to detect because they come from the throat.

Robert Dunn, the junior education minister responsible for schools for the physically handicapped, told The Sunday Times last night that he was studying the NUD's proposals for the reform of teacher training.

National Union of the Deaf begins the battle for British Sign Language

Thousands of profoundly deaf people leave school almost illiterate, with unintelligible speech and lipreading no better than most hearing people, claims the Nation Union of the Deaf, a pressure group of about 100 people.

Last month the union launched a campaign to bring British Sign Language back into the classroom and lobbied the Department of Education and Sci- [...] people being taught by deaf people but a teacher should be able to provide an oral model in school.

"The NUD plan certainly

Sue Surkes and Diane Spencer examine the main issue facing deaf children – whether they should be taught in sign language

Teachers urge GCSE tailoring

Teachers of the deaf are joining forces to negotiate with exam boards for GCSE syllabuses which will suit their pupils.

Deaf children are at a disadvantage under the new exam rules, their teachers say, because the GCSE requires a more complex use of language than GSE Mode 3.

More than 70 teachers and representatives of organizations concerned with deaf and hearing-impaired people met recently at Oak Lodge School in south London to discuss ways to help pupils.

Assessing needs — the gesture must be made

When Emma Tumim, who was born deaf, went to school sign language was discouraged.

By the age of five she still had minimal vocabulary, no grasp of syntax, and could not communicate with anyone.

While the residential school for the [illegible]

she points out.

Nowadays, many deaf youngsters with some residual hearing benefit from technologically-advanced hearing aids and a more natural form of language teaching that might, for example, use recitation of a nursery rhyme to convey rhythm.

[illegible]

Emma Tumim tells a police officer why she has joined a protest outside the DES on Monday asking for sign language to be taught in schools.

[illegible] fully integrated classes, she says, that if the child can't receive the communication naturally the child is not going to gain a great deal from being in integrated education.

● The National Union of the Deaf is demanding that deaf children should be treated as a linguistic minority and be taught sign language to improve their education.

In a response to the Department of Education document Better Schools, it calls for a radical re-think of training teachers of deaf pupils. Education courses in Manchester, Oxford, Wall hall and Moray House should be closed at the end of the 1988/89 academic year "provided that an acceptable alternative can be put forward." These are the main departments for specialized teaching for the deaf.

The NUD thinks it impossible for these departments to make the kind of change needed to produce teachers who can use British Sign Language.

[illegible] at some level, all without professional contact, represents the most appalling picture. This is about as good for deaf education as share cropping is for agriculture.

Among that number are some profoundly deaf children who understand so little of what they are exposed to that they have regressed almost to autism. Some of them can be found in residential schools, still quite traumatised, adds the report.

SIGN LANGUAGE

Deaf island

By Robin McKie

[illegible]

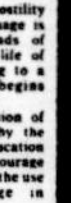

Experts turn deaf ear to signs

JUDITH JUDD
Education Correspondent

GOVERNMENT hostility towards sign language is consigning thousands of deaf people to a life of illiteracy, according to a campaign that begins tomorrow.

The National Union of the Deaf will lobby the Department of Education and Science to encourage officials to increase the use of sign language in schools.

The NUD blames education policy for 'alarming' levels of literacy among Britain's 50,000 profoundly deaf people. They have an average reading age of eight and a half and 90 per cent of them cannot speak intelligibly.

Many deeply resent the way that their desire to learn through sign language has been frustrated by their teachers. Some have even had their hands tied behind their backs to stop them 'signing.'

Helping hands: Mrs Riki Kittel says sign language has taught her son Piers to speak.

Yet 100 years ago sign language was widely used to teach the deaf. Its supporters contend that many more learned to read and write.

Since then the prevailing view has been that oral teaching offers deaf people the best chance to learn to speak, to lip read and to integrate into society.

A union spokesman said that most people did not realise that sign language was effectively barred from many classrooms.

Mrs Riki Kittel, whose son Piers was diagnosed deaf at the age of eight months, has challenged the officials.

At the time a teacher of the deaf instructed the Kittels never to use sign language to the child and not to gesture to him.

Mrs Kittel, of St Albans, Hertfordshire, says: 'The moment of diagnosis is when parents are most vulnerable and most accept advice without question.

'I'm a pushy lady and carried out some research. I was horrified to discover the illiteracy rate among deaf children who had not been taught with sign [illegible]

Opening up TV for the deaf

Television producer Eddie Montague and assistant Helene Grygar have been finding out the problems of being deaf the hard way.

They have been making an Open Door programme called *Signs of Life* for the National Union of the Deaf with five presenters – all totally deaf.

"It was no use saying to the group 'We'll ring you on Monday.' The telephone is a useless instrument to them," said Eddie.

He added: "Even the autocue in the studio is a problem. How does the operator know the speed of delivery of the presenters unless she can read sign language?"

Hopefully these problems will be sorted out by the time the National Union of the Deaf members go into the studios for the programme to be screened on Thursday next week on BBC2.

Signs of Life aims to show television companies how they could cater for the deaf in the future. It will include items on education, employment, communication as well as poetry and even jokes by a deaf comedian.

The National Union of the Deaf has told the BBC: "Not all the programme may work the way we want it to, but at least we know the problems at first hand and we at least are having a try."

Newspaper cuttings from the Press

Preface

The International Year of the Disabled, 1981, brought hopes and promises to the vast number of disabled people whom we meet every day in all walks of life. MPs and many authoritative people let out a constant flow of rhetoric, promising succour to ease their burden and to get them accepted in society. This was in 1981 and what we see now is damn all.

It would be wrong, however, to say that no action was taken. In a Private Member's Bill, Bob Wareing submitted the Anti-Discrimination Bill in 1983. The House was almost empty during the debate. Where were the M.Ps, some who were sympathetic to the cause of the disabled, at the time? In the bar or presumably with their mistresses?

When the call for voting came late in the afternoon, there was a rush on a Gadarene scale and soon there was only standing room in the house. The Bill was defeated, naturally. While the Government made it illegal to discriminate against the blacks, it legalised discrimination against the disabled. So when a Deaf person applies for a job any employer has a legal right to tell him to buzz off.

Tom Clarke's Amendment to the Disabled Person's Bill in 1986 again failed to get passed as the Government feared it would incur great expense and bankrupt the country. What about the numerous approved measures that are stretching the country's finances to breaking point? Arms expenditure and accommodating unwanted people from abroad in luxury hotels, for instance.

There appears to be some resentment in classifying the Deaf with the physically and mentally disabled. People, and even doctors, tend to regard Deaf people as physically disabled whereas they are only sensorially disabled with communication as their only handicap. It is felt that if they were correctly categorised, their success to legal rights and a number of concessions would be greatly enhanced. European activists HAVE succeeded in this approach and in 1981 the European Parliament unanimously supported a motion to recognise sign languages of member states.

It would take a few years to get the stolid British Government compelled to legalise sign language. When the law comes into force, would it result in teachers, who practise the craze in banning sign language getting hurled into jail? It would be justice after all these years of coercion! What effect would it have on the psychopathic head of a well known school who spends a lot of time prowling about in the hope of catching offenders using sign language and enjoying the experience meting out punishment? When this law comes into force, the NUD shall have a powerful tool to resort to when confronting the teaching and educational needs.

International Year of the Disabled People

Guildford. Opening Speech at a Seminar. 1981. A. F. Dimmock.

I thank you the Chairman, officials and members of the committee for allowing me to make some basic comments on the special needs of the Deaf. It is known that I am here as a representative of the British Deaf Association, for which I act as a branch secretary; it is a small role. I very much prefer to be regarded as an activist of the National Union of the Deaf, a pressure group which came into existence in 1976. The NUD hopes to use the International Year of the Disabled People as a platform to voice a number of proposals in an effort to ease handicapping agents in the lives of Deaf individuals.

First and foremost is the demand for legal recognition as an ethnic body of people with their own language, culture and mode of thinking. By the last remark, the meaning is that the thought process of the profoundly Deaf is different from the 'normal' and this is a major reason why I am experiencing difficulty in getting wholly involved in meetings where the language used is not my own. Concealed within many Deaf people is a strong desire to be freed from being forced to behave as if they were not Deaf at all. Deaf children at special schools are coerced to use hearing people's language and banned from using their natural mode of communication. This dangerous suppression is known to cause mental atrophy, and the long chapter of poorly educated Deaf people proves the point. The NUD wants you, the public and authorities, to become aware of this.

The Deaf have to live with an invisible handicap that is made worse by their being able-bodied. They are, as a consequence, misunderstood and denied sympathy. Their handicap is that of communication and this can be very severe and awesome. Among themselves the handicap does not exist as they have a common language, but in society they are extra-handicapped. Conditions imposed by society mean that almost everything is designed and learnt to be appreciated through the ears. They have to expend more in the form of time, money and energy to stay just within the verge of society. While the Deaf can compete with the hearing in sport and work alongside them, they can never be accepted socially.

Television is just a talking box, the theatre meaningless and the radio is not for them. But recent measures, thanks to pressure from the NUD and other bodies in connexion, have brought closed captioning services on TV. Demands for extending this service are now being aired. I would be grateful if all of you here could help with the petition organised by the Deaf Broadcasting Campaign (DBC). There are other beneficial introductions like the devices that enable the Deaf to use the phone and the Palantype recorder which transforms the spoken word into the written. But the Deaf are forced to pay huge sums for these things. I am able to appreciate to a great degree the mobility allowance and the financial assistance to purchase vehicles accorded to cripples.

I feel that Government funding should be made available for the Deaf as well to have the means in order to reap the benefits that are readily available to the hearing at little or no cost. The Deaf are tax-payers and in most cases good workers and law-abiding and should be entitled to funding. A great deal of tax-payers' money is used to provide sound effects for ignorant masses of boob tube watchers.

The House of Representatives in the USA is considering a law to compel all phone companies to use only phone receivers that work with an inductive coupler. This costs little and is designed to help people who use hearing aids. Our own government and the Post Office knew of this but they took a lethargic stance. I feel that it is our business to shake them out of their stupor. Tom Jackson, of the Union of Post Office Workers, had helped the NUD in the past on another matter and I am convinced that he would lend muscle if we approach him.

Up to now, I have singled out the Deaf for comment. This does not, however, imply that I am one-sided. The NUD has battled against laxity in imposing the quota system, implemented in 1944 by the Disabled Persons Employment Act. Many firms feel they are under no compulsion to take on disabled workers and an unscrupulous employer can hire anyone with a tip missing from a finger and claim that he had complied with his quota. The NUD has collected sufficient evidence to show that many employers are reluctant to take on the severely disabled, the blind and the Deaf. Some firms, notably the one where I am employed, are punctilious over the quota scheme and they should be commended. Perhaps, during this special Year of the Disabled, we should present awards to such firms in the area.

Deaf People's Problems in Job Opportunities and Social Integration

University of York. July 1986. A. F. Dimmock.

Employment and social integration are aspects of living in which Deaf people tend to be the losers. In the bygone days of traditional crafts the Deaf were able to compete with the hearing for job security and high wages. Nowadays they appear to be kept in jobs that are repetitive or associated with cleaning, jobs that have little appeal for most people. Even Deaf graduates experience severe difficulties in getting considered when applying for work. Employers seem to prefer people without qualifications who can communicate normally, so the Deaf person ends up with an useless degree and no work.

Others reluctant to employ Deaf people sometimes use nonexistent insurance conditions as an excuse to turn them away. The exploitation of the Deaf is widely known; they are paid less and given menial work. One, known to me for years, rose to become a company director through his own special talents but his salary was less than his fellow directors with lesser talents. It was because his firm had to hire a secretary to take his phone calls and interpret proceedings of the boardroom meetings. The Quota Scheme, designed to compel employers to take disabled people, is open to abuse. To give an example, an unscrupulous employer can hire someone with a tip missing from his finger, or something like this, not a real disability but more of a convenience, and so comply with his quota. This hits all types of disabled people; the Deaf more so. Another form of discrimination is advertisements inviting people to apply for work but only have phone numbers and no addresses. This clearly suggests that only hearing jobseekers can apply.

The English language, being the most difficult for the Deaf to learn, has effectively blocked them from training schemes and jobs where one would have to pass written tests. The skill and promise a candidate may have takes second place. Many Deaf people lost the chance of getting jobs through bosses' reluctance to communicate with them. Even when they have jobs, they are usually underemployed and not encouraged to upgrade themselves in order to take advantage of their intelligence, better talents and training.

There are organisations in which both the Deaf and hearing are brought to work together. It is interesting to see these two groups together but during breaks they separate into Deaf and non-deaf groups. These two groups do not seem to attract each other; they more or less repel the other. Socialisation between such groups is done at the barest minimum. Nevertheless, there are specialists who claim to know all about the Deaf and who are forever urging the Deaf to integrate with the hearing. These so called pundits all too often unwarily sacrifice the social and psychological wellbeing of the Deaf for the sake of physical integration. Do the Deaf intellectually, emotionally and spiritually mix with other their hearing peers? This question is in want of a satisfactory answer. Should a Deaf person find it convenient and sufficiently beneficial to be integrated and diffused into the hearing world with about the same effort extended by the hearing, he would naturally be expected to use the components of society which are designed to be learned and appreciated through the EARS. For the Deaf to pace with hearing in social intercourse can be very demanding. Straining one's eyes on moving lips or struggling to catch what is being said with the help of a hearing aid for long spells is obviously a very arduous task that defeats even the most phenomenal lipreader or the one with good residual hearing and even subjects such people to neurotic disorders.

There was a time when a syndicate of businessmen, who met regularly in Birmingham, had a Deaf person among themselves. They decided to learn the manual alphabet and use it as the sole means of communication when their Deaf colleague was present. In this respect the Deaf man was totally integrated in the company and they were all on equal footing. I have always felt that the hearing learning the sign language would be the ideal solution to the integration of the hearing and the Deaf. The sign language appears to have become respectable after years of being looked down on as grotesque and unintelligent. Sign language classes and tuition through television have been popular in USA. People were thus encouraged to have a second language. Now it is claimed that there is about a million hearing people who can adequately communicate in sign language with the Deaf in USA.

There is, however, one situation where the Deaf do not feel left out. It concerns sport. There are many clubs with Deaf members who contribute to their club's achievements and teams of Deaf players that are strongly competitive. But top league football clubs are unwilling to take Deaf players even if they have exceptional talents. To these clubs, coaching is of major importance and the Deaf are found to be difficult to coach. As a result Deaf footballers have not been able to distinguish themselves in the top echelons of the game since Cliff Bastin, who had a hearing impairment, played for Arsenal and England in the Thirties.

G..o.od mo..r..innngg..mmmMi..st..er..Org..a..li..st...

*Speak up! Say 'Hello' to your schoolmates....you ***?!!*

Preface

The late Frederick Schreiber once said, “As far as Deaf people are concerned, our Deaf rights are violated daily”.

More recently Rev. Jesse Jackson, said, “The problem is not that the Deaf do not hear. The problem is that the hearing world does not listen”. These sayings indicate that Deaf rights are just a thought, not a precept for legislation. This is probably due to people, Deaf or hearing, having no clear idea of the issue. The great misfortune today is that there is no published or formulated guideline of Deaf rights. The basic idea of Deaf rights is not just about getting media attention; it is converting the mind, heart and soul of hearing people - and that includes Deaf people who don’t have strong feelings - so as to share common goals of true equality, justice and opportunity for all. The great drawbacks in achieving these goals are discrimination and paternalism. People who practise the latter want to be benefactors and they are always refusing to give up. Harlan Lane commented on them as “The whole attitude to benevolence is that ‘I am better than you, and I am helping you’. That says, ‘I don’t need to learn your views, mine are better. I don’t need to hear your priorities, mine are better’”.

Our modern Deaf movement is almost 16 years old. During that time we learned a basic truth: there can be no reform of society’s discrimination against the Deaf unless we stand up for ourselves and fight back. Today, we continue to fight our own battles. There has been a phenomenal increase in the number of Deaf people defending and extending the rights of Deaf people. The significance is the improved accessibility to television, telephone and interpreting services. Another step was the European Parliament’s acknowledgement of sign language as the first language of the Deaf. These historic decisions do not, however, end Deaf discrimination and paternalism. Therein lies the long and hard road ahead to educate the public and to stand up against anyone and anything that tend to oppress us. There is a notable trend of support from some people and associations. These are our allies and in them lies a powerful weapon and here we must concentrate on gaining more strength for it. Changing laws or political decisions can never be enough. The solution, as mentioned earlier, is to change hearts, mind and souls.

Human Rights and the Deaf

Liverpool. September 1980. A. F. Dimmock.

The theme of my thoughts this day is "Human Rights and the Deaf". I have repeatedly asked myself what rights the Deaf have and what rights they have been denied. They certainly have rights like saying what they like, watching the television and doing what they like with leisure. I cannot recall any Deaf person being prevented from the pursuance of doing what one wishes. But we often hear of parents, teachers and counsellors taking a forbidding stance in the Deaf children's use of the natural language of their own, namely the language of signs. There is now a growing demand, unmistakable at length, for urging the public and authorities to recognise the Deaf as a legitimate linguistic and ethnic minority group with their own language, culture and mode of thinking.

There exists a trend that must date back to the dawn of civilisation. 'Normal' people perceiving 'different' people through their 'normal' frames of reference and making efforts to 'normalise' such people. They predetermine their concepts of normalcy and expect the 'differents' to fit within their definition of normalcy. Because of this trend, thousands of Deaf individuals are coerced into learning to normalise themselves. Two favourite devices used on them are the oral methods (speech and speechreading) and their placement in settings dominated by non-deaf people. These devices were dreamed up by speculating theorists who deemed these to be ideal for such purposes.

As a result, Deaf persons have been told to be open minded about it and to accept 'value' for mingling with non-deaf persons. There are some non-deaf people who have subscribed to this brand of theory and they have attained certain levels of credibility and influence to put this theory into use. Their well-meaning but paternal attitude enabled few Deaf persons to obtain some fluency in the oral method and the ability to intermingle with non-deaf people. When people hear of such rare successes there is an immediate wave of thinking that one and all in the Deaf world can be successfully 'made normal'. It takes a lot of hard work to reverse this fallible thinking and convince people that huge numbers of Deaf people can never hope to attain fluency in hearing people's language.

There are organisations in which both the Deaf and hearing are brought to work together. It is interesting to see these two groups working together but during breaks they separate into Deaf and non-deaf groups. These two groups do not seem to attract each other; they more or less repel the other. Socialisation between such groups is done at the barest minimum. Nevertheless, there are specialists who claim to know all about the Deaf and who are forever urging the Deaf to integrate with the hearing. These so-called pundits all too often unwarily sacrifice the social and psychological well-being of the Deaf for the sake of physical integration. Do the Deaf intellectually, emotionally and spiritually mix with their hearing peers? That is the question that is in need of a satisfactory answer. Should a Deaf person find it convenient and sufficiently beneficial to be integrated and diffused into the hearing world with the same amount of effort expended by the hearing, he would naturally be expected to use the components of society which is designed to be learned and appreciated through the EARS.

The English language, being the most difficult for the Deaf to learn, has effectively blocked them from training schemes and jobs where one would have to pass written tests. The skill and promise of the Deaf candidate often takes second place. Ironically the hearing applicant for employment in areas created for helping Deaf children or Deaf adults is not required to pass sign language competency tests. Another form of discrimination is advertisements inviting people to apply for work but only having phone numbers and no addresses. This clearly suggests that only hearing job seekers can apply. Many Deaf ones lost the chance of getting jobs through bosses' reluctance to communicate with them. Even when they have jobs, they are under-employed and not encouraged to upgrade themselves in order to take advantage of their intelligence, better talents and training.

The way to gain our rightful place as an independent and ethnic group is to get the Deaf to sit on boards of crucial decision-making and political processes in the area of deafness which affect their own lives. The bone of contention is that Deaf citizens are shut out and their rightful places given to people of influence who know nothing about Deaf people. What is long overdue in this old country is an Individual Rights Protection Act which already exists in America and several progressive countries. Such a legislation is designed to permit Deaf citizens to enjoy living without having to continue to struggle against intentional or unintentional environmental handicaps or attitudinal factors that become extra-handicapping agents themselves. Deaf people have proven abilities, pay taxes and raise their young to be fine citizens and yet they are denied a say in any legislation making decisions and are forced to stay on the outer fringe of society when they should be constituted as part of the general society. They are forced to expend more in the form of time, money and energy because of these obstacles. Even the buying power of the Deaf is lower than the average hearing because of additional hardship created by discrimination. So the Deaf must pay more in order to keep just within the verge of society. Authorities simply use the term 'disability' to defeat the struggle of the Deaf towards a rightful place. If one is disabled, one is regarded as one who must be helped to certain remedies; that automatically disqualifies them from having a say in decision-making. Are the Deaf really disabled? Handicapped, yes, but disabled? The handicap lies in communication with the hearing. The hearing themselves are equally handicapped in Deaf society.

Something catastrophic happened last year. A doctor examined the child of a Deaf couple and decided it was a case of child abuse. He did not ask the parents any questions and had the child taken away. Certain professionals had decided that this 12-year-old child did not have normal speech development and recommended his placement with foster parents. This effect definitely undermines the value of Deaf parenthood and takes away their basic human rights.

In this paper I have been trying to point out some of the instances that keep the Deaf within the bounds created by society's response to deafness. Of course, there are far more unwarranted circumstances that are not known to me. This concludes that it is really tragic to be Deaf in present-day society. Only a massive response from the masses of Deaf people can alter the course and establish 'Deaf Rights'.

Deaf People's Rights When Under Arrest

London. August 1978. A. F. Dimmock.

The NUD has received complaints from time to time about the special problems faced by Deaf people in their dealings with the police and with solicitors and courts. The latest case has brought us to the point where we must call for co-operation and resolution of the problems on a national basis. Here we detail one such case and as a result suggest ways in which improvements can be made.

Mr D was arrested and taken to a police station. He was questioned for several hours and his request for an interpreter skilled in sign language was refused from the start, as was his request for a solicitor. As Mr D can hear nothing at all and is unable to speak, considerable difficulties were experienced. Communication was carried out in writing but Mr D ran into difficulties several times in either understanding the written word or conveying it. Since he was not guilty of many of the charges (nine were later dropped), he had an even more urgent need to discuss them. It must be stated that many Deaf people have great difficulties in using the written form of communication and that this is due to poor schooling, not to intelligence factors. Because this piece of information is not widely known amongst the guardians of the law, the mistake is made of relying solely on the written form - often by the practice of writing out a statement and asking the accused to sign it, which they do, feeling quite intimidated by the whole process.

During the period of statement taking, Mr D was struck on four occasions. Two were with the open hand, one with a fist and one incorporating a pulling action which ripped the buttons from his shirt. This could have been avoided if Mr D's request for an interpreter had been granted.

When the court appearance was due, Mr D met his solicitor and interpreter for the first time 15 minutes before the case was due. The solicitor did not know anything regarding the case and this lack of communication led to Mr D's being quoted as asking for 12 charges to be taken into account, which was quite untrue. In addition to this, his plea for anonymity was turned down by the magistrates because the solicitor and court were unaware of the nature of the Deaf world, which is so small that news like this travels extremely thoroughly. This was the more alarming since he was eventually given a conditional discharge, yet will not be able to shake himself free from suspicion for the rest of his life because of the 'no smoke without fire' syndrome. In addition to this, he was unable to follow his supposed interpreter but had no time to protest this as the 15 minutes time lag was not sufficient to make his position clear to court.

A further result of this case was that his daughter has been put in a children's home. This decision was arrived at by the social worker and the probation officer, neither of whom can speak sign language, a situation which is the more scandalous since all the four members of the family are Deaf. This aspect of the case is more involved than we need to deal with here, and is on-going, but it is fair to say that it could have been avoided if so simple such a thing as an interpreter had been available at the start. The NUD suggests that certain basic guidelines are laid down to prevent these incidents from happening, and these include the following points:-

> A Deaf person should not be questioned or a statement obtained from him or her without the presence of an interpreter approved by the Deaf person concerned. (The last clause is added not in order to obtain preferential treatment, but because there are many ways of interpreting BSL and these may not always tally closely enough with the Deaf person's own use of it. Local dialects are particularly strong in the Deaf world at the present time).
>
> When a Deaf person has contact with a solicitor, an interpreter must be present at all times. Extra time should be allowed before a court case to ensure that briefing takes place to its fullest extent. Again the interpreter should be approved by the Deaf person.
>
> The Deaf person in court should have an interpreter in whom he or she has the fullest confidence in terms of communication, rather than an ad hoc interpreter.

Certain basic guidelines including the above 3 points to be printed on a wallet-sized card which can be carried by as many Deaf people as possible. This would greatly ease the task of the police in ensuring that these recommendations were carried out evenly across the country.

Preface

I gave this paper shortly after the NUD TV programme, "Signs of Life", broadcasted in May 1979. Today we have had television programmes in sign language for eleven years. A great deal has changed in this time. Deaf self-advocacy has affected the major Deaf organisations which now employ Deaf people. The Signs of Life has continued but the fundamental powerlessness of Deaf people described in this paper remains the same. We have no status or rights as a linguistic minority in Britain and the miseducation of our children continues. But our thinking and analysis of our oppression has developed considerably and our greater contact with the international Deaf community has led to a certain amount of co-ordinated activism on the world scene.

We do not, as yet, have the level of control which is our right in education, Deaf organisations and Deaf television, but it has been a decade in which we have achieved much in getting nearer these goals.

Signs of Strife - Signs of Life

Bradford. May 1979. Maggie Woolley.

I have got two problems here. One is that although I can hear my own voice with the help of this hearing aid, I'm never sure how loud or how soft I am talking. There have been times when I've told my political views to a whole restaurant; when a whole tube train has been enthralled with my life story because no one bothered to say that my noise was Deafening. If I am not loud enough, wave your arms. If I am too loud, put your hands over your ears. That's sign language; it works wonders. The second problem is that I am wondering how I'm going to hear your questions when they come. Maybe I'll use an old Deaf trick and talk so much that there won't be time left for questions.

Seriously, we are rarely given this time - a chance to talk like this. I can count on the fingers of one hand the number of Deaf people who have been invited to an university to speak. Imagine an university audiology department where people spend three or four years or more training to be audiologists, teachers of the Deaf and what have you; where no Deaf person is ever seen, ever heard (and certainly ever read since our views are rarely represented in the academic literature in this country). We do not pretend to know it all, far from it, but we do have a personal investment in these issues; a subjective and growing objective awareness which should not be ignored to this extent.

However, I have seen a gradual change in the 1970s and believe we have much reason to hope. Deaf people are beginning to speak out, to sign out and professionals and academics are beginning to listen to us and some are becoming what Deaf people in their own way call (in signs, friends of the Deaf). I have chosen to dwell on the profoundly Deaf section of the population today because they are the people who are the most often denied the chance to present their case. If you want to talk about the hard of hearing, the adult deafened and the partially deaf, I will gladly discuss them afterwards. You will be seeing the programme, "Signs of Life", later. It was written and produced by the National Union of the Deaf which is an organisation, in fact the only organisation in the Deaf world which is run by Deaf people themselves. I want to expand on some of the themes in the programmeto discuss the signs of strife and the signs of life.

Deafness is a social handicap to a degree that no other form of handicap is. Because it is invisible, it seems that people rarely meet a Deaf person in their everyday lives. Such is the low level of public understanding of the disability that a person meeting a Deaf person might mistakenly think she had encountered someone who was mentally deficient. Other disability groups have made great inroads into gaining acceptance and understanding of their needs during the past twenty years or so, but the Deaf remain a largely unknown, misunderstood and forgotten race. We are disadvantaged because of communication difficulties and the isolation resulting from this, both on inter-personal and society levels. We are disadvantaged also by an educational and social conditioning that renders us impotent to take initiative in bringing about change. These are the signs of strife but I firmly believe that these disadvantages are not intractable and that Deaf people in this country are waking up to the beginning of a new era, and that the signs of life have already begun to emerge.

Any explanation of the situation of Deaf people must begin with an examination of childhood experiences. The extent of the role of childhood experience in human social development is a matter for debate which I do not want to go into today. However, when we look at Deaf people I think childhood experience is very significant and I leave you to draw your own conclusions as to its relevance. Considerably more Deaf children are born to hearing parents than to Deaf parents and it is these hearing parents who suffer the heartache and struggle of bringing up a Deaf child.

It is virtually impossible to diagnose the degree of Deafness at the statutory 3-month and 6-month hearing tests. We can tinkle spoons in cups or shake rattles and assess what response we get, if any. There is some sophisticated EEG type equipment which can be used to monitor electrical charges in the auditory pathways of the brain in a new-born baby. But few hospitals have this and the pictures we get are still far from accurate. When the child reaches a certain age, we can give an audiogram. Let's look at an audiogram and see what different responses mean in terms of what the child can understand.

An audiogram is an useful tool-however its value is limited. It tells us only what volume and frequencies the child can hear. It does not tell us anything about the quality of that sound and in some forms of nerve Deafness that quality is severely distorted. It tells us nothing of the child's functional ability. It does not tell us what the Deaf child could tell us if she could, if we gave her a way - if we really wanted to listen and know. And yet this audiogram determines what hearing aid the child will have, what education she will receive and ultimately what job she will get. As far as the medical profession is concerned, the child is the audiogram.

A recent survey by the National Children's Society, whose membership is comprised of hearing parents of Deaf children, found that 30% of the parents were not shown the child's audiogram and many others had to insist on being shown it. Of those who did see it, little more than half had it explained to them. Many parents did not know if their child had seen an educational psychologist who also plays a big role in determining the child's needs and future - and only 40% of parents were present when these tests were carried out. Many did not have the results of these tests explained to them. Parents therefore expect too much of their children and feel they fail, or expect too little and fail to make the most of the child's abilities.

As soon as Deafness is confirmed, it seems that parents begin an ever spiralling journey of mystification at the hands of the "experts". The most frequent visitor, if you live in an urban area, is the peripatetic teacher. She encourages parents to talk to the child as much as possible to encourage lip-reading and provides an auditory trainer. The peripatetic teacher emphasises the importance of lip-reading, hearing aids and perseverance. She tells parents to discourage signing and gestures with the threat that if the child signs she will not speak. Conscientious parents get taken in by this and mothers take on the role of the teacher - hardly the most natural role for this first essential relationship in the Deaf child's life. This method with its emphasis on speech at all costs can work with children who are partially hearing and whose hearing aids amplify what they can already hear in speech frequencies. But what about the profoundly Deaf child?

Lets leave the parents and look at the child for a bit. Her residual hearing is so little that she will hear only unpleasant sounds such as loud bangs, perhaps a pneumatic drill or a jet plane at close quarters. But to her naked ears, these sounds are not disturbing. They are perceived as muffled thuds which are largely vibration. But remember it isn't until the baby is a little girl that we are sure of the extent of her Deafness. So in the cradle she gets wired up with a hearing aids that amplifies her muffled thuds to a frequency of a jet plane at take-off and the distortion at this amount of amplification is horrific. And yet we do this to babies in cradles and wonder what kind of monster we have produced when she tears at the wires and screams in pain. Parents turn to the peripatetic teacher for advice and are told to persevere, keep on with the training, talk to her and one day your child will speak to you. But will she? Lets look at the facts.

Partially Deaf children will speak. 10% of profoundly Deaf children will speak. 0% of totally Deaf children will speak. 10% may sound good to you but you have got to remember that even though they speak, their speech is unintelligible to the woman in the street and even to some of their own teachers. Yet parents are conned into believing the fairy story and must feel they have failed miserably when the child is 16. (Montgomery 1978).

More important than speech is language for its internal function of thinking and its external function of communicating. If you do persevere, you may get your child to lip-read, say, 300 words by the time she is 4 years old. But what about sentences? What about a language that puts the richness of the world into words? How do you prepare your child for a trip to grannies, her first day at school, a measles vaccination or a tonsillectomy if you can't communicate with her? What about a language that is a two-way process - which allows the child to respond and express herself, to tell you about the slug in the back yard, her tummyache, the funny man who stopped her in the street and offered her a sweetie? How can you feel close to your child? All the money and hours spent on this method fail to establish closeness between human beings - between parents and children. Closeness comes from meaningful exchanges of information and feeling and from understanding and empathy. (McCay Vernon. 1971). As it is, many a Deaf child and her parents are strangers in the same house and this gulf widens as she grows and starts school.

Have you ever meant to say something and forgotten what it was? It was on the tip of your tongue - a thought which returned unembodied to the realm of shadows as one poet put it. That realm of shadows is where the Deaf child is at all the time.

She lives, she feels but cannot tell us about it, or rather she is not allowed to because we deny her a most fundamental right - a right to language.

Deaf parents of Deaf children don't have any more heartache and struggle than hearing parents of hearing children. They have a language - a first language of signs. Countless studies have shown that a Deaf child exposed to sign language at an early age has the potential to develop intellectually and emotionally at the same rate as a hearing child. In acquiring a first language, she is more highly motivated to learn a second one - spoken and written English. She already has a language to think with and to communicate with and it is only a small step then to the language that the rest of the world speaks and writes. But the child denied the first language has no concept of language. The only input she receives is distorted sounds and funny shapes on the lips. OK for me. I lip-read but I know what I am looking for. I learned English as a hearing child and retain an auditory memory of sound. But how can you learn a - language from lip-reading when you don't even know the meaning of the words?

What does the oral method mean for the social development of the child? The effect of being without a language in the early years is profound. All children go through a period of infant rebellion but eventually it is quelled as they are socialised and language plays a big part in this process. The Deaf child's rebellion is greater. Unable to express herself, she throws violent tantrums, engages in bouts of stubborn negativity, cuts herself off from attempts at communication, which can lead in some cases to a form of autistic withdrawal. Casualties of this order are to be found in many a mental hospital (Denmark. 1972). Many parents are driven to hitting their child when they have never punished hearing siblings in this way; "All she understands is the flat of my hand." Their feelings of guilt and failure must be considerable. Peripatetic teachers can't help much here. Parent counselling just does not feature in their training. But the rebellion is quelled here eventually. The child gives in and her tantrums decrease and her rage becomes a smile. She becomes dummified. I'd like to quote some pertinent remarks from McCay Vernon here: - "When the Deaf person smiles, it usually means he has chosen to conceal his embarrassment and dismay at not being a full participant in the conduct of human affairs. Thus he gets the hearing person and himself 'off the hook'. The Deaf person has discovered all too often that to say 'What?' or to ask for an explanation results in the hearing person's anger, impatience or rejection."

In school, signing is banned. She spends hour after hour, year after year plugged into distorted sounds, pretending to lip-read her teachers, nodding and smiling. Technical equipment is improving all the time and it does help the partially hearing child but not the rest. A favourite technique now is for the teacher to hold a piece of paper in front of her mouth and get the child to listen through an aid and repeat what the teacher says. I have tried this experiment on a group aid. I am not profoundly Deaf; I have a 70/80db loss. I failed this experiment. Imagine my humiliation when I was told I wasn't listening hard enough. Imagine how the Deaf child feels when she gets told this every day. For talking to friends she uses a primitive sign argot peculiar to her particular school, but when no one is looking.

How would you have felt if you could have only spoken to your childhood friends when no one was looking!

Those early childhood experiences are the common heritage of many Deaf people. I teach the end products of this system. Deaf students have left school at 16 but are so socially immature that they are not ready for the world outside and work. Somewhere along the line someone forgot to teach them about life. They can't read much, can't write intelligible English, can't speak and can't sign much either. When I try to work out what has been happening to them in the last 16 years I am stumped! Non-verbal intelligence tests show that they have normal IQs and they do think. I have taught drama for 4 years and have never ceased to be amazed at the Deaf child's imagination and powers of observation. Like most people, I had grossly underestimated Deaf people's potential. Despite the many deprivations they have suffered in their young lives, working with them is an interesting and exciting experience. It is when a Deaf child acts out her experience or paints it that you really see the richness inside her head. She loves and lives like all of us but in such incredible isolation and even solitary confinement.

In the National Union of the Deaf (NUD) we are campaigning for the adoption of Total Communication (TC) in all schools for the Deaf. TC is speech, lip-reading, hearing aids (where they are of use), signing and fingerspelling all used simultaneously. Everything that will give a Deaf child a language. Why should we make things so difficult for her as we do at present? Some schools are experimenting with TC and more will if we shout and sign loud enough. Infant rebellion is common in all human beings. It is the first sign of struggle for autonomy; the first impulse towards revolution and change. In many Deaf people this first sign of life is never seen again, but in the NUD I think we see the special circumstances under which that common potential for change can be mobilised.

I have spoken at length about education but I believe that this is the fundamental injustice that lies beneath all the other sources of Deaf people's oppression. If we can crack the oral myth, then we can set about causing the rest of our oppression to crumble. What happens when the Deaf child leaves school? Discrimination in employment is rife as you will see in our programme. Deaf adults are separated from Deaf children and are kept out of schools. Children never meet them and think they will grow up to be hearing like all other adults they know or, worse, that they will die when they are 16. We are kept out of professions, even those that deal with the Deaf although there has been a slow leak into social work with the Deaf.

We are kept out of television and other media. The journals of the British Deaf Association (BDA) and the Royal National Institute for the Deaf (RNID) seem to operate a type of censorship on articles which express the views I am giving today.

Which brings me to organisations for the Deaf; "FOR" being the operative word. The RNID is run completely by hearing people. Their headquarters in 105 Gower Street employs its quota of Deaf people but none have a say in the running of the organisation and hearing employees do not know how to communicate with them. The journal of the RNID refuses to mention the NUD and refuses to print articles written by our members. A non-controversial article on the making of the Open Door programme was rejected before the editor had seen either the programme or the article itself. And yet they have published a six-page spread on a recent BBC series on lip-reading. The BDA is geared towards the needs of the signing Deaf. It provides holidays and further education summer schools and weekend courses. It has one or two paid interpreters who have saved the lives of a handful of Deaf people who have braved the world of further education. However, not all the people on the executive committee are Deaf. The BDA holds annual delegates conferences where hundreds of Deaf people meet to discuss their views and pass resolutions. Every three years it holds Congress where thousands attend to discuss their views and pass resolutions. These resolutions land in the hands of a group of hearing people who try vaguely to influence the world at large on our behalf. The BDA, despite some aspects of its work, operates a censorship similar to the RNID with regard to the NUD.

These organisations grew out of the 19th Century upsurge of charitable organisations. The first friends of the Deaf were missionaries who sought to save the souls of Deaf people by bringing Christianity to them. They did a good job in their time in many ways, but their 19th century brand of paternalism is with us in abundance still.

We are denied access to technological aids such as teletypewriters (TTYs) and you will see a discussion of this on the programme. We are even denied aids which will help us in the home. Some local authorities provide free baby alarms which translate the baby's cry into flashing light, and flashing doorbells, but many don't. But even where LAs do provide these facilities many Deaf people are not aware of their existence; such is the pitiful absence of communication among people who provide a service of some kind for the Deaf. In areas where there are Deaf clubs, few are run by Deaf people themselves. Missionaries for the Deaf and social workers do that. It is in these clubs that the Deaf school leaver comes into contact with their own subculture and sign language. But social workers find it easier to cook themselves rather than to teach others to cook, as one Deaf person put it. (Ladd. 1977). Deaf people are often criticised for their apathy and for not taking initiative but no one ever gives them a chance. They have been denied the right to take part in decision making ever since mummy and daddy and brother and sister got together and decided to go to the seaside for the day and then told the Deaf child to eat her breakfast and get ready to go out somewhere.

Deaf people who cannot have children are not allowed to adopt Deaf children. But what about the things that you take for granted? Here you choose to listen to the lectures or fall asleep. The Deaf don't have that choice. There is an appalling lack of interpreters in this country, not for want of people who could be interpreters but for want of training facilities and finance for that. How can a Deaf person join an evening class, go to a tenants meeting, become active in a community group? We desperately need interpreters and the few we have love their work. Next time you see President Carter on television or Jane Fonda addressing the masses on her latest cause, look carefully and you'll see someone near with flying fingers - the interpreter. It could and must happen here.

I have been receiving letters all week about our programme. Many of the hearing correspondents ask where they can learn to sign. I am overwhelmed with joy at the response and also sadness that there are so few places where people can learn to sign. But there are thousands of Deaf people who could organise classes given the encouragement.

Such is the weight of Deaf people's oppression that they have tended to internalise the negative image of themselves that society reflects. The NUD was established in 1976 to change all that - to encourage Deaf people to speak out, to sign out, to develop an awareness and self-respect which will enable them to participate in their own affairs. We have in the past three years started very slowly to do this. The television programme, I think, is a fine achievement - never mind the quality, feel the width.

I started to go Deaf when I was 17 or 18 and my hearing has continued to deteriorate over the past 12 years. The initial experience was traumatic. I bluffed my way as a rather scatty hearing person. When the bluffing had to stop, I entered a no man's land where I felt at home in neither the hearing world nor that of the world of flying fingers. I took a hearing person's conception of the Deaf as rather dumb and daft people with me on my rare journeys into the Deaf world. But gradually the stigma began to evaporate as I began to know Deaf people on their own terms. I love their language. It is a warm and emotional way of communicating. We communicate face to face and the eye cannot lie, nor the body - only words do that. Has this something to do with the universal fear of Deaf people and sign language - the fear of non-verbal self-disclosure?

I am an exile in the Deaf world. I came here to speak on behalf of the natives. Next time, perhaps you will ask a native to come and if he or she accepts your invitation, then that will be one more sign of life - one more reason to hope.

Deaf Broadcasting Campaign

Linz, Austria. September 1981. Maggie Woolley.

The Deaf Broadcasting Campaign was established in January 1980 with the aim of pressing for an improvement in broadcasting provisions for Deaf and hard of hearing people in Britain. We recognised that technology had the potential to make much more of television broadcasting accessible to us through teletext subtitling. However, at the time the output of teletext subtitling amounted to a few hours per week and hardly justified the expense of the necessary equipment - teletext sets or decoders. We also recognised that even if the total output of television were subtitled many Deaf and hard of hearing people would still be unable to benefit. There are two reasons for this. Firstly, additional visual handicaps, particularly those which comes with age, mean that subtitles are difficult to see. Secondly, people in Britain who are either born profoundly Deaf or who lose their hearing before learning to speak are unable to read sufficiently well to understand subtitles due to the poor education they receive. A study by Dr Conrad in 1979 revealed that the Deaf 16 year olds have a reading age of 8 and their speech is unintelligible even to members of their own family. The language of the profoundly Deaf population in Britain is sign language. We therefore recognised that as a minority language group these people had a right to receive and put out information via television in their own language.

The aims of our campaign tried to encompass all these issues and were as follows:

1. To increase the output of subtitled programmes through teletext.
2. To obtain a reduction in the cost of receiving teletext.
3. To have at least one news bulletin per day interpreted in sign language.
4. To have sign language interpretation and subtitles on all programmes giving important information.
5. To have at least one weekly magazine programme for Deaf and hard of hearing people that would be intelligible through the use of subtitles, sign language and clear speech.

I do not wish to dwell further here on the subject of subtitling through teletext. Much good information has already been given to this forum about the advantages which teletext have to offer us. Suffice it to say we applaud the work which is being done and we want to see more subtitles now. I would like to devote most of this paper to the needs of the profoundly Deaf people and the issue of sign language and television. This is because I feel that born Deaf people are the people who least often get the chance to be heard and understood. Because of the additional handicap of poor literacy levels these people are in greatest need when we look at what television can offer.

I have said that the Deaf Broadcasting Campaign began in January 1980 but its genesis can be traced to the emergence of the National Union of the Deaf in 1976. This was a group of born Deaf people whose language was sign. As the only organisation which was run by Deaf people themselves, they soon gathered supporters from all over Britain.

When the NUD looked at the history of the Deaf people they could see that there were two versions. There was the history written and told by hearing people which seemed to be a story of hearing people's achievements in improving the quality of Deaf people's lives. We were told that Deaf people posed problems which were being solved, as never before, by good social services, good special education and increasingly sophisticated hearing aids. The second history was known to few hearing people and was unwritten. This was the story of Deaf people's experience of oppression, despite all that hearing people have done to improve the quality of our lives. Whenever conferences were arranged, books written or television programmes produced about us, the voice of Deaf people themselves was unheard and totally absent. Perhaps the most unjust factor in our oppression was the suppression of sign language and the suppression of Deaf people's culture.

Profoundly Deaf people were viewed as failures by teachers who had failed to teach them to speak intelligibly and as mentally retarded by the general population. Branded as failures and "dummies" and seeing their language prohibited and even punished in schools, Deaf people experienced a more insidious form of oppression, that which is self inflicted through feelings of inferiority. The National Union of the Deaf realised that Deaf people needed a public voice so that their history and experience could become common knowledge. This public voice must come from Deaf people themselves and in sign language. They needed to raise the consciousness of Deaf people to a level where they could take pride in their language and culture - to a level where they could achieve the self-respect and self-confidence necessary to take their rightful place in society.

Sign language is a visual language and therefore requires a visual medium. Television is the one medium through which Deaf people can reach the rest of the population in their own language with subtitles and voices giving instant interpretation. Britain is now a multi-racial society in which other minority language groups such as Asian and Welsh people have their own programmes. The NUD realised that Deaf people also had a right to have their language and culture reflected to them from their television screens. Indeed, given that sign language has to be seen to be understood we felt we had a greater claim than those of languages which can also be written. In May 1979, the NUD made a pilot programme for the BBC 'Open Door' series. Open Door is an access programme in which ordinary people are invited to produce their own programmes. *"Signs of Life"* was the first programme to be broadcast in sign, voice and subtitles by Deaf people themselves. The reaction from Open Door viewers was overwhelming.

Hearing people, particularly, were enthusiastic and many asked where they could learn sign language. We were overjoyed to realise that it was possible to be accepted by hearing people on our own terms.

As the year progressed we learned that hard of hearing people too were not content with television provision. After meeting with several organisations for the Deaf and hard of hearing, we launched the Deaf Broadcasting Campaign (DBC) in an attempt to cater for the needs of all hearing impaired television viewers. In the beginning television people said, "We appreciate your needs but there are so few of you and what you are demanding is so expensive." In fact, there are some ten million hearing impaired people in Britain according to the latest survey. One in six Britons have some level of hearing impairment. All minority groups are given to understand that because they are in a minority they are not important enough to merit the changes they deserve. However, in the DBC we had been oppressed by feelings of insignificance for too long. We were determined to convince programme makers that we were important enough to be acknowledged.

We staged publicity stunts. We inundated members of Parliament and television company directors with well constructed arguments. We handed in a petition to Margaret Thatcher in 10 Downing Street. We attended public meetings about the fourth television channel and put our interpreters on the platform where all could see them. Wherever we went, we made news because Deaf people and sign language had so rarely been seen in public before. To the media we seemed to have a novelty value and we exploited this as much as possible. As newsmakers, we were interviewed on television. Needless to say we demanded subtitles and sign language interpretation for these interviews. By September 1981, we gained an interview at the Home Office and 55 members of Parliament tabled a motion in the House of Commons which echoed our demands. What had begun as a voice of dissent amongst a small group of profoundly Deaf people in the NUD had become a subject for debate amongst the most important decision-makers in the land.

I want to pause here to mention our hearing allies. These have ranged from ordinary members of the public to people in public life and professional people working in the Deaf world. Perhaps our greatest allies have been our interpreters. Without exception, all our allies have firmly resisted any attempts to make them our spokesmen. Television producers have sometimes wanted to avoid communication difficulties by negotiating with our hearing friends but this they have steadfastly refused to allow. This is a remarkable achievement after years of being kept in the background, hardly knowing what was said about us whilst hearing people held court with the outside world. Of what changes have we seen so far? Several regional companies are now giving sign language interpretation on their news bulletins and weather forecasts. In Wales, interpretation was tried for three weeks as an experiment and then the little interpreter box was withdrawn from the screen. This removal was met with a public outcry not least from hearing viewers. It emerged that the interpreter had become a kind of television personality in his own right and viewers looked forward to his appearance. Furthermore, hearing people had been learning signs and were beginning to talk to Deaf people for the first time in their lives. The interpreter panel was restored and is now a permanent part of news broadcasts. Progress with teletext subtitling is slowly improving and in July we were treated to instant subtitling for the first time for the coverage of the Royal Wedding. This event was greeted with acclaim and Deaf people are now anxious that they need not wait for another Royal ‘super event’ before instant subtitling is used again.

Interpreters on television have encouraged the Deaf to demand interpreters elsewhere and more and more events now have sign language interpreters. Where interpreters go, Deaf people follow and gradually become more involved in the hearing world.

On October 11th this year, the same department of the BBC which gave us “Signs of Life” will broadcast “See Hear” - the first in a twenty programme series for Deaf and hard of hearing people. Sign, subtitles and clear speech will be used throughout. “See Hear” promises to be the public voice we have been demanding. But not only this. It aims also to put Deaf people in touch with the mainstream culture by covering current events in a way which they can understand. This “See Hear” team recognised that more of television could be enjoyed by Deaf viewers if more information was available. Thus, part of the programme will be devoted to trailing some of the following week’s programmes and explaining them in subtitles and sign.

Researchers and production teams have had to work directly with Deaf people in order to bring this series to the air. Before work could begin they had to learn how to communicate with Deaf people. Everyone involved has learned basic sign language and the special needs of lipreaders. People working in the studio are equipped with signs for studio jargon. The result of this is that Deaf people now have a team of people within the BBC who are as committed to improving the rest of television as they are. I sincerely believe that attitudes are already changing towards Deaf people. Television can be instrumental in this change of attitude. I am talking here not only about changes of attitudes among hearing people but changes among Deaf and hard of hearing people themselves. The literature of the psychology of deafness has abundant references to our low self image, fear of the hearing world and crushing isolation. The casualties of such experience are to be found in many mental hospitals. Even those of us who manage to stay sane have experienced the psychological oppression of inferiority and hopelessness at times. I make no secret of the fact that as a Deaf person I have also known isolation. However, I believe it can be defeated by a process of coming together. Deaf and hard of hearing people coming together and hearing people and Deaf people coming together. Television can be our most vital tool in this coming together. In our discussions and resolutions at this forum, this is something we must bear strongly in mind.

I wish to thank you for inviting me here and helping the Deaf Broadcasting Campaign and the Deaf people of Britain towards a better life in which we can reclaim our language with pride - in which we can claim our right to be respected and to self-respect - our right to be part of this world.

Preface

The following paper is known in the NUD as 'The Bulgaria Paper'. It was presented by John Hay, Murray Holmes and Dr. G. W. G. Montgomery at the World Federation of the Deaf Congress at Varna, Bulgaria in 1979. This paper inspired the NUD to develop its *'Charter of Rights of the Deaf'* and from there to lay the foundation that both the repression of sign language and the closure of schools of the Deaf in favour of mainstreaming was (and still is) a genocidal move to destory the Deaf community, their culture and their langauge.

Like 'NUD 1976' five years previously, 'The Bulgaria Paper' created for the three authors numerous enemies and critics, but this was to be expected when people get a massive dose of shock. The NUD, at the time. was probably the only organisation to welcome this historic paper, giving it a front page praise in its Newsletter. Historic indeed it was; this paper, in spite of receiving all the wrath and fury of world-wide organisations and people who condemned it, was the originator of the current trend to respect sign language and Deaf culture in Britian.

Bicultural Adaptation and Survival: Integration or Disintegration

Liverpool. September 1980. A. M. Holmes.

When two cultures, economic systems, religions, races or language groups meet on common ground there are several types of interaction possible, none of which are inevitable in the sense that they are uninfluenced by the human choice of peoples involved. The Napoleonic threat to German culture last century focused the attention of philosophers of genius upon the problem and many theories of cultural interaction were propounded such as those of Hegel on national groups, Marx on economic class, Treitkschke and Herder on race and Fichte on culture. Most theories implied confrontation, clash and struggle and at times a thesis-antithesis-synthesis, mother-father-child model suggested a reductionist simplification more appropriate to the resolution of forces in elementary dynamics than to the complexities of human interaction as they appear in modern experimental social psychology.

The first broad type of interaction, which we shall call the Mohican model, is that of simple dominance and total replacement of the 'weaker' culture by the 'stronger.' Examples of this are the replacement of the Celtic language, once the communication mode of all Europe from the Black Sea to the Atlantic but now reduced to a few outlands and islands in the British Isles and Brittany. French linguistic orthodoxy constantly threatens the very existence of Amoricain, the Cornish language has disappeared in England and Gaelic is making a rather artificial recovery in Ireland and Scotland after being proscribed for centuries. Such was the linguistic self-centredness of the Saxon invaders of Britain that the number of Celtic loan words from the original Welsh language may be counted upon one hand. In the religious sphere we can cite the lasting replacement of the protestant Hugenot community in Normandy and North France with the majority state-approved religion. More recently the complete annihilation of the native Tasmanian peoples by immigrant Europeans has been recorded for British television. Even more recently we have seen the total replacement of a capitalist economic alignment in Vietnam, followed closely by the expulsion of racially deviant sub-cultures. In Uganda, the mass deportation of those of Asian descent was based on the legal technicality of possession of formal nationality.

The second type of interaction, which we shall call the McGregor model, occurs when the weaker culture refuses to submit to replacement and embarks on a struggle for recognition which may result in mutual attrition for centuries. A sorry example is the wars of religion which set back European civilisation for decades, and which still have their echoes in the disturbances in parts of Ireland and the United Kingdom today. The Basques still await their Ayatollah but our favourite example was the way in which the Scottish Kings tried for centuries to obliterate clan McGregor, confiscating their wealth, lands and rights and making their very name illegal. McGregors, however, are unsuited to oblivion and not only declined to co-operate in their own extinction, but sang defiance: “If you rob us of name and pursue us with beagles, It’s your roofs to the flame, your flesh to the eagles. While there are leaves in the forest and foam on the river, McGregor despite them will flourish forever”.

The attitude, of course, comes easier from the vantage point of a mountain stronghold as every Scot, Yugoslav or Afghan would confirm. The resilience of proscribed languages puts them in this interaction category. Basque survives centuries of competition from neighbouring Latin languages. In England, the native language survived and emerged 200 years after the conquest by Norman French, while ironically Norrois has itself suffered dialectisation and replacement by ‘proper’ French. The Bulgarian language was the precursor of the Bulgarian nation ensuring the survival of national identity in the face of Ottoman assimilation.

The third broad type of interaction which we shall call the Symbolic model, is that of co-existence of cultures which are clearly separable and co-operate without endangering their separate identity. The tolerant recognition of difference and a mutual understanding of demarcation areas with an explicit absence of hostility marks this kind of separatism. But this arrangement depends upon power-sharing at the political level as cultures cannot always maintain an equivalence of power and efficiency as they develop along their different courses. Without some genuine power sharing, a fairly devised apartheid may easily become a formal mark for simple dominance.

It is the fourth type of interaction which we call the Integration model that interests us most in our work with the Deaf community and its relationship with the general populace in Scotland. Although the word Integration means many things to many people, we see it as a social grouping of people with common interwoven communication and friendship networks. Friendship is incompatible with the doctrine of strife, struggle and dominance and respects cultural identity rather than seeks to replace it with a ‘better’ or ‘stronger’ pattern: assimilation is not integration, the extreme exploitation of cannibalism does not constitute an acceptable integration from the victim’s viewpoint.

Integration of Deaf and Hearing Communities.

At a time when the schools for the Deaf in Scotland have now accepted Total Communication and when the integrational function of the Scottish Workshop gives valuable experience in self-education, organising and leadership to Deaf adults, it is sad to have to report that a reaction has set in some areas.

Inspired by a one-sided interpretation of the recent government report (Warnock) on integrating children with special needs, some education authorities have decreed that profoundly Deaf children must be placed in ordinary schools, putting instant integration before the eventual integration which is the aim of special schools. As King Jordan explained in an Edinburgh workshop, such dispersal and proximity is pseudo-integration, and without communication this kind of integration is about "as meaningful as the relationship between a dog and his fleas" (Young. 1978). In their naivete the new integrationalists assume that (one hour per day peripatetic?) teaching of language suffices to develop language in a profoundly Deaf person, not realising that the problem of ACQUIRING a first language demands a radically different approach to TEACHING literacy to children who already have a spoken language. Without total communication and forbidden sign language such children grow up 'integrated' with neither Deaf, hearing nor Deaf-hearing communities - not even with themselves. There are alternatives to an integration based on ignorance and isolation.

The philosophy of such maltreatment of Deaf children is the shallowest gut-feeling which, albeit in ignorance, accepts the Mohican solution to the problem of the Deaf cultural minority, i.e. replacement of the 'weaker' culture. What these ill-conceived integration plans overlooked is the fact that schools for the Deaf are organic linguistic communities where hearing staff learn sign language, thus enabling a realistic integration to take place at an appropriate time. They also teach children to swim in the school pool rather than expecting them to learn instantly by throwing them overboard from a North Sea oil rig. The genocidal implications of 'integration' which destroys Deaf communities should not be overlooked and, although the comparison may at first seem far fetched, the similarity of technique to that employed by the fascist genocides in occupied Europe should be a cause for concern. Lemkin (1944) coined the term genocide for Churchill's 'crime without a name' and thought it to consist of two phases - first, the destruction of the pattern of the oppressed and second, the replacement of the pattern of the oppressor. This was not solely a matter of simple military annihilation. "There are many ways", said Hitler, "systematical and comparatively painless, or at least bloodless, of causing undesirable races to die out." (Rauschning 1940). In fact a co-ordinated attack upon all aspects of group identity was carried out, simultaneously in the social, political, economic, cultural and biological fields as a calculated strategy.

Deaf people are not racially foreigners in the land of their birth, but they are realistically seen as a minority with a foreign linguistic tradition. The United Nations in general guard the rights of minorities within a nation and often formally guarantee those rights by law as with the educational rights of sub-cultures in regions of the USSR (Holmes 1977) and the outlawing of racial discrimination in employment in USA and UK. But constant vigilance by national Deaf organisations is required if their minority identity is not to be subjected to 'kid-glove genocide' on many fronts.

On the social front, the genocide removed natural leaders and reduced a people to a structureless rabble. If educated intelligent Deaf people of ability are separated from Deaf children and adult groups, then disintegration will follow. Deaf persons offered sinecures in oralist establishments can thus effectively be isolated from the rank and file. Deaf children brought up in a school setting without other Deaf children often think of themselves as hearing children temporarily out of order. In the absence of Deaf adults they think of themselves as becoming hearing on leaving school or even in extreme cases of dying then, because they never see a grown Deaf person. If none of their teachers are Deaf, they do not have any appropriate adults upon which to model themselves and come to think of themselves as second class citizens, condemned to the bottom of the (hearing) class long after they leave school.On the political front, legislation became an agent of genocide and compulsory sterilisation for congenitally Deaf people was legalised in occupied Europe until 1945 but remained in Finland much later (Savisaari 1968).

Less physical, but equally hostile,pieces of legislation against the Deaf may be found in many national codes of law and professional practice. The English association of teachers of the Deaf, for example, is 'unbelievably reactionary' in its hostility to any form of manual communication in schools and to the admission of Deaf people to professional status: they say, "The Association's certificate is awarded on the ability to teach by the oral method, so the examination can only take place in a class which has been taught by the oral method." The secretary of the Scottish Workshop (Hay 1977) called this "the most cool, dictatorial insolence to be imposed on any group of children in the records of our democratic educational system", going on to say that the ruling is "wholly unacceptable to the Deaf community, to those many teachers of the Deaf who identify with us and to Deaf children whenever they are allowed to express a preference." The Scottish teachers of the Deaf largely accept total communication following recent researches showing some 90% of profoundly Deaf children are unable to speak and lipread intelligibly. The oral method has been supplemented by manual communication in the USSR, USA, Scandinavia, much of North England and Scotland. "Unfortunately", as Hay puts it, "the latter still have as a millstone round their neck the most unenlightened part of Europe on this issue - South England." Not to be outstripped by English legislative malevolence, however, the Scottish General Teaching Council registration rules for teachers clearly states "if a candidate cannot hear the ordinary conversational voice at twenty feet, he should be in general rejected." These educational-communicative restrictions are called medical rules and make the medical fraternity sound somewhat professionally isolated and in need of integration with the rest of us. But the Teachers' Association had even more policies to let loose and in March 1978 let this dinosaur escape: "This association believes that hearing impaired persons should not be debarred from qualifying as Teachers of the Deaf because of their hearing impairment, providing that no concessions are made to their hearing impairment and they qualify as teachers and teachers of the Deaf in the normal way." This sounds as if it is firmly rejecting discrimination against Deafness and then firmly endorses it. The logic reminds us of a Chief of Police accused of racial bias in recruiting, who retorted that he had no objection to immigrant policemen and would recruit Congo pygmies - provided that they conformed to the usual height requirements.

The recommendation produced a situation where Deaf children who understand sign must be taught by hearing teachers who do not, and at the same time hearing children who do not understand sign are to be taught by Deaf teachers who do. The logic is the logic of the strategists of genocide - deny the minority group social, economic and professional status and deny them identity by refusing to admit their differences in order to help them, and to admit this difference in order to restrict them. The only consistency is that they are heartlessly restrictive against the Deaf community they profess to serve - at one annual general meeting, the proposal to amend the rules currently excluding Deaf persons from becoming Deaf teachers of the Deaf was dismissed "in a few ill-considered minutes" (Woodford 1979). At their worst, zealous integrationalists seem bent on making it against the law to be Deaf and after years of this 'normalisation' in Denmark, we can sympathise with Jorgen Hvit who demands the freedom to be handicapped (Vognson 1976). How paradoxical that misguided idealists, who seek to normalise handicapped people by legislation, often leave the door open to parents who mutilate the growing child's psyche by irrational denial of the handicap and to less idealistic, less altruistic groups who impose uniformity at any price, and like the masses according to Hitler, "want the victory of the stronger and the annihilation or unconditional surrender of the weaker." (Mein Kampf. Vol 1 Ch 12). On the economic front, Scotland has little to criticise as the employment of Deaf persons has always been very high and ahead of the hearing employment rate. Underemployment has never been eradicated, but has not arisen from repressive moves against the Deaf community. On the contrary, much effort from careers and rehabilitation services has gone into understanding and correcting underemployment. Only recently, however, with the increase in places in higher education for the Deaf and the inauguration of a tutorial residential college in Donaldson's, Edinburgh, does the problem of underemployment look like receding now that Deaf students can take a fully integrated role in local colleges and universities with supportive tuition via total communication available at their residential base. The threat of the cultural identity of the Deaf community is mainly directed towards their sign language. Like the Welsh minority in Britain, the Deaf community regard their language as symbolic of their identity and defend it accordingly with all the conviction of a McGregor at bay. Lane and Battison (Gerver & Sinaiko 1978) have recently outlined the sorry consequences to Deaf language of linguistic solipsism on the Mohican model. Their exordium quite unconsciously parallels the co-ordinated strategy of genocide described above. "They are a linguistic minority..... from this fact, so often overlooked or denied, follow the major givens of the Deaf condition; their cruel ostracism and oppression by the oral language majority, their low standing economically and socially, their effective exclusion from the most higher education and their segregation in compulsory education; likewise, the concerted effort, for nearly a century, to annihilate their languages." These commentators trace the historical oscillation between the many unsuccessful attempts to replace Sign outright and to reduce its status to that of dialect.

Total proscription and dialectisation are no strangers to the Scottish linguistic scene where Gaelic was for centuries eroded and replaced with English and the old Scots form of English - an official language when French was the official language of England - reduced to the status of dialect. Thus after some forty years of formal banning of sign language in schools in Scotland, we are fascinated to observe almost immediately, consequent on the acceptance of total communication in schools, that the dialectisation of Sign swings into action with the introduction of Paget-Gorman in Grampian and the rapid adaptation of British Sign Language into a form of Signed English in Strathclyde and Lothians. The intention here, however, is not so much to impose the linguistic solipsism of the linguists but the educationalists' recognition of problems beyond the narrow concerns of language, namely the fact that occupational advancement at virtually all levels in Scotland correlates not with speech (we have thousands of unemployed people with perfect speech), not with sign language (almost all Deaf people work solely with hearing workmates), but with written literacy in the English language and as the poet Burns said just before dialectisation, "Facts are chiefs that winna ding." Nevertheless, all Scottish schools respect BSL and encourage its use between pupils for social interactions and in senior lessons, if not always in the initial stages of learning English. And most of our educationalists would applaud the clarion cry with which Lane and Battison finally dispose of linguistic imperialism; "Let us set right in 1977 what was set wrong in 1880. Let us.... confirm that no language is incontestably superior to any other, that every language is equally the priceless heritage of all mankind, and that we particularly cherish the free use and development of minority languages precisely because they are subject to repression in the hands of the majority." Yet the most disconcerting threat to the Deaf community is not in the cultural sphere at all and it is the most difficult to evaluate because it is poised on the biological front by people who are convinced they are well intentioned and sometimes are. Here is a world of difference between the application of surgical skills to heal or to destroy individuals but this distinction can become dangerously blurred when we refer to groups rather than individuals. We have already mentioned the eugenic legislation of Axis Europe in 1933 which was the precursor of the racially based genocidal legislation of 1935 and 1938. We further note that the explicit legal anti-minority biological licence of this sort is not unknown elsewhere, for example, in USA where castration was incorporated into the penal code of some states until quite recently. An English eugenicist, Professor Ruggles Gates, opined as late as 1946 that American schools for the Deaf were educating grandchildren of previous students and thought that this justified sterilisation of those with the wrong grandparents. In the current climate of opinion in the region of Fife in Scotland, not only is blanket normalisation in ordinary schools imposed on all Deaf children by their authority, but less responsible opinion has publicly proposed blanket euthanasia for all handicapped babies in the first five years of life as a more eugenic alternative to abortion (Dunfermline Press. May 1978). Apart from the admirable record of psychiatrists, whose stock-in- trade is communication with patients, medical authorities are too often concerned with defective ears than effective brains (Montgomery. 1980). Thus genetic counsellors dealing with Deaf families may easily overstep ethical boundaries by using the authority of their calling to persuade parents at risk to accept sterilisation or abortion. Where eugenically minded advisers employ this travesty of genuine counselling (which by contrast gently respects the rights of the client) they are practising a form of genocide by suggestion and, where a national medical complex has a monopoly of services in a given area, then the stage is set for the 'final solution' of the problems of Deafness. The decrease in the number of Deaf people born in Scotland may be welcomed as a medical advance until one talks it over with a good friend who after all is only a grown foetus and has the uncomfortable feeling that he would not now be allowed to live beyond the foetus stage because his parents were Deaf. At least one London clinic is professing the diagnosis of Deafness before birth with the explicit option of abortion if the test shows Deafness. At least three cases of a travesty of genetic counselling (one vicariously through a hearing sister) leading to the sterilisation of Deaf women have recently come to our notice. To be sure, this is a subject difficult to approach objectively and one's attitude is necessarily coloured by which end of the knife one is at. Whether this is a reasonable purification of the race or the extermination of a minority may be debatable, but the difference between these cases and the deliberate mass attack on the biological front in Axis Europe is only academic as far as the victims are concerned.

The difference between acceptable eugenic progress and professional genocide by public or private practitioners lies in the attitude to the consumer and where genuine consent to genetic advice is obtained, then few ethical objections remain. But to legislate, educate or operate in the absence of consumer consensus is not only foolish but is downright barbaric, no matter how pure the intentions. The 1933 eugenic code prescribed compulsory sterilisation for Deaf people and alcoholics amongst others, but at least in one other case a similar effect was achieved by a well meaning paternalist prohibition of aberration from the dominant culture pattern. This classical example was the Australian government's rehabilitation of the near-alcoholic culture of Pleasant Island near the equator in the Pacific. Regular brewing and drinking of palm wine by Island mothers who shared it with their infants resulted in a social norm whereby the 'hard stuff' was literally imbibed along with mother's milk; a lifelong habituation to alcohol was an integral part of the culture pattern at all ages. Yet this culture pattern tolerated a 7% infant mortality rate until, against local opinion, prohibition of the fermentation of the sap of the local toddy palm was imposed. Now while it is a matter of moral conjecture whether or not any group of people have the right to enforce 'betterment' on any other group, it is much less conjectural to notice that prohibitionists are history's losers. Attempted genocide forged Israel. Sign languages thrive on repression, subject people burst free from decades of enslavement, and McGregors flourish untrammelled. Which brings us back to Pleasant Island. The confident, well- intentioned legislators had overlooked one small aspect of the socio-biological problem, which was that palm wine was the islanders' almost sole source of vitamin B1. Without it the 7% mortality rate leapt to 50% in just six months: it is no longer called Pleasant Island but Nauru.

If this paper, written jointly by colleagues who are respectively Deaf and hearing, had but one theme to leave with you, it would be to insist that Deaf/hearing integration is a noble aim, provided that it is not imposed prematurely and only with the full consent of and consultation with the consumer minority. Good health to you all: May your reserve of vitamin B1 never run dry. Nazdrave.

Preface

Most of the ills of Deafdom are due to not understanding the mind of the Deaf. Authorities in the field of medicine, education and counselling tend to think that the Deaf and hearing do their thinking along identical lines. Only the Deaf themselves know this is not the case. As one of these people and able to describe the mind of the Deaf in written and signed forms. I was asked to submit a paper about it at Stirling University in 1982 and a shortened version of the same at Manchester University in 1985.

The latter was an attempt to convince educators and teachers that the Deaf, having different thought processes, need a different method of imparting instruction from the general approach. In other words, what is good for the hearing is no good for the Deaf. Failure to respond has some bearing on the low language attainment that is widespread in the Deaf world. I venture to think that educators who are aware of this conception tend to ignore it as it would mean a great upheaval in Deaf education and, of course, it would render integration a valueless project. But there was a number of teachers at the Manchester congress to whom the contents of the paper served as an impact. They asked for copies and about a hundred were hastily printed and some were sent overseas.

The third and final version is insterted in *"Beyond Hobson's Choice"* published by the Scottish Workshop Publications. Owing to lack of finance and facilities for further research, a much wider and more convincing version is not available. I applied to Durham University for a three-year bursary but was turned down because the subject was strange to the authorities and they thought such revelations of the Deaf mind would serve little or no useful purpose.

The only work that mentions my observations is Reuben Conrad's book, *"The Deaf Schoolchild"*. I can assume that someday someone would be assigned to do some real research into the introspections on the mind of the Deaf for the sake of reforming Deaf education.

Thought Process: Introspections on the Mind of the Deaf

Manchester. August 1985. A. F. Dimmock.

The subject of my address is something rarely or never thought about or made accessible to clinical assessment or deep research. This failure contributes to the state that refers the Deaf as a deprived group. Thought Process is the way people do their thinking but almost all of them, Deaf or hearing, find it difficult to describe in a clear form this practice that is in constant use. Although no authority, my views are based upon my 60-plus years of association with people similarly afflicted as I am. This lengthy space of time enabled me to analyse their thinking through the mode of communication and behaviour and bring it into comparison with my own which is not very dissimilar to that of the prelingual or those who went Deaf at an early age. The postlingual, those who acquired spoken language before becoming Deaf, are a different class but through integration into Deaf society could have their thought process evolving into that prevalent among the prelingual.

Much written material on thought process is in existence but none covers the field of Deafness. It was produced by philosophers and psychologists and was subject to lengthy debates and disagreements. There appears to be two main schools of thought among these specialists holding different views that are poles apart. One group holds to theories that fit within the broad scope of the behaviourist school which believes that thought is nothing more than sub-vocal speech, or in other words silent speech. Some experimental findings on transpositional behaviour and concept forming in relation to language give general support to this behaviouristic position. The opposing school sees thought as pure and unrelated to language. In fact, they believe that thought is distorted by words. This schools provoke research, debates, surveys and assessments involving vast amounts of time and money and equally vast amounts of printed material that yielded no accepted resolution to the issue.

The idea of thought being pure and unrelated to language corroborates with my own findings of the general thought process of the Deaf. They are related to a common usage of a simple form. We often hear of the wonders of the mind that knows no barriers. While conventional thinking known as internal speech is the main, and in some cases the only form of thinking in normal people, the Deaf are inclined to a more varied form composed of pictorial, imagine and symbolic thinking. As for myself, words are seen as printed or finger-spelled, never as sounded since I am non-oral. I am also able to think in gestural language and do not regard myself as unique since many Deaf people think along identical lines. Internal thinking used by the Deaf may be ungrammatical or consist of words incorrectly pronounced or syllabled. This implies that unheard internal expressive speech, although important in itself, does very little to enhance verbal language mastery.

However, it is well known that the Deaf do well in art and mathematics. This is because these subjects do not rely fully on words and it shows that the Deaf are not word thinkers. A word itself is not meaningful; that characteristic lies in the perception of the meaning of the word. Language is an instrument for human reason but language itself is not necessary for reason. It is a system of symbols and conventions which are dependent on each other and which act in a predictable manner. This shows that the mind can function without language as I stated earlier. It appears that the brain has different departments for different forms of thinking. Very often mind visions are fleeting illusions. Aspects of interest are vividly thought about and committed to memory. The Deaf appear to remember pictures, signs, objects and visual words better than sounds and lip movements. The latter seems to be so lifeless that what is recorded by this means appears easily forgotten. This is apparently some form of disinclination of the mind to deal with matters that are not conspicuous or touching to the feelings.

It is quite possible for the prelingual like myself to be trained to speak and this would inevitably lead to the acquisition of internal speech. This was open to me but, probably through preference or habit, I stuck to the thinking I was accustomed to, and which I found over the years to be quite efficient. I felt that it has given me the advantage of a wider conception of a thought at an instant without having to skip from word to word as internal speech induces. Thinking in pictures is also a quick way of getting a wide coverage of a subject provided that all points needed to know are seen in the mind. The transposing of pictures to words soon became smooth after practice and then it became a habit. Some cannot or, as in my case, prefer not to break a habit that comes naturally to them.

The oral system of teaching most certainly forces ordered thinking upon children. In time they acquire conventional thinking which sometimes does not click well into their natural thinking and gets them into confusion. Ordered thinking forcing the Deaf to think differently from their natural inclination may be responsible for certain mental and nervous strains which are evident in the oral-orientated Deaf. This is made more apparent by the difficulty of lipreading and attempts to articulate words correctly. During infancy, the non-deaf child is talked to and given orders verbally. This goes on all his waking hours till basic understanding is established but logical reasoning is notably absent. This comes later and in some cases never at all. The Deaf child is dragged along this routine till frustration at not understanding anything induces him to use gestures of his own imagination in an effort to communicate with his parents. This type of imparting meaning is purely spontaneous and these non-verbal acts are formed into an effective and flexible combination. This puts the Deaf child ahead of the hearing one in non-verbal intelligence and, indeed, above the average in the whole population. This is rather a remarkable biological phenomenon. The child's thoughts should be exploited rather than condemned as it seems to be done recklessly.

I believe I have shown that the mind of the Deaf so strikingly differs from that of the hearing. The failure of the Deaf in conventional education is largely due to lack of understanding of their mind and mode of thinking, resulting in their being given methods of education designed for the hearing that are not fully accessible to minds not of the masses.

PART FOUR

The 'Integration' Battles

Preface to Section

By the early 1980s, success was visible. Deaf schools were changing to use sign language. But as fast as the schools changed, so too did the oralists succeed in having them closed down in the name of integration; little heeding or caring how those now-orphaned Deaf children coped in large hearing schools. In these infamous deeds they were assisted in four ways; first of all by the Warnock Report which consciously and deliberately chose to reject Deaf people's views, and secondly by disabled people themselves. The latter, in their haste to achieve integration for themselves, they refused to listen to the NUD's pleas. The NUD's offers to support the disabled people's campaigns if they would support Deaf people's campaigns to keep their schools open fell on..... disabled ears.

The third obstacle was the Left. Instead of listening to Deaf people's views, many people on the Left chose instead to push ahead, labelling Deaf views as "segregationalist" or "separatist", and patting themselves on the back for their "radicalism". The fourth difficulty arose when local authorities saw a chance to cut education spending and be seen as "right on" at the same time. If a Deaf child were to be truly integrated into a hearing school, it would cost far more than to continue to send them to a Deaf school. But if they were to be merely flung into the water and left to sink or swim, ah, that cost least of all....

Thus at the very time when Deaf organisations could have relaxed the struggle and turned their full attention to the new needs of converted Deaf schools, they were forced to spend all their time fighting to keep this very schools alive - schools which had been established as far back as the 1820s, and which were proud centres of Deaf pride and history. Despite all the campaigns of the last ten years, and the quality of some of the papers included here, the picture looks as bleak in 1992 as it did in 1982.

Preface

These first two small papers are typical of numerous short papers and pamphlets which the NUD used in its campaigns and group discussions. Papers like these were distributed when campaigns against school closures were in effect and also at meetings when discussions for closures of Deaf schools in favour of integration of Deaf children into mainstream schools were taking place. As usual, heated arguments with pro-integrationists were generated, but victory usually belongs to the oralists in that Deaf schools more often than not were closed down.

Open Letter to All Parents of Deaf Children

Wheatley. September 1981. Education Sub-Committee.

1. We, Deaf and hearing people who are here today, ask you to try and keep an open mind to realise that there are two sides to this picture. We are very worried about the philosophy of the National Aural Group and can see many dangers that lie ahead from our experience. We cannot say everything here, and hope you will write to us to find out more.

2. 'We' are Deaf people from all walks of life; Deaf people with degrees, people who mix with hearing people all day, who have many hearing friends and who went to hearing schools all our lives. 'We' include hearing people too; headmasters, judges, professors, social workers, doctors and parents of Deaf children like yourselves.

3. 'Oralism' has been used in this country for over 100 years, and we have heard these same views on hearing aids for generations. Please listen to the voice of our experience:- You cannot eliminate deafness by giving people hearing aids, just as you cannot make blind people see by giving them sticks.

4. People who advocate natural oralism are on record as saying that "in future there will be no more Deaf people." This is a terribly dangerous lie. We know that there are thousands of situations in life that no hearing aid will overcome - sitting in groups like families, clubs, pubs, sport activities, hobbies, parties, meetings, conferences, community activities, meeting the opposite sex and all social activities. This leaves very few situations; imagine your own lives and you will see just how few.

5. The only way we can genuinely integrate is through sign language, used where appropriate with speech, residual hearing, fingerspelling and lipreading. Through Total Communication, with hearing people meeting halfway.

6. The only way in which this current integration idea can work without causing severe mental damage to Deaf children is through these four points:

a. Total Communication (TC) at home and at school.

b. Teaching hearing children to sign.

c. Using Deaf culture in school assemblies, etc.

d. Involving the Deaf community in helping with your child.

Without these, your child will be lost in the world with no identity at all. We need both the Deaf and the hearing world for balance. It is NOT an either/or choice as the National Aural Group (NAG) infer.

7. All Deaf people want to talk as well as they can. Make no mistake about that. But we know that sign language does not impair speech development - if anything, it improves it through growth of confidence and identity.

8. A final cautionary note about the NAG. It include people who have made it impossible for Deaf people to teach Deaf children. Is that not in itself cause for suspicion?

9. If you would like to know why we want to be first class Deaf citizens, not second class hearing citizens, please write to NUD at address given below.

Best wishes to you and your children ......

Deaf Community in Danger

London. June 1985. NUD Education Sub-Committee Pamphlet.

All over Britain, oralists and educationalists are putting more and more Deaf children into hearing schools and forcing Deaf schools to close. If they are not stopped, there will be no Deaf community left in the future when these young Deaf children grow up.

WHY IS DEAF COMMUNITY IMPORTANT?

1. Like the various communities in the hearing world, Deaf people need to meet each other to share their common participation in their own language and culture. Most ethnic groups have their own communities - the Asians, the blacks, and so on.

2. Deaf people need the association and moral support of other Deaf people within their own community to give them the strength, pride and determination to succeed and survive in a predominantly hearing world.

3. Should the oralists get their way, there will be many Deaf children classified as oral failures, and having never met any Deaf adults inside or outside of their schools, where will they fall back on to seek help from the Deaf themselves to enable these young Deaf oral failures to survive and succeed in the hearing world?

4. If there is no Deaf community, there will be many Deaf people who would end up as living wrecks. This is dangerous and must never occur.

Oralism is the biggest single contributing factor to the destruction of Deaf individuals as first class Deaf adults, and oralism instead makes Deaf people third class hearing persons, one class below other ethnical and disabled groups. The oralists have an impossible dream, to make Deaf people 'normal' like hearing people. They have repeatedly failed in their crazy quest for the last 100 years. Those Deaf people the oralists claim to demonstrate the success of their dream were in fact hard of hearing - not profoundly Deaf.

People are starting to study the language of the Deaf, British Sign Language (BSL), and so far linguists are amazed to find that our language is indeed a language - not merely a collection of gestures and mimes. BSL has its own structures, features, rules and grammar. This is the language of all the Deaf communities in Britain, and it is the language that helps the Deaf to live on in the world in which they would otherwise have given up 'living for'. BSL gave to Deaf people what oralism and the oralists cannot give - a base for language acquisition in the early pre-school years.

Deaf people and hearing friends of the Deaf community are trying to bridge the gap between the Deaf world and the hearing world. They are trying to do this through Total Communication, which means the simultaneous use of signing, lipreading, writing and amplification. A lot of Deaf schools are using Total Communication and these schools have reported that Deaf pupils are much more brighter, more interested in lessons, progress quickly and are much more advanced than those who were taught by the oral-only method.

Total Communication helps the Deaf to forge a link with the hearing world and thus helps them to take active participation. Oralism does precisely the opposite - it creates isolation, and what's more, it destroys a good number of Deaf individuals. The oralists do not like signing and do not show any respect for the rights of the Deaf to use and develop their language. They are interested in their impossible dream - no matter at what cost. This is dangerous. They are phasing out fine Deaf schools, which is attacking the roots of the British Deaf community. They are setting up partially hearing units in hearing schools and herding Deaf children like cattle into these units. We must stop them from doing much harm to these Deaf children. We are fighting these moves which are slow and systematic destruction of the Deaf community. If any of you, Deaf or hearing, care for Deaf children, their education, their future and their rights, please try to give your help and support. The NUD will be pleased to get in touch with you, and supply further facts and information.

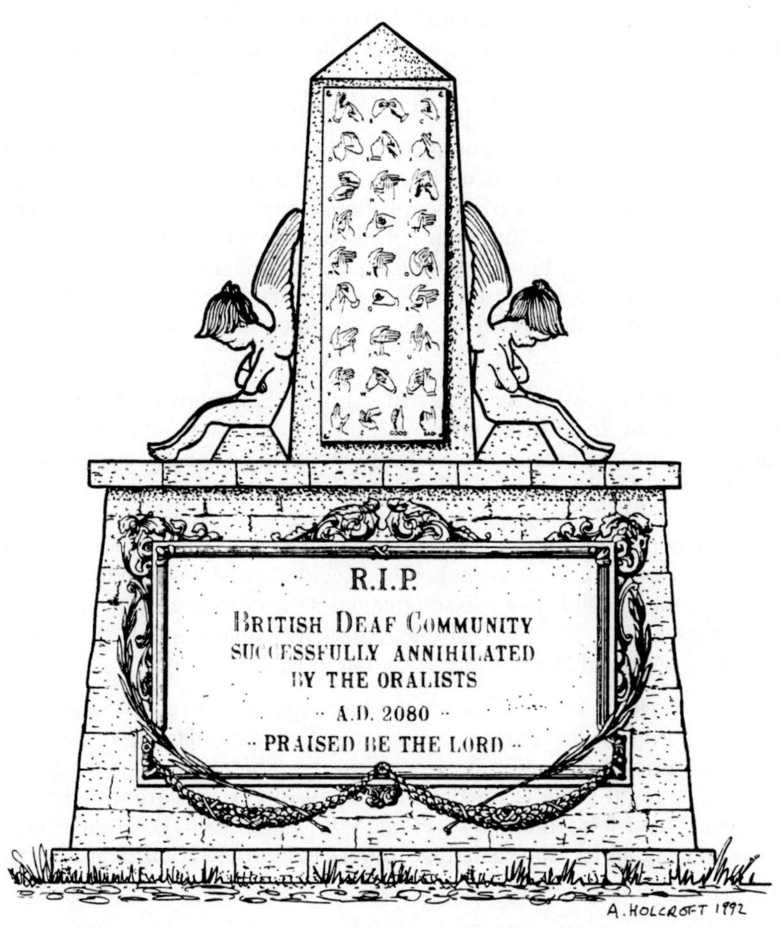
R.I.P.
BRITISH DEAF COMMUNITY
SUCCESSFULLY ANNIHILATED
BY THE ORALISTS
· A.D. 2080 ·
· PRAISED BE THE LORD ·
A. HOLCROFT 1992

Preface

Almost two decades have passed since herding Deaf children into schools for the hearing in the hope that they would end up as hearing children. The ludicrous phantasy was foreseen by those who knew something about Deaf people and Deafness as a disaster but it appealed to parents of Deaf children who thought this type of education would enable their children to grow up and be like themselves. When they realised too late that most, if not all, did not succeed, they began to regret being led up the garden path by dishonest counselling.

Since the advent of the National Deaf Children's Society (N.D.C.S.), much has been done to advise parents on the pitfalls and what steps should be taken. The society is comprised of hearing people but a number of Deaf are activists in it. The director, Harry Cayton, and many of his backers are users or supporters of sign language and strong believers of total communication as instruction for Deaf school children. Every day they use sign language as a communicative medium for themselves and their children. This welcome trend is due to the gospel preached by the N.D.C.S.

If NUD is to be effective in its campaign for better education and the defeat of illiteracy, some form of alliance with the parents must be cemented and an all out-war against dishonest counselling must also be fought. A case of misjudgement occurred at Malta in 1957 when the first school for the Deaf was opened. The parents of the Deaf pupils were taught English or Maltese, a basically Arabian language corrupted with Italian. The children were not consulted as it was thought they do not know their own minds. They decided on Maltese and when the children grew up, they found them disadvantaged as access to better jobs depended on knowing English. Now the parents admit they made a daft decision that subsequently deprived their children of good jobs.

When the legal recognition of sign language, assumed to be inevitable thanks to jurisdiction of the European Parliament, comes there is bound to be a big upheaval among educational authorities and educators. Sign language may be mandatory in all schools for the Deaf, even in PHUs (Partially Hearing Units). They may have to mend their ways and if they do not NUD should arm itself with the respective legislation so that the union can remind authorities and school heads when they are out of step.

Dr Reuben Conrad's survey among Deaf school children, published in 1979, most obviously caused a lot of embarrassment among the Government and authorities. Since then no new survey has cropped up. The reason is obvious - they do not want another embarrassment - and they prefer to sweep the mess under the carpet.

Integration of Profoundly Deaf Children into Partially Hearing Units

Guildford. October 1982. A. F. Dimmock.

The integration in question was implemented by the Government and educational authorities after a study of the recommendations in the Warnock Report. Warnock invited comments from specialised bodies and individuals whose knowledge of the Deaf was fragmentary, and contacts with them almost nil. Former consumers of Deaf education, people who experienced the problems of Deafness all their lives, welfare workers and missionaries who had years of association with the Deaf, were not asked to give advice. Recommendations from national associations of the Deaf were ignored. The possibility of using sign language as an educational tool was never considered. Literally all that which concerned the Deaf and Deafness was swept under the carpet. How then could the Warnock Report have had authoritative status? There was unmistakable evidence to show that its reporters took pains to bend over backwards to make provision for those with a minority auditory language. It all sums up to the fact that the Government and educational authorities are pursuing a policy of high bias and outright discrimination.

Since 1945 a new form of syndrome became apparent. School leavers from oral-only schools and Partially Hearing Units (PHU) stared blankly when questioned by the means of speech, writing or sign language. This is now known as the 'Dummification Process'. This result affects not only language development but emotional maturity and self-respect. Dr John Denmark, a psychiatrist at Whittingham Hospital, Preston, noticed that victims of the process were emotionally disturbed and prone to suicidal tendencies. The cure was to expose them to sign language and Deaf adults at Preston Deaf Club. Another major fault in PHUs is that small children are schooled alongside older ones. The daily procedure is to teach the lowest elements because of the presence of small children. This form of teaching is a repetition to the older ones and is repeated all over again when there are new admissions of smaller children. How then could older Deaf children progress educationally?

Mrs Morag Rosie who is with us here today was subjected to this form of sub-standard education. By all means she should be a moron. But she had the great fortune to have Deaf parents who knew exactly what to do. Her father took off his coat, rolled up his sleeves and forced her to write English correctly. Her sister underwent the same parental treatment and has become a successful businesswoman.

The National Union of the Deaf (NUD) conducted a survey among profoundly Deaf school leavers. The highlight of the survey was that semi-literacy, depicting a reading age of eight years, was found to be greater in PHU leavers than in others from special schools by a staggering 40%. The absence of State Reports on PHUs in a way confirms the evidence, and it is also a clear admission that all is not well with PHUs. About 60% of all oralists who were tested had voices that resembled farmyard brayings and 75% of that number were products of PHUs. According to the given figures, speech teaching at these units is lagging just as far behind as education. Concluding the report on the survey, the NUD declares that to send Deaf children to PHUs is a disservice.

An interesting account of the consequences of educating Deaf children in public schools took place at the Jericho Hill School for the Deaf and Blind in British Columbia, Canada. The Ministry of Education in the area issued an order to mainstream the Deaf children of the school into the public education system, in spite of a report recommending the school to be more autonomous that was submitted by a local educator who had a mandate to look into the school's records and problems. The report was ignored and the mainstreaming stepped up. This reflected a general feeling in the Ministry that handicapped children should be integrated into society. At first glance, the idea might appear to make sense. Why should children be separated from parents and forced to live in a distant school that is unfamiliar to them?

Several years were to pass before parents found their so-called integrated children were just dummies. They displayed all the symptoms of the Dummification Process and stared blankly when spoken to. Frustrated parents and angry adult members of the Deaf community joined in alliance and declared war on the mainstreaming. Seeing the evidence, the authorities relented and stopped mainstreaming. The Jericho Hill School was restored to its former prestige. It was given more money and allowed to expand. But there remained one unfortunate aspect to the saga. Those exposed to mainstreaming may remain dummies for life, so damage was done because of a mistaken ideology. Had the authorities listened to the people who knew best, the Deaf themselves, so much damage would have been averted.

Government circles and education authorities have been constantly claiming that the number of born Deaf and profoundly Deaf children are dwindling. This is held in grave doubt since no official census of the Deaf population was carried out. Furthermore a research paper submitted by Dr Andreas Markides, of Manchester University, states that the population is getting Deafer although it does not contain ample reference to the degree of Deafness in children. It appears that the advancement of medical knowledge and techniques cannot stop the increase of Deafness. It tends to be obvious that the authorities have crammed Deaf children into PHUs and thus dried up the incoming roll for special schools. This is a deliberate ploy designed to close such schools and save money that, according to financial reckoning, generally results in meagre savings. Now we are seeing schools being closed at a time when they are finding greater success in educating the Deaf through the introduction of total communication.

The authorities managed to gain support for their scheme from hearing parents of Deaf children by bludgeoning them into the belief that PHUs are best for their children. An extract from a report by the West Scotland Region of the NDCS is as following:-

"It will be said that many parents are perfectly satisfied. It is certainly true that if too many parents assume that if their child is out of the house from 8.30am till 4.30pm he is receiving adequate full time education. They only become alarmed when the child leaves school and it then transpires that the child is almost unemployable as he has not acquired the basic skills of reading, writing and arithmetic. Often he cannot communicate adequately in sign language since in some schools signing is still frowned upon. Too late to do much about it. Too late that is for some, but not for all, for many of our Deaf children have greatly improved on their academic standards after leaving school, by their own efforts and with the help of understanding adults. This would seem to indicate that the fault often lies within the system and not always with the child."

If PHUs are to be made successful, the introduction of total communication or sign language interpreters is essential. This is the principal recommendation of all major associations of the Deaf like BDA, RNID, RADD and NUD. The latter has published *'The Rights of the Deaf Child'* in which emphasis is given on Deaf children's rights to be educated by a system most suitable to them which turns out to be total communication.

Preface

The NUD's 5th Convention was held at St. Joseph's Centre for the Deaf in Manchester on September 1984. It provided the lowest turnout of NUD membership and attendance was indeed very poor. Little did the NUD know that its guest speaker, Harlan Lane, was going to set alight flames of change, passion and history of the Deaf community of Britian on that day.

'Who is Harlan Lane?' was the general remark. And beacuse he was unknown, some members decided that he was not worth the trip. But when he delivered his paper, he generated an interest and atmosphere that was both engrossing and electric. Never before had Deaf people heard about their history.... a history which all Deaf thought was forever erased from the face of the earth. Harlan Lane gave Deaf people inspiration and hope. And more, he gave Deaf people pride and confidence. He made Deaf people realise that it was not impossible to delve back to the past to create a picture of Deaf people's own history.

Great things began in humble beginnings and it is true to say that from the humble beginning in St. Joseph's Deaf Club in Manchester, Harlan Lane has both blazed a trail and set a course for members of the British Deaf Community to direct their lives.

The NUD is pleased to report that wherever and whenever Harlan Lane gives talks in Britain, he attracts large audiences ......

Why the Deaf are Angry

Manchester. September 1984. Harlan Lane.

When I began, ten years ago, to study the history of the Deaf and their languages, visiting schools and libraries, gathering documents, I was intrigued, full of questions. I wondered, why has no one written a history of the Deaf, and why hasn't a Deaf person done so? The Deaf are, after all, a sizable minority: in the United States alone some two million people rely on manual rather than oral communication in their everyday lives. Why do the sketches of Deaf history in textbooks for educators of the Deaf refer mainly to hearing people and rarely to Deaf people? Why do they mention the writings of hearing persons and almost never those of Deaf persons? Once there were many Deaf intellectuals - for example, Laurent Clerc, who founded the education of the Deaf in the United States in 1816, was cultivated, well-informed, fluent in several languages - but now few Deaf people graduate high school; there are no Deaf college students in most of the world; most Deaf adults read little if at all, and they are usually unskilled labourers. How did this major change come about? Why did the Deaf and their hearing friends let it happen?

Today there is a vast hearing establishment, trained at great cost to the nation, to serve the Deaf: speech therapists, audiologists, special educators, and rehabilitation counsellors. Yet this establishment excludes the Deaf from its ranks and the counsel of the Deaf from its plans. It proceeds with a purely medical conception of what it is to be Deaf, a medical model that tidily blames all the ills of the Deaf on a cruel nature, and calls on the health professions to deal with them while disturbing the rest of society as little as possible. Deaf people themselves, however, seem to have a social rather than medical model of what it is to be Deaf; they mention the social ties and language that binds them together into a community; when asked about their handicaps, they cite educational loss, job loss and not hearing loss. I wondered, how has it happened that the very professions created to serve the interests of the Deaf are totally at odds with what the Deaf perceive as their interests?

As I examined the writings of hearing and Deaf people across the ages, the history of the Deaf began to reveal the answers to these questions. Where I began intrigued, I have ended up angry like many Deaf people themselves. For the history of the Deaf is a history of cruel and stupid oppression. It is a history of bigoted hearing people who could not tolerate the diversity of humankind, who have sought to interpret it as deviance and who have used the schools to force their spoken language and their pathological conception of deafness on Deaf children.

Throughout this history, the open-minded reader hears the voice of the oppressed and largely powerless Deaf protesting their treatment by the hearing majority, pleading with the fair-minded among them to respect the views and language of the Deaf. Listen to Pierre Desloges, the first Deaf author, writing in French in 1779: "It would be a serious mistake to think of us as dumb animals whose fate is only to vegetate.... Our language is highly appropriate for giving us accurate ideas and for enlarging our understanding." Listen to Isaac Goldberg, an American Deaf chemist writing at the turn of the century: "Pure oralism has not a leg to stand upon. It is a menace to the Deaf mentally and morally, and robs them of happiness and peace of mind. If I can do anything to combat this foolishness and this crime, please call on me".

Yes, the Deaf have been angry and are still angry. Listen to Murray Holmes, writing from Scotland in 1981: "Now is the time to restore Deaf people to the positions of responsibility denied to them by the oralists and to throw away the oralist package along with other repressive doctrines such as fascism, (slavery), and other forms of human sacrifice ...."

And listen to John Hay in the same volume: "(We should be aware of) the genocidal meaning of 'integration' which destroys Deaf communities and (be concerned by) the similarity of its techniques to those (of) the fascist genocides in Occupied Europe".

The history of the Deaf justifies such anger for it accuses hearing society, and especially the hearing establishment serving the Deaf, of four serious charges:

(1) You are committing the fraud of oralism.

(2) You are trying to wipe out the language of the Deaf.

(3) You disregard the views and abilities of the Deaf.

(4) You are currently engaged in a program aimed at destroying Deaf language, marriage, education and culture by eliminating specialized schools for the Deaf.

CHARGE 1. THE ORALIST FRAUD:

What is generally presented as the history of the Deaf nowadays is in fact an oralist fraud. It is a record of the efforts of hearing people to replace the language of the Deaf with their language, to replace signs with speech. It calls itself the history of the Deaf - yet it is a history not of Deaf people but of their hearing "benefactors", who claim that the only proper route for elevating the Deaf is oral instruction.

Neither history, nor method, nor progress is here if by method we mean a reasonable procedure that generally succeeds. How do you teach speech to those who never spoke? These hearing histories tells us: be patient; use every device you can think of. All of the methods across the ages come down to this: some observations on how we make various speech sounds, some suggestions on which sounds to teach first and some prejudices on what the Deaf child should be doing with his hands (hold the teacher's throat, his jaw, his tongue or his mirror).

Patience instead of a method. A day, a week, a year amount to nothing in the struggle to twist your tongue around a vowel. The truly Deaf need so much diligence, in fact, to make the least progress in articulation that many writers recommend the choice of a teacher whose mind is not too active. Monks like Ponce de Leon, who first taught speech to the Deaf in 16th century Spain, also make good teachers for they have much time and patience in worldly matters such as tongue positions.

If the history of oral education of the Deaf reveals not a single principle for making a successful pupil, it reveals many for making a successful teacher. Principle first: the rich need your help as well as the poor and the rich can pay for it; the history of oralism glitters with jewelled aristocracy. Secondly: teach a few, carefully chosen pupils. When a teacher's pay depends on contented parents, he must select pupils with favourable characteristics: the greater their intelligence, the later the age when they lost some hearing and the more hearing they still have, the better. Deny your pupil's unique qualities: only teachers vary in intelligence; there are no degrees of deafness nor diverse ages at which it begins - none worth noting. Disregard your pupil's earlier teachers and exaggerate your own accomplishments: one of your pupils can sing, another recite from the Bible, a third can speak some words in a foreign language he has never studied before. Teach only a few students but give the impression of teaching many. Be patient, the job will take years: ideally you should live in your pupil's home, or make him pay to live in yours. Swear your pupils to secrecy; permit no one to observe you; the more you make your method a secret, the more people will believe in its power. To keep your method secret, you must hire only your relatives. You must publish: suggest that you have a method; mention your famous predecessors in this art, for that makes the profession seem more grand but claim that your method is completely original and that you learned about their works after your book was written. Get testimonials from your pupils - they will surely co-operate - and from other oral teachers who may ask the same of you.

Am I fair to the oralists? Consider with me the English tradition that began with John Wallis in the mid-1600s and continues with Thomas Braidwood in the 1700s. Certainly Wallis was intelligent: he was a founding member of the Royal Society, a distinguished group of scientists. Wallis was professor of geometry and librarian at Oxford, and he wrote an English grammar with an introduction to phonetics. However, the other professors at Oxford described him as "a liver by rapine", "a liver by perjury", "a breaker of oaths who could always make black white and white black", "so extremely greedy of glory that he steals feathers from others to decorate his own cap .... writes down their ideas and publishes them without giving credit to the authors".

Wallis had read about how the Deaf children of Spanish nobility were taught speech so he decided to try the same thing with some English children. Soon he announced in a letter to the Royal Society that he had taught a Deaf and dumb child to speak and understand language. The pupil, Deaf since he was five, was Daniel Whaley, son of the mayor of Northampton. Wallis took Whaley in front of the Royal Society and the boy pronounced distinctly various words put by the members. They concluded by applauding Wallis' achievement, which led to an audience with King Charles II. The fact that Whaley had some hearing remaining, and was recovering speech and not learning it for the first time, went more or less unnoticed in the general enthusiasm.

Wallis also mentioned a second pupil. This boy, though Wallis did not say so, had received speech lessons for three years from another member of the Royal Society, William Holder. But when the first teacher moved away, the boy's speech deteriorated and his father, an admiral, brought him to Wallis, who took credit in his letter for the boy's accomplishments. When Holder came across Wallis' published letter, he sent a complaint to the Society: the title of the first English teacher of the Deaf belonged to him, as Wallis well knew. Wallis called Holder a liar, but his contemporaries judged Wallis the plagiarist.

Wallis' instruction, in any event, had no enduring result; the admiral's son stopped speaking once again. The famous philosopher, Thomas Hobbes, knew Wallis very well and had this to say about his method: he who can make a Deaf man hear deserves to be honoured and enriched; he who can make him speak only a few words deserves nothing; but he who brags of this and cannot do it, deserves to be whipped.

In the last years of his life, Wallis stated in another letter to the Society that teaching speech to the Deaf does not lead to permanent gains, so the teacher should emphasize written language, not spoken. He also said that the Deaf are extremely able in expressing their thoughts by signs and that the hearing must learn this language of the Deaf in order to teach them their own by showing them which words correspond to which signs. The instructor would first write a few clear simple sentences and then explain them by signs to give his pupils an understanding of simple propositions.

In view of the evidence that Wallis was a plagiarist, abandoned speech teaching and used sign, it is astonishing that the whole shaky edifice of British oralism cites him as its foundation.

A few decades later, the most successful oralist of them all, whose family monopolised education of the Deaf in Britain for a century, was inspired by reading Wallis' letters to go to seek his own fortune as a teacher of the Deaf. His name was Thomas Braidwood and he was a mathematics teacher in Edinburgh. A rich merchant from Leith brought him his son, Charles Shirreff, to educate; this boy had become Deaf when he was three years old. This was 1760 and about the same time that the Abbe de l'Epee took his first pupils in Paris; both men found it necessary to learn sign language to communicate with their students. Braidwood taught primarily rich hard-of-hearing pupils. The Abbe de l'Epee taught, housed and fed large numbers of poor Deaf children at his own expense and he used manual language to instruct them. For him, speech was an ancillary skill, education the all-important goal.

Over the course of a few years, Braidwood taught Shirreff, then fifteen, to speak a little again and to read and write. He advertised his success and soon he received other pupils from families that could afford his high fees. In the end, Shirreff chose a profession that made few demands on the speaking skill so painfully restored: he became a successful painter of miniatures. One acquaintance of his denied that he ever did recover much speech: "More than a hundred inhabitants of Cambridge would admit," he wrote, "that they could never understand a single sentence of Mr Shirreff's."

Braidwood's fame grew in Britain but when Samuel Johnson and James Boswell visited his school they helped to establish his reputation throughout Europe. Thomas Braidwood's school in Edinburgh gave birth to many more throughout the British Isles, making up a tight-knit monopoly. As with most other oralists, the principle of secrecy imposed on Braidwood the necessity of hiring relatives to manage the growing business. First, Braidwood's school moved to Hackney near London. Son John and his mother ran the school until John's death, when his wife took control. John's eldest son accepted the invitation to re-open the Edinburgh school but was said "to take little interest in the instruction." This grandson of Thomas Braidwood, named John like his father, left abruptly after a year for America. It was rumoured that he misused school funds; he died an alcoholic shortly after leaving a debtor's prison in New York. He was succeeded by Robert Kinniburgh, a minister, who was sent to the Braidwood academy at Hackney for training, then placed under a bond never to teach anyone else how to teach the Deaf. Eventually, however, he was allowed to take private pupils of his own provided that he pays half the fees received to the Braidwood family. It was about this time that Kinniburgh refused to reveal the secret of Braidwood's craft to Thomas Gallaudet, who had come from America to learn how to teach the Deaf. It is a happy irony that Kinniburgh's refusal sent Thomas to the Paris school and thus was indirectly the cause of sign language instruction coming to America.

To their schools in London, Birmingham and Edinburgh, the Braidwood clan added yet one more. The parents of a Deaf boy attending a Braidwood school, unhappy about the cost of his tuition, organised a school for the poor Deaf in Bermondsey under the direction of a local minister. So synonymous with Deaf education had the name Braidwood become that when Joseph Watson, Thomas Braidwood's nephew, offered to instruct the pupils, he was hired and after about two decades the school moved to London where Joseph's son took charge. All in all, the Braidwood oralist monopoly on British Deaf education lasted six decades.

There are several indications that the Braidwood clan soon became aware of the futility of efforts to train speech, as had John Wallis before them. Indeed, the report of the Edinburgh school in 1822 affirmed: "Signs are the only language the Deaf can comprehend and they must be taught by its means."

Nowadays, we are told that the art of teaching the Deaf to speak has a glorious history and long experience that "substantially in all cases" Deaf children can thus be restored to society.

But what are the facts? In America, only one in ten Deaf adults can read a newspaper. Their average Deaf seventeen year old is six years behind in arithmetic - their best subject - and eight years behind in reading. And those among them who became Deaf before learning English, the language of the schools, are doing even worse. In England, these prelingually Deaf high scholars, after ten years of strict oral training, read at a level typical of hearing students half their age. they leave school at sixteen with a reading age of eight. In short, endless efforts to teach the Deaf child to see on the lips the messages of a language he never knew or no longer uses are completely frustrated. Meanwhile, the classroom teacher continues to speak English, with or without few isolated signs. Under these conditions very few of the thousands of students with limitless ability to learn in their primary manual language can get through high school, not to mention university. No wonder that 80% of the Deaf in America work in manual or unskilled jobs.

Now, the hearing benefactors of the Deaf tell us that oral instruction is the oldest and best established method for educating the Deaf, that the one absolute requirement of oral instruction is that the teacher and pupil must never use sign, that oralism gives the Deaf easy intercourse with the rest of society, discourages Deaf congregation and intermarriage, helps the Deaf read in English while cultivating their minds and aids in making them "as precisely as possible like other people".

History, however, true history gives us a different understanding of oralism. In fact, the oralist tradition is a story of greed, plagiarism, secrecy, trickery - but not education. Its aim is speech. In the pursuit of that illusory goal, a few Deaf sons of wealthy noblemen were also, almost incidentally, taught a few things. Nothing has come down to us from this tradition except one more reason to distrust those who style themselves the benefactors of the Deaf for their own gain. One man, a silent monk in 16th century Spain, Pedro Ponce de Leon, had an idea: using sign language, the Deaf could be taught some speech. One man, one idea - an idea that was plagiarised, published, translated, rationalised, propounded, cited, footnoted, cross-referenced, capitalised - but still the same idea. This is the final dirty secret of the history of oralism: it is not a history at all. Should we now refuse to recognise this fact and follow instead the preaching of the hearing establishment, I fear we will but repeat past mistakes, condemning the friends of the Deaf to sterile efforts and the Deaf themselves to lives of ignorance, poverty and isolation.

CHARGE 2: THE ANNIHILATION OF SIGN LANGUAGE:

Our daily newspapers record the struggle of various minorities for acceptance of their difference and especially their language. Spanish speakers protest their oppression in the United States, Basque speakers in Spain, French speakers in Canada, Tamil speakers in India, Georgian speakers in the Soviet Union - the list goes on and on. But this is not a modern development: language and power are intimately related. Language policy has long been a tool of oppression, an instrument of empire, used to create homogeneity and obedience to a central power, used to minimise or eliminate diversity. first among the rights demanded by language minorities is typically the conduct of their children's education in their own language, at least in part.

In America, the community using the manual sign language of the Deaf has been at odds with the surrounding community speaking English for over a century, ever since the Deaf Frenchman, Laurent Clerc, and his American colleague, Thomas Gallaudet, created a family of residential schools for the Deaf throughout the land where a single language, evolving from the manual language of the Deaf in France, served all the purpose of a daily life, including worship and instruction. And once again the struggle centres on education: shall the children of the signing community be educated, at least in part, in their minority (manual) language or shall spoken English exclusively dominate? Thus the history of the Deaf in the United States is the history of a struggle in which, by a bitter irony, the community of signers is opposed to their would-be benefactors, the English-speaking establishment charged by the nation with improving the situation of the Deaf.

Speakers of a majority language commonly view those who use another language in their midst as deficient; to be thus demeaned is the unhappy lot of the French community in Canada, the Basque community in Spain and the signing community in America - to cite a few examples. The oppression of the American Sign Language of the Deaf and its users, however, has been particularly severe because in the first place this language has appeared so exotic to English speakers and, in the second place, because the varying degrees of hearing impairment of most of its users seemed to validate the tendency to view them as deficient.

The Deaf community itself, however, has historically rejected this pathological model of its situation. The Deaf are too familiar with what their manual language does for them to ever reject it. And they are too injured by the sacrifice of education in the name of rehabilitation to ever embrace rehabilitation as their main goal in life.

It is no accident, then, that Deaf history is mainly a struggle between the pathological and social models of the Deaf condition - mainly a struggle for the acceptance of their sign language which forces a choice between these two models. The struggle has involved wide swings between these polar conceptions of the Deaf condition; hearing action and deaf reaction have see-sawed back and forth ever since the 18th century in which European societies first took an interest in the signing communities in their midst. The long-term trend, however, has been unmistakably against signing communities and their languages. Consider France: in the middle of the last century there was 160 schools for the Deaf and the manual language of the signing community was the language of instruction in all of them; by the beginning of this century, it was not allowed in a single one. Similarly, in mid 19th century there were 26 schools for the Deaf with the American Sign Language (ASL) the language of instruction in all; by the dawn of this century, there were 139 schools and in every one ASL was forbidden. When the dominant group in society sets out to destroy a minority language, replacing that language in schools is not its only means. It can also seek to convince the users of the minority language - especially the children - that they speak an inferior dialect of the majority language; that they must replace their "low" Spanish with "high" Spanish, or their "low" sign with "high" sign. "Low" sign in this smear campaign is the language of the Deaf community - ASL in the United States, BSL in Britain. "High" sign is manual English, a hodgepodge of signs invented for various prefixes, suffixes, prepositions, conjunctions and so on, merged in a befuddling order for the Deaf child with his sign vocabulary and contributing nothing to his comprehension or understanding of English. Although signing at Deaf children in English word order - whether in manual English or in Total Communication - is hailed as a technological innovation, in fact it was all tried before in America and in France and was dismissed in the end as a dismal failure.

The banishment of sign language continues to this day. Our institutions defame and broadly prohibit manual language; they seek to take it away from Deaf children so it cannot be passed on. Our institutions try to force signers to assimilate, to replace sign with spoken English and lipreading; faced with the failure of that undertaking, they treat the Deaf as constitutionally inferior. Our institutions do not allow signing adults to teach in the schools, nor signing children to receive their education in their most fluent language. As a result of this language policy, our society continues to condemn generation after generation of Deaf children to intellectual impoverishment and a life of manual labour.

"What monstrous crime," asked the first President of the National Association of the Deaf in the United States, Robert McGregor - Deaf orator, writer and school principal - "What monstrous crime have the Deaf been guilty of that their language should be thus forbidden?" And he continued: "By whom are signs forbidden?" By a few educators whose boast is that they do not understand signs and do not want to; by a few philanthropists who are ignorant of the language; by parents who do not understand what is necessary for the happiness of their Deaf children and are inspired with false fears by the educators and philanthropists .... And worst of all, (these people) ignore the Deaf themselves in their senseless and mischievous propaganda against signs. Claiming to have no goal but the benefit of the Deaf, they show an utter contempt for the opinions and desires of the Deaf:

"And why should we not be consulted in a matter of such vital interest to us?"

CHARGE 3: CONTEMPT FOR THE VIEWS AND POTENTIAL OF THE DEAF:

Long after many other nations accepted education as a fundamental right of all its citizens, hearing and deaf, Deaf education remained in Great Britain a matter of private charity rather than public responsibility. Late in the last century, however, the Crown created a commission to consider these issues. At first it was charged with investigating the education of the blind and feeble-minded but an influential barrister, member of Parliament and father of a Deaf girl, St. John Ackers, managed to have himself appointed to the commission and to have its scope enlarged. Ackers wanted his daughter to speak although she had become Deaf at only a few months of age, and he hired a teacher from the United States. "I would call upon all interested in the success of the (oral) system," he wrote, "to unite together resolutely to refuse admission into their schools of any who can converse by signs." The chairman of the commission had recently opened a new wing of the Manchester school for the Deaf with the claim that "if only the education of children were begun at an early age, in 99 cases out of 100 the Deaf and dumb could be taught to speak by the oral system". No one on the commission was an expert on teaching the Deaf and there were no Deaf people on the commission. In short, the combining of Deaf issues with those from the blind and feeble-minded, guaranteeing a medical model, and the make-up of the commission, left little doubt that it would recommend oralism for the Deaf.

One of the leading witnesses before the Commission was Edward Milner Gallaudet, son of Thomas Gallaudet the Protestant minister who, with Laurent Clerc, created a network of residential schools in the United States. The leader of his profession in America, and son of a Deaf woman, Edward Milner Gallaudet believed that sign language was the irreplaceable vehicle of educating the Deaf and that speech and speechreading were valuable supplementary skills when they can be acquired. Opposing him was the most famous British subject alive, a professional teacher of speech and inventor of the telephone, Alexander Graham Bell. Bell was the leading figure in the attack on the Deaf community in the United States. Bell sought to banish the sign language; to scatter the Deaf and discourage their socialising, organising, publishing and marriage; to have Deaf children educated in and use exclusively the majority language. To this cause he devoted his great prestige, personal fortune and tireless efforts; thus he became "the most fearful enemy of the American Deaf, past and present", to quote the president of the National Association of the Deaf.

The report of the commission was called a victory by both sides. It concluded: "All children should be, for the first year at least, instructed in the oral system; those who cannot profit should then be taught manually". Of course the adult Deaf may disagree with putting signs in the second place, using the language only with those who fail speech. But the report explains that signs tend to isolate the Deaf with the result that they "are not at all competent witnesses as to which is the best system; those that have lived in cages all their lives are so much attached to the cage that they have no desire to fly outside. The children themselves may prefer the sign system as more natural to them and the parents of poor (Deaf) children are sometimes indifferent and careless".

The most flagrant and destructive disregard of the views of the Deaf in history is to be found, however, in the international congresses organised by hearing teachers of the Deaf that finally sealed the unhappy fate of the Deaf in Europe and America to the present day. It all began at the French Exposition of 1878 when a meeting of hearing instructors of the Deaf was hastily convened. Only 54 persons attended, half of them instructors, and all but two of these from France. No Deaf people were allowed to attend, although a majority of the instructors of the Deaf in France were themselves Deaf. Nevertheless, the hearing group grandiosely proclaimed themselves the First International Congress on the Education and Welfare of the Deaf, affirmed that only oral instruction could fully restore the Deaf to society and chose Milan the site of the second congress to be held in 1880.

In fact, the Milan meeting was a brief rally conducted by opponents of manual language. The congress amounted to two dozen hours in which three or four oralists reassured the rest of the rightness of their actions in the face of troubling difficulties. Nevertheless, the meeting at Milan was the single most critical event in driving the languages of the Deaf beneath the surface; it is the most important single cause - more important than hearing loss - of the limited educational achievement of the modern Deaf man and woman.

Writing from Milan, a British teacher raved, "The victory for the cause of pure speech was gained before (the) congress began". And the headmaster at the Royal School for Deaf children reported that the congress "was mainly a partisan gathering. The machinery to register its decrees on the lines desired by its promoters has evidently been prepared beforehand and to me it seemed that the main feature was enthusiasm (for) 'oral pure' rather than calm deliberation on the advantages and disadvantages of methods". The location chosen, the make-up of the organising committee, the congress schedule and demonstrations, the composition of the membership, the officers of the meeting - all elements were artfully arranged to produce the desired effect.

The Italians made up more than half of the 164 delegates and there were 56 from France; the committed delegates from these two countries were seven-eighths of the membership. Of the eight British delegates, six were brought by St. John Ackers.

The British delegation included, apart from the Ackers group, Rev. Thomas Arnold, author of a monumental oralist history of Deaf education. Arnold was shortly to become the intellectual leader of his profession in Britain. "Articulate language is superior to sign", Arnold told the congress, "because it is the method employed by nature. Modern science teaches us that what is natural ends up with the upper hand". And: "No doubt signs are often animated and picturesque but they are absolutely inadequate for abstraction". And much more of the same.

The officers of the Milan congress - like the location and the membership - were chosen to ensure the oralist outcome. The organisers selected Guilio Tarra, a rabid oralist, as the president by acclamation. "Let us have no illusions", Tarra preached to the congress. "To teach speech successfully we must have courage and with a resolute blow cut cleanly between speech and sign .... Who would dare say that these disconnected and crude signs that mechanically reproduce objects and actions are the elements of a language?" "Oral speech is the sole power that can rekindle the light God breathed into man when, giving him a soul in a corporeal body, he gave him also a means of understanding, of conceiving and of expressing himself .... While, on the other hand, mimic signs are not sufficient to express the fullness of thought, on the other they intensify and glorify fantasy and all the faculties of the sense of imagination .... The fantastic language of signs magnifies the senses and inflames the passions, whereas speech elevates the mind much more naturally with calm, prudence and truth, and avoids the danger of exaggerating the sentiment expressed and provoking harmful mental expressions".

When a Deaf mute confesses an unjust act in sign, Tarra explained, the sensations accompanying the act are revived. "For example, when the Deaf person confesses in sign language that he has been angry, the detestable passion returns to the sinner, which certainly does not aid his moral reform. In speech on the other hand, the penitent Deaf mute reflects on the evil he has committed and there is nothing to excite the passion again". Tarra ended by defying anyone to define in sign the soul, faith, hope, charity, justice, virtue, the angels, God .... "No shape, no image, no design", Tarra concluded, "can reproduce these ideas. Speech alone, divine itself, is the right way to speak of divine matters".

All but the Americans voted for a resolution sanctifying the dominant oral language and dismissing the sign language whatever the nation: The congress, considering the unarguable superiority of speech over signs for restoring Deaf-mutes to social life and giving them greater facility in language, declares that the method of articulation should be used instead of the method of signs in the education of the Deaf and dumb. Considering that the simultaneous use of signs and speech has the disadvantage of injuring speech, lipreading and precision of ideas, the congress declared that the pure oral method should be used.

In the closing moments of the congress, a delegate from the French government cried from the podium, "Vive la parole!" This has been the slogan of hearing educators of the Deaf down to the present time. But an American Deaf leader has written: "1880 was the year that saw the birth of the infamous Milan resolution that paved the way for foisting upon the Deaf everywhere a loathed method; hypocritical in its claims, unnatural in its application, mind-deadening and soul-killing in its ultimate results."

The Milan resolution for the replacement of sign meant that Deaf professors would be gradually eliminated and so it came to pass. The fraction of Deaf teachers in the United States fell from nearly half in the mid 1800s to one-quarter when Bell testified to the Royal Commission, to one-fifth by World War 1, to an eighth in the 1960s. And most of these few remaining were teaching manual trades. Things had indeed changed since the days of Laurent Clerc. At the Convention of American Instructors of the Deaf in 1890, there was this characteristic exchange:

> A hearing headmaster: A teacher in a pure oral school who understands the sign language is out of place .... He might demoralise the school in a very short time. Only insofar as he would suppress his inclination to use sign could he be useful ....
>
> The Chair: I would like to hear from a Deaf educator.
>
> A Deaf teacher: The Chinese women bind their babies' feet to make them small; the Flathead Indians bind their babies' heads to make them flat. And the people who prevent the sign language being used in the education of the Deaf .... are denying the Deaf their free mental growth through natural expression of their ideas and are in the same class of criminals.

Nevertheless, the educated Deaf, taught under the old system in American or French sign language, were not silent. They expressed their views in periodicals addressed to the Deaf and in congresses of their own.

The Deaf press labelled oralism the method of "violence, oppression, obscurantism, charlatanism, which only makes idiots of the poor Deaf-mute children". A Deaf leader urged the authorities to "stop tying the hands of the Deaf, forbidding the colourful language which alone can restore them to moral life and the bosom of society." The international congresses of the Deaf were set up to resist the banishment of their language decreed by the hearing in Milan. The first was held in Paris, on the centennial of Epee's death, under the presidency of one of the French Deaf professors forced into retirement a few years earlier. "Suppress the language of signs", said the president of the National Association of the Deaf in the United States, "and the Deaf man is excluded from all society, even that of his brothers in misfortune; he will be more isolated than ever". Likewise, an American Deaf journalist argued, "Everywhere we see Deaf-mutes associating exclusively among their own society and almost never in that of the hearing society. It is natural for the Deaf man to seek the society of those .... who have the same means of communication and approximately the same tastes. I doubt he can ever be forced to change". The congress of the Deaf ended with quite a different set of resolutions for promoting their welfare than those voted in Milan. Here is the first Deaf resolution:

> "The congress declares the infallibility of the method of the Abbe de l'Epee which, without excluding the use of speech, recognises manual language as the most suitable instrument for developing the intellect of the Deaf".

The congress closed to the cries of "Long live the emancipation of the Deaf!" But the views of the Deaf were ignored. In the final congress - held in Paris in 1900 - that gave us our present legacy of oralism they were again excluded by the hearing leadership. The president of the meeting, an otologist, wrote in a textbook on speech training, "The Deaf-mute is by nature fickle and improvident, subject to idleness, drunkenness, and debauchery, easily duped and readily corrupted".

Since the Deaf had demanded that they participate in future congresses concerning their welfare and planned to participate in the Paris congress of 1900, the otologist president decided to separate the Deaf from hearing sessions, on the pretext that the sessions would be too long and that the translation between sign and speech would produce confusion. The Deaf leaders then proposed a compromise, a common meeting of all delegates merely at the end of the congress to debate and vote on the resolutions. The presiding octologist rejected that as well. Then the Deaf planners met to decide whether to acquiesce or attempt to block plans for the congress; they chose to acquiesce and convene a separate Deaf section.

Right from the first session of the hearing section Edward Minor Gallaudet and Alexander Graham Bell, the leaders of the manualist and oralist camps, traded blows. Bell agreed with excluding the Deaf from the congress deliberations: "It goes without saying that those who are themselves unable to speak are not the proper judges of the value of speech to the Deaf". Gallaudet rose to call the Milan declarations a great error. He showed how unrepresentative that congress had been, yet "its decisions have been cited for twenty years as if they had the weigh of a judgment of the Supreme Court". Now this congress, he said is no more representative: anyone with ten francs can vote. Milan decided nothing, for the controversy rages. He then moved a resolution calling for an open exchange of ideas with Deaf leaders. At this, the president declared - while giving no one else an opportunity to express an opinion, and without submitting the proposal to a vote - that the proposition was rejected by the congress, which was adjourned until the afternoon.

At the start of the next session the French government delegate asked the congress to reaffirm that the right to vote was reserved for hearing delegates and any speaking Deaf. "This principle is no doubt already in the minds of everyone", he said, "as it is inadmissible to grant the right to vote to people who cannot follow the discussions". The third session opened with a paper by Gallaudet. He asked to read it to a joint session of the two sections; the leaders of the Deaf section supported this request but the president refused. Gallaudet claimed that oralism had not lived up to its promises and he raised the question of whose testimony should carry the most weight in determining whether it had kept its promises or not. The teachers? But they are partisan and too familiar with their own pupils' speech to make an accurate judgment. Friends and acquaintances of the Deaf? But they, too, adjust to the poor speech and gestures of the orally taught pupil. Strangers? Their testimony is more important. But the greatest weight should be given to the views of the Deaf themselves. You can imagine how those remarks were greeted by oralist teachers who had repeatedly excluded the views of the Deaf! But even harsher words were to come: Gallaudet raised the question whether oralist educators were defective morally. He stated that they were engaged in a cover-up. It was hardly possible that these teachers were deceiving themselves about the poor fruits of oralism, so it must be that they intended to deceive everyone else.

Oralists and their opponents fought back and forth. The French delegate appealed for "the same cry that rang out twenty years ago in Milan: Long live speech!" The vice-president of Gallaudet College presented a resolution in behalf of the combined system: choose the method to suit the pupil but teach speech to all who can profit. The director of a French oral school read the conclusions of the Milan congress and then presented a resolution of his own reaffirming pure oralism. When the question was called, the combined system received only seven votes while nearly everyone else voted for the French resolution:

"The congress, considering the incontestable superiority of speech over signs for restoring the Deaf-mute to society and for giving him a more perfect knowledge of language, declares that it maintains the conclusions of the Milan congress".

Wrote an American Deaf leader, "These hearing men were too obtuse, too self-satisfied, too blind, to see what consummate fools they were making of themselves". Said another Deaf leader, "Government derives its power from the consent of the governed - but not when it comes to the affairs of the Deaf". Here there are two congresses and two conclusions; the governed demand one thing, the governing authority, another. "We protest in vain. Our petitions addressed to governments receive no response, our resolutions at national and international congresses are ignored .... If you ask hearing educators how they can act in utter disregard of the wishes of the Deaf, they answer that we do not know our own best interest. If that were true, then they have failed in the first objective of education, which is to enable the student to think and judge for himself... In fact, the Deaf are in a better position to judge these issues than the hearing. They know what it is to be Deaf, they know what it is like to have only a single method available for education and they know what it is to be forever blocked in their legitimate demands".

"Let us join together as one", he appealed, "to protest these educators who would fix our destiny without consulting us, without hearing us. Here in the greatest republic of the Old World, the delegates from that in the New World ask all present to join together to affirm a declaration of human rights, the right of the Deaf to life, liberty, the pursuit of happiness and the education of their children on a plan they accept. Let us declare to the entire world that the Deaf will not be crucified on the cross of a single method".

But the Deaf did not have - and do not have - the final word. To quote a major professional journal reporting on the Paris congress, "The oral method has been weighed in the balance .... and it is not found wanting". Whereas Milan was a hope, it said, Paris was a conclusion - a verdict after the trial. "The action of Paris will have the chief effect .... to confirm the faith of those who practice .... oral education of the Deaf .... The question of methods", it concluded, "is practically retired from the field of discussion".

And silence fell.

CHARGE 4: DESTROYING DEAF COMMUNITY AND CULTURE:

Under the banner of "integration" or "mainstreaming", the hearing establishment continues to pursue its historic goals of undermining Deaf marriage, language and culture. In the process, it is further undermining Deaf education.

In America, Deaf children came to the schools for the Deaf to find their place as Deaf people among the Deaf, to develop as individuals and citizens, then to return to their villages, towns and cities to farm, to teach, to manufacture, to write, to paint, to preach, to publish, to defend the nation and more.

Only schools for the Deaf can provide the social contact necessary for the continued evolution of manual language. Only schools for the Deaf can provide the bath of language and culture that develop the child's mind - especially the unfortunate child of hearing parents who is surrounded by a second culture he cannot understand. Only schools for the Deaf can ensure the transmission of Deaf culture on a large scale, for most Deaf youths learn nothing of their language and culture at home, find there no elaboration of what it means to be Deaf and find there only a void. Only schools for the Deaf can provide the wider social contacts that allow a discriminating choice of a partner for life. Only schools for the Deaf can provide effective instruction in the pupil's primary language. Schools for the Deaf provide the noblest of careers for talented Deaf men and women, the instruction of Deaf children. Schools for the Deaf stand proud and impressive before society. They say: "Our society is made of many people. We are the Deaf people: we have a language and a culture; we have a past, a present and a future".

Only specialised schools for the Deaf can provide all this; state schools cannot. The state schools prevent the Deaf child from developing a sense of community and identity. In the state schools the Deaf child finds no peers and no role models; there are no shared sports and other activities and there are few, if any, friends. The Deaf child is isolated and lost among a hundred or a thousand hearing students. Yet the law in the United States does not require this "mainstreaming". It classes the Deaf as handicapped and states that handicapped children must be educated in "the least restrictive environment." Now, which is more restrictive, a school for the Deaf where the Deaf child can communicate freely with his peers and find a sense of himself, or an ordinary state school where he cannot? The absurdity of calling isolation "the least restrictive environment" reveals the real motive of the hearing establishment for embracing "mainstreaming". It is the most ambitious attempt yet to eradicate Deaf culture and community. History has taught us repeatedly that if the goal is educating the Deaf child, mainstreaming will not work. The plan was tried on a grand scale once in France and again in Germany in the last century. Both times it failed miserably and for obvious reasons. Even that arch-enemy of the Deaf, Alexander Graham Bell, recognised that it is impossible to educate Deaf children integrated into an ordinary school. But educating the Deaf child is not the primary concern of the hearing establishment. The goal is, instead, to efface that child's identity as a Deaf person.

Let the hearing establishment concerned with the Deaf be brought before the bar and charged with these indictments. We cannot wait for history to condemn them. Too many present lives, hearing and Deaf, are at stake. It is high time to put education in the schools and speech lessons in the clinics. It is high time to embrace sign language and to begin educating Deaf children in this - their primary language. It is high time to allow the Deaf full realization of their potential and to reopen the career of teaching to the Deaf.

It is high time to stop wholesale forced mainstreaming of Deaf children, without regard to their needs, talents and language skills. It is high time, in short, to listen to the Deaf. For the terrible deafness, wrote Victor Hugo, is deafness of the mind. "What matters deafness of the ear," he asked, "when the mind hears? The one true deafness, the incurable deafness, is that of the mind".

Preface

The following paper was presented at the International Congress on the Education of the Deaf in Manchester, 1985.

The paper tried to emphasise the importance of employing the Deaf in education if Deaf education is be changed for the better. For years, Deaf education has been controlled by our lords and masters, the hearing people. We are being told by our lords and masters what is good for us, what to do and even how to live. These hearing people, the oralists, even went a stage further to demonstrate to society that they know everything about deafness and the Deaf more than the Deaf themselves - they even say they know the needs of Deaf children more than the Deaf themselves. If they are sons of God, how come they could not work miracles?

As usual, the response to the appeal for the Deaf to share equal participation and co-partnership in the education of Deaf children has been nil. In fact, the oralists stepped up their campaign for integration and individualised integration. This made the NUD all the more determined to fight and campaign against the oralists.

The Need for Integration of the Deaf in Education

International Congress of Education of the Deaf Manchester. August 1985. Raymond Lee.

In this paper I would like to stress the important need for the integration of Deaf adults in all areas and levels of Deaf education. As every person here today is aware, the education of the Deaf is one long history of chaos, failure and conflict in providing education for Deaf children. Many Deaf children at present are still leaving schools with poor or no educational qualifications which are vital when they apply for well paid employment. The causes for the poor and sub-standard schooling of Deaf children are attributed to three important facts and these are:

1. Severe imposition of oralism in schools for the Deaf.

2. Hearing people's continuing monopoly in Deaf education.

3. Lack of participation and co-operation with Deaf adults in education.

The first fact is very familiar with many of us and I do not intend to indulge in this subject any further other than to condemn the current trend towards integration and individualised integration. Mainstreaming of the Deaf has not been a proven success and to present there are no official statistics or evidence to show for the success of integration. On the other hand, the lack of such evidence is a measure of failure of the integrationalist policy. Deaf people know that and they still look askance why the educational authorities are continuing to carry out this terrible experiment and thus destroying the education of the Deaf.

Secondly, hearing people's continuing monopoly on the education of Deaf children, beginning from the 1880 Milan Congress, shows us all why there is that need for monopoly. Oralism is no longer merely a method of education. It is not a replacement for articulation. That word, "Oralists", means in the language of the Deaf, people or groups who are concerned in their endeavours to make every Deaf person hearing. In pursuit of this aim, these people, the oralists, have taken to implementing cruel experiments and processes such as forcing both articulation and auditory training on Deaf children at the expense of providing education itself. Who knows we may see the oralists recommending imposing cochlea implants on Deaf children in the very near future. Hearing authorities and their speech-obsessed allies are, through implementing the current policy of integration, committing genocide against the roots of the Deaf community. To carry out these experiments, the oralists need a free hand and a smooth course without obstacles and objections. Having Deaf adults sharing an important role in Deaf education would interfere with the aims of oralism - hence the monopoly.

Another need for the hearing to maintain a strong monopoly in the education of Deaf children is that they have a great fear of being proved wrong should Deaf people become successful as teachers, turning out brilliantly educated Deaf pupils. This kind of thing is not impossible - it is only the hearing who are making it impossible for Deaf adults to become teachers or to get involved with Deaf children in schools.

Lastly, for the past one hundred and five years since the infamous Milan Congress, the education of the Deaf has been in chaos and conflict. Chaos, because many schools (and partially hearing units) adopt a medical approach in the education of the Deaf. These schools and authorities fail to understand (or deliberately ignore) the fact that educational ethics dictate that the Deaf child be helped to acquire language, literacy and other skills as a part of a socialisation process for life. Educational ethics do not dictate that teachers restore faulty parts of the body to a fully functioning order - yet this medical ethic is what oralist education is based on at the expense of vital language acquisition, education and socialisation that every Deaf child needs. Conflict, because no one has ever agreed unanimously on an ideal method of communication for the Deaf in schools. It is important to bear in mind that hearing people are the cause of all these troubles. If Deaf people who were themselves former recipients of the education meted out to themselves by hearing people, were allowed to work together on equal participation basis with hearing people to improve the education of the Deaf, that move could not but reap great benefits in three ways:

1. Deaf adults, having lived in the world of work, can show hearing people what is needed for every Deaf child in schools to prepare them properly for the world outside after leaving school. Proper preparations also mean warning the children of the many obstacles they may encounter because of their deafness. They too must be alerted about the various forms of discrimination in existence and given advice on how to overcome these.

2. The Deaf adult can be a great asset in the role of both teacher and advisor. Deaf adults can show hearing teachers that their responsibilities, amongst others, also include moulding every Deaf child under their care into a first class Deaf adult, able to become a fully contributing, participating and useful member of society, as opposed to making every Deaf child a second class "hearing" citizen which is the best most Deaf schools do at present. The co-operation and participation of Deaf adults can help greatly in other ways in that they, sharing common language, culture, attitude and approach, can get closer to the children. In this way Deaf adults would make excellent teachers and this must be viewed positively. Perhaps the chaos and conflicts in Deaf education would never have occurred if Deaf teachers and adults were not banned from Deaf schools since 1880.

3. The experience of every Deaf adult is a must to those whose occupation it is to study ways of improving the education of the Deaf. The importance of having Deaf people in the area of research and study has yet to be fully realised and I urge this Congress to give this urgent thought.

Speaking of research in Deaf education, for years research and studies have been carried out by hearing people - a good proportion of those knew a little or nothing about the Deaf. It is true to say that the disgraceful educational situation, both past and present, has its root cause in the classic "Observer and Observed" situation. To explain this briefly, the observer (i.e. researcher) in his quest for perfection notes, analyses, calculates and concludes what is best or needed for the observed (i.e. the Deaf child). The observed is merely an object of study for the observer and the observed has no connection or involvement with the observer, and vice versa. What this implies is that any recommendation resulting from research or study would be the result according to one person's, or one group's, findings - the "one" deciding what is good for the others. Whenever there is a situation such as the Observer and the Observed, where the observed has no equal participation with the observer, there is always division, disagreement and conflict.

It is only when the observer becomes a part of the observed that rapport and harmony can be achieved; both the observer and observed becoming "one." To do that, the involvement and participation of the observed - in that case, Deaf adults representing Deaf children - is vital to enable the observer to get fully involved with and thus understand the needs of the observed. Deaf adults in the role of the observer, as well as representing the observed in an indirect way, are the best persons to take on research work on Deaf education. If only hearing people could have allowed Deaf people to work with them on co-partnership basis, Deaf education would have in no time be improving for the best.

Although I do not hold too much hope of this , it is hoped that some of the things mentioned here will make some of you to reconsider your approach, attitude and standing. Deaf people have had enough of being left out or ignored and they are appealing to every one of you here today to try and understand their viewpoints and experiences. Deaf people can help every one of you to understand what it is like to be Deaf and also help you to understand anything connected with deafness, its language, community and culture.

Most important of all, Deaf people can contribute and help in improving not only research and studies, but also the whole education of the Deaf itself through working on a co-partnership basis with hearing people. Please do give us a chance to participate and to show what we can offer; and to create improvements in Deaf education which is at present getting still worse.

Preface

The International Congress on the Education of the Deaf (Manchester, August 1985) had 'Cochlea Implants' as its main theme. The actual Congress itself was boycotted by both the NUD and the North West Regional Council of the British Deaf Association (BDA). Both the NUD and the NWRC (BCA) got together and organised an Alternative Congress which took place during the week in Manchester Deaf Centre. One evening, the NUD invited Harlan Lane to present his paper, 'On Language, Power and the Deaf'.

The massive club hall was packed and even standing room was extremely scarce... hearing and Deaf people alike from countries all over the world sat, rivetted and enthralled as Harlan Lane delivered his paper alongside him three or four interpreters signed and sweared themselves to keep in pace with Mr Lane's delivery. The atmosphere was truly electricit will be quite a while before the Deaf see someone of Lane's calibre come along.

On Language, Power and the Deaf

Manchester. August 1985. Harlan Lane.

Language and power are so intimately related that an interpreter cannot translate a single word, or cannot even appear on the scene, without communicating messages about group loyalty. Much of what the interpreter mediates between the two cultures, explicitly and implicitly, is a struggle for power.

Our daily newspapers record the power struggle between the world's various language minorities and the language majorities that engulf each of them. French speakers protest their oppression in Canada, Breton speakers in France, Tamil speakers in India, Georgian speakers in the Soviet Union, Armenian speakers in Turkey, Turkish speakers in Denmark, Basque speakers in Spain, Spanish speakers in the United States - the list goes on and on. Each entry on the list stands for lives taken and for countless more lives enfeebled by needless suffering and ineffectual education.

Listen to Cesar Chavez describe the common experience of Spanish-speaking children in the United States. "In class, one of my biggest problem was the language. Of course, we bitterly resented not being able to speak Spanish, but they insisted that we had to learn English. They said that if we were American then we should speak the language, and if we wanted to speak Spanish, then we should go back to Mexico. When we spoke Spanish, the teacher swooped down on us. I remember the ruler whistling through the air as its edge came down sharply on my knuckles. It really hurt. Even out in the playground, speaking Spanish brought punishment. The principal had a special paddle that looked like a four-by-two with a handle on it. The wood was smooth from a lot of use. He would grab us, even the girls, put our head between his legs and give it to us".

Modern studies in multilingual countries such as Canada show that excluding minority teachers and their language from the schools and thus attempting to force the assimilation of minority children like Chavez carries heavy penalties. Educators do indeed become disciplinarians as they pursue the aggressive steps required to stop the child from using his or her primary language - grades are lowered, physical punishment is inflicted, friends are separated - and the school becomes a place of incarceration. An Alsatian student: "When I was in primary school it was forbidden to speak Alsatian both in and out of class. Children were punished if they were caught." An Arab student: "In my boarding school the nuns forced us to speak French to one another, even when we were playing. We had a special dog collar that every violator of the rule had to wear."

Language oppression is not, however, a contemporary development. Language has long been an instrument of empire, used to create homogeneity and fealty to a central power to minimise or eradicate diversity.

Queen Isabella of Spain, for example, ordered that her American colonies were to abandon their "crude barbaric tongues" in favour of Castilian Spanish so they would become subject to God - and the crown! Under Charles II, the Indians were ordered to learn Spanish and "other good habits of reasonable men." They were to be schooled only in Castilian, which was to become the one and universal idiom since "it belongs to the monarches and conquerors." "This universal knowledge of Castilian", the decree continues, "is necessary in order to facilitate the governing and spiritual guidance of the Indians, in order that they may be understood by their superiors, conceive a love for the conquering nation, banish idolatry and be civilised for the purpose of business and commerce.... The natives' inclination to retain their own language impedes their will to learn another foreign language, an inclination accentuated by their somewhat malicious desire to hide their actions from the Spaniards and not answer them directly when they believe they can be evasive."

Likewise, at the end of the Enlightenment when the first French Republic supplanted the monarchy, its legislators were told: "Governments do not realise, or do not feel keenly enough, how much the annihilation of regional speech is necessary for education, the true knowledge of religion, the ready implementation of the law, national happiness and political tranquillity .... Federalism and superstition speak Breton; emigration and the hate of the republic speak German; the counter-revolution speaks Italian, and fanaticism speaks Basque." So much for Liberty, Equality and Fraternity. The renowned Encyclopedia defined a patois as "a degenerate tongue such as is spoken in all provinces .... The language of France is spoken only in the capital."

Few communities have as long and as tragic a history of language oppression as Deaf communities in the western world. Let us trace that history briefly and see where it has led us today. Many centuries went by before the world even recognised manual languages. At the dawn of Deaf education in the seventeenth century, its founder in the German- speaking world, Jan Conrad Amman, could write: "The breath of life resides in the voice. The voice is the interpreter of our hearts, and expresses its affections and desires .... The voice is a living emanation of that spirit that God breathed into man when he created him a living soul." And because signers did not use voice, "What stupidity we find in most of these unfortunate Deaf", Amman wrote, "How little they differ from animals."

Civilisation had to wait until the middle of the French Enlightenment before the education of Deaf children was undertaken systematically using the language of the Deaf. Even then, the founder of this education, the Abbe de l'Epee and his successor, the Abbe Sicard, thought their pupils' manual language to be without grammar or method and sought to reorganise it along the lines of French - articles, genders and all. Said Abbe Sicard: "We all know the kinds of sentences in use among the negro tribes; those used by the Deaf and dumb are even closer to nature, even more primitive."

It mattered not a whit that Pierre Desloges, in what was probably the first book ever published by a Deaf man, had given a ringing defence of sign language, showing how it served the needs of the Deaf community of Paris, so that "no event in Paris, in France, or in the four corners of the world lies outside the scope of their discussions."

The leading medical authority on the Deaf in the following decades, resident physician at the National Institution for the Deaf in Paris and the renowned teacher of the Wild Boy of Aveyron, Jean-Marc Itard, likewise vilified sign language as "the barbaric language without pronouns, without conjunctions, without any of the words that permit us to express abstract ideas, which provides only a vague collection of adjectives, nouns and a few verbs, without determinate time and always in the infinitive."

The decisive victory in the struggle to supplant the sign languages of the western world with majority languages was gained some decades later at the infamous Congress of Milan in 1880. In the opening address the Italian host enjoined the delegates to remember that living speech is the privilege of man, the sole and certain vehicle of thought - the gift of God, of which it has been truly said:

> *"Speech is the expression of the soul*
> *As the soul is the expression of divine thought."*

The congress of the educators of the Deaf, from which the Deaf were excluded (although one slipped in), elected a rabid enemy of sign language as its president, an Italian priest named Guilio Tarra. "The kingdom of speech", Tarra began in what would prove to be a two-day peroration, "The kingdom of speech is a realm whose queen tolerates no rivals. Speech is jealous and wishes to be the absolute mistress. Like the true mother of the child placed in judgment before Solomon, speech wishes it all for her own - instruction, school, Deaf-mute - without sharing; otherwise she renounces all.... Let us have no illusions", Tarra continued. "To teach speech successfully we must have courage and with a resolute blow cut cleanly between speech and sign.... Who would dare say that these disconnected and crude signs that mechanically reproduce objects and actions are the elements of a language? I know that my pupil has only a few imperfect signs, the rudiments of an edifice that should not exist, a few crumbs of a bread that has no consistency and can never suffice for nourishing his soul - a soul that cries out for moral and social existence."

The congress president eventually came to what he called his fundamental argument. "Oral speech is the sole power that can rekindle the light God breathed into man when, giving him a soul in a corporeal body, he gave him also a means of understanding, of conceiving and of expressing himself.... While, on the one hand, mimic signs are not sufficient to express the fullness of thought, on the other they enhance and glorify fantasy and all the faculties of the sense of imagination..... The fantastic language of signs exalts the senses and foments the passions, whereas speech elevates the mind much more naturally with calm, prudence and truth, and avoids the danger of exaggerating the sentiment expressed and provoking harmful mental impressions."

When a Deaf-mute confesses an unjust act in sign, Tarra explained, the sensations accompanying the act are reawakened. For example, when the Deaf person confesses in sign language that he has been angry, the detestable passion returns to the sinner, which certainly does not aid his moral reform. In speech on the other hand, the penitent Deaf-mute reflects on the evil he has committed and there is nothing to excite the passion again. Tarra ended by defying anyone to define in sign language the soul, faith, hope, charity, justice, virtue, the angels, God.... "No shape, on image, no design," Tarra concluded, "Can reproduce these ideas. Speech alone, divine itself, is the right way to speak of divine matters."

All but the Americans voted for a resolution exalting the dominant oral language and disbarring the sign language whatever the nation:

1. The congress, considering the incontestable superiority of speech over signs for restoring Deaf-mutes to social life and for giving them greater facility in language, declares that the method of articulation should have preference over that of signs in the instruction and education of the Deaf and dumb.

2. Considering that the simultaneous use of signs and speech has the disadvantage of injuring speech, lip-reading and the precision of ideas, the congress declares that the pure oral method ought to be preferred.

In the closing moments of the congress, the French delegate cried from the podium, "Vive la parole!" This has been the slogan of hearing educators of the Deaf down to the present time. But an American Deaf leader has written: "1880 was the year that saw the birth of the infamous Milan resolution that paved the way for foisting upon the Deaf everywhere a loathed method; hypocritical in its claims, unnatural in its application, mind-deadening and soul-killing in its ultimate results."

In the aftermath of Milan, "pure oralism" washed over Europe like a flood tide. Many people and schools were swept up in its advance. There is no single explanation for such tides in human affairs. In my history of the Deaf, "When the Mind Hears" I have discussed the confluence of nationalism, elitism and commercialism that led to the Congress of Milan and to its deadly legacy. Another contributing cause was the educators' desire for total control of their classrooms which cannot be had if the pupils sign and the teacher knows none. The teacher then becomes the linguistic outcast, the handicapped. Nor can he or she acquire the necessary skill in a year, or even two, any more than an Anglophone teacher can so rapidly prepare himself to teach in French. This understandable reluctance of hearing teachers to master a language radically different from their own continues to have the greatest weight in what are misrepresented as pedagogical decisions. There was a time when teachers of the Deaf could not practice without a knowledge of their pupils' primary language. But the vast expansion of schools for the Deaf in Europe and America late in the last century created more professional positions than there were educators and administrators fluent in sign. Increasingly, people with few ties to the Deaf community dominated their education.

Teachers who used sign language were increasingly forced into retirement; whereas most of the teachers of the Deaf had been Deaf themselves, by the turn of the century only a handful were. Before Milan, American Deaf teachers had founded the Florida School, the New Mexico School, the Kansas School, the

Oregon School, the North Dakota School, the Arizona School among others. Many more Deaf teachers taught in these and scores of other schools, and some developed widely-used teaching materials. Some published learned articles and appeared on the international Deaf scene, shaping the future of their profession world-wide. Within a decade after Milan, however, the fraction of teachers who were Deaf fell from one-half to one-quarter; by World War 1 it was down to a fifth, and most of the fifth were in the south teaching manual trades in just a few schools. Nowadays the fraction is about one-tenth.

With the forced retirement of signing teachers, and the quarantine and then graduation of the older signing students, sign language could be totally banished from the schools. There were 26 American institutions for the education of the Deaf in 1867 and ASL was the language of instruction in all 26; by 1907 there were 139 schools for the Deaf and ASL was allowed in none. The French figures provide a comparable glimpse of ruthless linguistic imperialism. In 1845, 160 schools for the Deaf with FSL the accepted language; by the turn of the century, it was not allowed in a single French school.

Of course, the signing community protested. At the Convention of American Instructors of the Deaf in 1890, a decade after the Congress of Milan, there was this characteristic exchange:

> A Hearing Principal: "A teacher in a pure oral school who understands the sign language is out of place.... He might demoralise the school in a very short time. Only insofar as he would suppress his inclination to use sign could he be useful.... "
>
> Chair: "I would like to hear from a Deaf educator."

J. Schuyler Long, a Gallaudet graduate and superintendent of the Iowa School for the Deaf, rose to respond. He was a poet, a journalist and author of the first pronouncing dictionary of American Sign Language published in 1908. Long said:

> "The Chinese women bind their babies' feet to make them small; the Flathead Indians bind their babies' heads to make them flat. And the people who prevent the sign language being used in the education of the Deaf.... are denying the Deaf free mental growth through natural expression of their ideas and are in the same class of criminals."

At the dawn of this century, the first president of the National Association of the Deaf, Robert McGregor, cried out against the oppression of sign language in these words:

"What heinous crime have the Deaf been guilty of that their language should be proscribed? .... The utmost extreme to which tyranny can go when its mailed hand descends upon a conquered people is the proscription of their national language.... By whom then are signs proscribed? By .... educators of the Deaf whose boast is that they do not understand signs and do not want to; by a few philanthropists who are otherwise ignorant of the language; by parents who do not understand the requisites to the happiness of their Deaf children and are inspired with false fears by the educators and philanthropists.... Worst of all, these (people) ignore the Deaf themselves in their senseless and mischievous propaganda against signs. Professing to have no object in view but the benefit of the Deaf, they exhibit an utter contempt for the opinions, the wishes, the desires of the Deaf. And why should we not be consulted in a matter of such vital interest to us? This is a question that no man has yet answered satisfactorily."

But the Deaf did not have - and do not have - the final word. The final word, as always, came from their hearing benefactors. As the new century dawned on Deaf education, a representative view was articulated by the principal of the Nebraska School. "The oral method has been weighed in the balance," he wrote in the Alexander Graham Bell Association Review, "and it may be believed weighed conscientiously and with all fairness - and it is not found wanting.... (Experience) confirms the faith of those who practice .... oral education of the Deaf ...." The question of methods, he concluded, "is practically retired from the field of discussion."

Today, more than a century since the congress of Milan, the oppression of languages of the Deaf communities in Europe and America continues unabated and in the crucial realm of education that oppression is becoming worse. The attempt to educate Deaf children with teaching methods appropriate for hearing children continues to prove a failure, decade after decade. In a classroom where spoken and written English are the basic means of communication, Deaf children are baffled and withdrawn, the more so as nine out of ten in the schools today become Deaf before they could learn English at home. These children lack the knowledge of English and the skills of articulation and lip-reading required to succeed: studies have shown that speech teachers find two-thirds of their own Deaf pupils hard to understand or utterly unintelligible, and Deaf high school students can lip-read no better than the man in the street - that is, scarcely at all.

An educational disaster has thus resulted from using English to instruct Deaf children: the average twelfth-grade Deaf student reads at fourth-grade level and does arithmetic (his best subject) at sixth-grade level. Only one Deaf adult in ten readily reads a newspaper or holds a professional post; most are employed in the obsolescent manual trades, and that is where we are consigning the futures of Deaf children in large numbers.

Why this staggering and disastrous rate of English-illiteracy among the Deaf? The relation between language and power accounts for much of it. I submit first that the English-illiteracy of the Deaf, far from being the unwanted calamity educators claim, is in fact the state of affairs desired by the prevailing institutions. It is in the interest of the establishment, and especially Deaf education, to undermine critical thought and the acquisition of bureaucratically acceptable language because if the Deaf had these abilities once again as they did in the last century, they would once again enter the teaching profession in large numbers, reform that profession and make obsolete the present teachers' training, endangering the employment of many.

The Deaf are English-illiterate, further, because their own extensive language skills are not acknowledged in the schools; they are demeaned or worse. Nothing is said of the manifold forms that Deaf literacy takes: the narrative traditions, the poetry, the handshape games, the pantomime and so on. The Deaf are English-illiterate because the systematic oppression of sign language shuts out the most effective strategy for teaching a second language: namely, conduct a contrasting analysis of the student's first language skills and second-language goals, and develop an instructional strategy based on that analysis.

The Deaf are English-illiterate because the written language is taught orally and they are Deaf, or it is taught using written English, which is just the language they do not know and are trying to learn; it is never taught nowadays using a language in which they are fluent. The Deaf are English-illiterate because the middle class white style of language their hearing teachers present as the only correct English is quite alien to whatever English their Deaf pupils have use for. The Deaf are English-illiterate because the schools treat language as an a cultural formal skill whereas language accords with and reinforces a host of cultural patterns, including group loyalty, problem solving, recreation, perception of space and time. The Deaf are English-illiterate because standard English is presented as an aesthetic and moral norm, not as a practical necessity for rapid transfer of information. In this era of information technology, the price the Deaf are paying for the alliance between language and power gets higher every day.

As a remedy, many leaders among the Deaf minority are urging the revitalisation of the residential schools for the Deaf and the re-introduction of sign language and Deaf teachers in their classrooms - successful practices in the last century when American Deaf children studied all their subjects in their most fluent language, the American Sign Language of the Deaf (ASL). In a residential school with Deaf teachers and a signing community, the Deaf student is able not only to understand and respond to the instruction, but also to get help after class with course work, to discuss local, national and international events, to participate in student activities, to develop friendships with other Deaf students (nearly all Deaf people choose a Deaf partner when marrying), to emulate older students and Deaf teachers and to acquire self-respect as a Deaf person.

Although none of these advantages is available to the Deaf child in an ordinary public school where sign language, Deaf teachers and a Deaf community is absent, that is just where Deaf children are being sent in large and growing numbers. More than half of the estimated 80,000 Deaf schoolchildren in the United States have now been "mainstreamed" to some extent, and the specialised schools for the Deaf they would have attended are starting to close.

Granted that the conditions in the local public school for the Deaf child's social and emotional growth are quite poor, is the child receiving a better education in the "three R's" there? Not at all. The first report cards on mainstreamed Deaf children show no improvement in their blighted English or mathematics attributable to mainstreaming (even though the first to be mainstreamed were the children with the best speech and hearing)

The Deaf children who do best in school are - note it well - the fortunate ten percent who learned sign language as a native language from their Deaf parents, the core of this linguistic minority. These "native signers" outperform their Deaf classmates from hearing homes in most subjects, even in learning to read and write English. They are also better adjusted, better socialised and have more positive attitudes. The superior performance of Deaf children of Deaf parents highlights the changes that most need to be made in the education of Deaf children, namely a return to sign language, Deaf teachers and Deaf administrators. These changes have long been advocated by the Deaf community itself.

Unfortunately, the very professions created to serve the interests of the Deaf have been totally at odds for over a century with what the Deaf perceive as their interests. These professions have vainly pursued the assimilation of Deaf children into the hearing majority at the expense of their individual growth; thus many special educators embraced mainstreaming precisely because it would help to close the residential schools the Deaf hold dear. In passing the Education for All Handicapped Children Act ten years ago, Congress was wiser, recognising (in the words of the Supreme Court) that "regular classrooms simply would not be a suitable setting for the education of many handicapped children" and providing for alternative placements. But educators have largely ignored this provision of the act.

Confronted with a similar tragedy in England, members of the British National Union of the Deaf (NUD), rather more political than their American counterparts, have formally charged their government with a violation of the United Nations Convention on the Prevention and Punishment of the Crime of Genocide. That treaty prohibits inflicting mental harm on the children of an ethnic group and it prohibits forcibly transferring them to another group. According to Deaf leaders in Britain, mainstreaming will gravely injure "not only Deaf children but Deaf children's rightful language and culture." Their published Charter of Rights of the Deaf asserts that "Deaf schools are being effectively forced to close and therefore children of one ethnic/linguistic minority group that is Deaf people are being forcibly transferred to another group that is hearing people."

To achieve intellectual and emotional maturity and full participation in society most Deaf children require an education conducted in their primary language, American Sign Language, with the participation of Deaf adults in the setting of a specialised school.

In the Bilingual Education Act of 1968 Americans institutionalised the premise that children are best educated, transitionally at least, in their most fluent language. The laws of most of the states soon came to require that schools impacted with more than a certain percentage of children whose primary language is Navaho or Chinese or whatever language, must offer a portion of their instruction in that language. Yet it has never been possible to add ASL, one of the more populous minority languages, to that list. Several possible reasons for the particularly severe oppression come to mind. One is that the hearing impairment of most users of ASL plays into the hands of a large segment of our society that would Deaf with social problems by medicalising them. From this point of view, the hearing impairment of the signing community is more salient than its shared language. This is precisely the posture of our government where the same agencies that support research and training for the education of retarded people do likewise for Deaf people, and the agencies that address the needs of minority language groups refuse to have anything to do with the two million or so Americans who use some form of manual communication.

Yet another reason for the singular oppression of ASL must be its unexpected mode, manual and visual, giving rise to the well-known fallacious beliefs that ASL is inherently pictorial, concrete and primitive. For example, in a recent book on thinking and language, the author remarks on "the crudity of sign language.... Even Deaf and dumb humans who rely entirely on sign languages find it cumbersome to make complicated abstract statements because of a lack of subtle grammatical inflections."

Let us not dismiss the difference in modality of signed and spoken languages, just because it has been at the source of so much sign language oppression. I think we might have something to learn from turning the table on the English snobs and claiming: ASL is not only as good as any oral language, it's better! The argument goes like this: our species, in common with all the mammals, is much concerned with three dimensional space. In fulfilling our needs, both biological and social, we move about in space. Commonly those movements are co-ordinated among the members of a pair or group of people and they relate to an arrangement of people or objects. Consequently much of human communication is explicitly about spatial arrays. How do we get to the swimming pool from here? Where shall the interpreters stand? Where are you going to put the new couch? Where did you leave the car? Countless similar everyday questions and their answers require us to talk about space.

But so spatial an animal are we that we also chose to talk about non-spatial matters in spatial terms. Lists start at the top and end at the bottom. Political alignments range from right to left. The future is ahead of us, the past behind. Power relations extend from the high and mighty to the lowliest of us. Comparatives in general are expressed in spatial metaphor, above all other means.

Let us see how adroit oral language really is, then, in this fundamental task of spatial description. How well does English convey arrangements and distances of people and things in three- dimensional space? Both literally and metaphorically, we will need to refer to left-right, in front-behind and above-below.

I look at two adjacent people in the audience, say Will and his wife. In English I might say "Will is to the left of his wife" but in that case I can also say he is on his wife's right, that is, "Will is to the right of his wife." So I have been quite unclear. Which is it? Is Will to the left or the right of his wife? Anna who is seated behind them disagrees with me; Will was never to the left of his wife. If you followed that and think that English is clear although complicated about left and right, try this one: Arrange Will, his wife and Anna so that Will is to the left of his wife, his wife is to the left of Anna and Will is to the right of Anna. (Anyone who solves that by tomorrow come see me and I'll give you a pat on the back - from in front.)

I have tried to illustrate that in English we must give different accounts of the same array, depending on two things: first, the speaker's point of view and, second, whether the speaker is using verbal pointing or intrinsic reference. Verbal pointing, called deixis, requires the English listener to know where the speaker is. The intrinsic system requires an interpretation of the scene and an intrinsic orientation. It applies to people and houses but it will not work for trees, tables or heaps. To illustrate, lets go for a picnic. If I ask you to put the little picnic table in front of the tree, you can comply with my instruction by putting it anywhere on the planet earth; I have been quite unclear.

There's a nearby dogtrack and we take our seats at the start line. As they leave the gate, the only dog I can see is the dog closest to me, which is, of course, in front of the other dogs - but he may be behind them as well, especially if I bet on him. The rabbit that runs around the inside rail of the track is behind all the dogs up to the turn, even though it is always in front of all of them.

My dog loses and the sky darkens. "The sun is behind the clouds", you say. When the sun comes out from behind the clouds is it then in front of the clouds? Of course not! So the sun is always behind the clouds. Actually, the sun is only behind the clouds when there is no sun.

I have brought two balloons to the picnic and tie them to a branch so that the red is above the green. You, however, are lying on your side on the grass, looking at the vault of heaven and the red is to the left of green - or to the right of green, depending on which side you are lying on. Unless of course you can see the horizon, in which case the red is above the green. "My friend", I tell you, "there's a spider dangling above your head." You go to brush it away but where to swing? Is it close to you or far? Is it year your cheek or near the top of your head? Who knows.

Will is to the left of his wife. The table is in front of the tree. The black dog is in front of the others. There's a spider above your head. All of these sentences are ambiguous, but they are like those we use all the time. Then we must be rather poor at communicating in English, that most essential of human messages, spatial arrays. I decided to do an experiment.

I bought a doll house - my first - that came with a few pieces of plastic furniture and, most important, a picture on the box showing where to arrange the furniture in this split level home. There was a sofa, a TV, a stereo, a picnic table and two chairs, and a barbecue. A graduate student in my laboratory, Dana Ginsberg, and I asked a pair of English speakers to assist us, as follows. With the house set up and the furniture in a pile in front of it, one of the pair was to look at the box and tell the other where to place each item of furniture in an effort to reproduce the arrangement shown in the photo on the box. We asked the furniture mover not to talk and we tape-recorded the speaker. Seven pieces of furniture to place in common ways - should be easy. Here is an average transcript by a graduate student, native speaker of English. "Okay Moti, we'll start with the table and the chairs on the bottom floor. In front of the house, um, there's a patch of green, like a patio, and the round table goes in the - in the, uh, top corner of the pa - of the green square. Okay. And in front of the - at - in front of the table - um - between the ladder and the table - goes one of the red chairs. Okay. And across from that red chair, on the other side of the table, goes the second red chair. Okay. Now, the barbe - the barbecue goes on the strip of patio between the green square and the house. Um, um, over to the left, almost in the left corner. Not quite. Okay. Now lets go upstairs. Oh, excuse me, we have to go back downstairs. I forgot the record player. Now we're in the house, and as you face the house, it's at the right, your right corner okay, that's where the record player will go. Against the wall, well, against the wall in the corner. Okay? Now lets go upstairs, Moti. Okay, now on the second floor - the floor's divided into a terrace and a bedroom and just where the terrace and the bedroom are divided there's no - there's a frame but no wall there and the couch or the little red seat goes in that frame, at an angle, so it's mostly in the room but it seems to stick out onto the terrace just a little bit. Okay. And the television goes - okay the floor in that room is separated by - there's a little ridge that sticks out of the floor, so the couch is on one side of the ridge - the television goes in the area that's separated with the other side of the ridge - and it's facing so that the person who is sitting on the couch can't see the TV screen - in other words, the TV screen is facing into the - is facing out of the house. Okay. Sort of facing the ladder. Okay. So we're done."

Because American Sign Language is a spatial language, it can communicate arrangement and relative distance of things and people in quite a different way from English or, indeed, any oral language. This makes interpreting sign into oral language and vice versa unique among translation tasks in that the interpreter must mediate between spatial and linear languages, utterly restructuring spatial discourse as he or she interprets from the one language into the other. ASL, instead of conveying a spatial array by a linear chain of words, can map that spatial message right into its surface form. Moreover, once ASL establishes a location for an object, it need not be re-established in order to refer to it. When I asked pairs of signers to do my experiment, they were not only quicker at it than English speakers, they followed a different strategy. Let me try to convey that by reading the transcript - not a translation - of their signing, prepared with the help of Judy Shephard-Kegl.

"OKAY. TABLE, WHITE, ROUND TABLE. OUTSIDE. OKAY, FRONT-OF-HOUSE, PUT-ON GREEN SQUARE FLAT-AREA. PUT THERE. CHAIRS, TWO-OF-THEM, ASSOCIATED-WITH-TABLE. OKAY. TABLE HERE CHAIRS ONE-HERE ONE-HERE IN-FRONT. NOW GRILL, COOKING, YOU KNOW, BLACK, HOOD-OPENS. TABLE HERE, HERE GRILL. TABLE HERE, ROUND, CHAIRS HERE, HERE, GRILL HERE. NOW STEREO - CAREFUL HEAVY. NOW YOU-KNOW LIVING-ROOM, WALL, BOOKSHELVES ON-WALL, OKAY, THERE, CORNER, MIRROR, THERE, PUT- THERE. NOW TV - YOU-KNOW DRESSER THERE, ALL-THAT, PICTURES, LAMP THERE, PUT TV THERE. NOW CHAIR - FOLDS OPEN

LIKE BED, RED, WHITE, SOMETHING, OKAY, THAT - GO UPSTAIRS, SEE WHERE TV, WHERE DRESSERS, THEN LAMP, THERE PUT-THERE. FINISHED."

So is speech, in the words of the Milan resolution, "incontestably superior to sign", or is it the other way round? My point, of course, is that no language is superior to any other and none is beneath you if you look up to it. Languages have evolved within communities in a way responsive to the needs of those communities. ASL is attuned to the needs of the signing community in the United States; English is not. And the effort to replace sign with English these last hundred years will get a chapter all its own in the history of human ignominy.

The renewed application of a cultural pluralism in our society today invites us to re-examine the assumption that others should speak as we do. Many Americans can recall their initial shock when they realised fully for the first time that other people were conducting their lives in an entirely different language. Perhaps that shock reflects a kind of egocentricism that it is in our mutual interest to overcome; for the growth of social consciousness, like that of the child, is largely a series of triumphs over egocentricism.

As I am not less but more when I recognise that the earth revolves around the sun and that man has evolved from the apes, so I am not less but more when I recognise that there are other languages, manual and oral, on par with my own. This humility is the enemy of forced assimilation; it is the friend of bilingualism and mutual respect; it is the only sure guide to a better day for Deaf people and their friend.

38 Victoria Place, Carlisle CA1 1HU Telephone 0228 48844

Date

For immediate release

INTERNATIONAL CONGRESS ON THE EDUCATION OF THE DEAF:

DEAF COMMUNITY CHALLENGES AGENDA

In an unprecendented move, members of two voluntary deaf organisations today (Monday 5th August) challenged the agenda for an International Congress on Deaf Education taking place in Manchester from 5th - 9th August, 1985.

The Organisations are: THE BRITISH DEAF ASSOCIATION and the NATIONAL UNION OF THE DEAF.

Deaf groups fall out over ear implants for children

by Peter Wilby
Education Correspondent

GROUPS representing the deaf have called for a boycott of an international conference on deaf education which starts in Manchester tomorrow, claiming it has been taken over by supporters of the experimental implantation of electrodes in children's ears. The agenda has been rigged, they say, to keep out supporters of sign language.

The international congress is a five-yearly event whose deliberations carry great weight in deaf schools throughout the world. Because of their doubts, the British Deaf Association and the National Union of the Deaf, the national organisations in Britain, are holding an "alternative congress" in the Manchester Deaf Club.

They are angry because the main conference session will be devoted to a discussion of experimental cochlear implants, in which electrodes are put in the inner ear to give the very deaf a crude impression of speech and sound. The main congress speaker will be William House, a Los Angeles surgeon who has tried the implants on more than 100 children.

The dissenters say the implants are "fringe experiments". "We don't know enough about the long-term effects," said Paddy Ladd, secretary of the national union's human rights committee. "It is quite wrong to make a medical matter, con-

publicity given to the electrodes damages the deaf child's self-esteem. "Despite their disability," says Jonathan Phillips, chairman of the society's education committee, "deaf children can lead a full life using other forms of communication such as sign language. They shouldn't get the idea that the thing is to become more like a hearing a person at any cost."

Deaf educators are split over sign language. Phillips describes it as "a legitimate language, like French or Spanish, which can cope with complex and abstract ideas," and it is widely used in the United States and France. But most British schools concentrate on lip-reading, arguing that it makes it easier for deaf people to carry on a normal life. The deaf people's union says this attitude is responsible for poor academic performance in deaf schools.

It claims that 90% of speakers at the conference are opposed to sign language and that papers favour it, some from leading international authorities, have been censored. Neither deaf people nor the parents of deaf children have been involved in planning the conference, the union says.

Ian Taylor, chairman of the organising committee and professor of audiology at Manchester University, said yesterday: "These allegations are lies. 500 people will be contributing, nobody has been stopped from doing so and nothing has been censored. Some people have submitted several papers and we have had to restrict them to

Storm over deaf split

By Peter Harris

A BOYCOTT of a major international congress on deaf education in Manchester today was described as "lunatic and absurd" by a leading professor.

Professor Ian Taylor, of the audiology and education of the deaf department at Manchester University said the rebel

He was speaking at the Manchester Palace Theatre before giving his keynote address to more than 1,500 delegates from 70 countries at the congress.

As he spoke, the two breakaway organisations — the British Deaf Association and the National Union of the Deaf — were planning a series of events of their own at the Manchester Deaf Club in Booth Street East although some

They are complaining that the congress is focusing too much on "fringe experiments" while the urgent educational needs of deaf children are being ignored.

They also claim that sign language should be more widely used in the educational process to help hearing-impaired children to communicate with the outside world.

Professor Taylor said: "Everyone was invited to

make a point they would have been most welcome to do so at the main congress. It is lunatic and absurd that they should exclude themselves if they have something to say on the matter.

Mr Elwyr ... congress ... the break... were oppo... of cochlear ... including d...

Progress for deaf lost in welter of words

Ministry to be warned that sign language is the way forward, reports Sarah Boseley

HOME NEWS 5

Deaf push for sign language in schools

When Emma Tumim, who is profoundly deaf, was once caught using sign language at school, and was chastised in front of fellow deaf and partially deaf pupils.

Now Emma, aged 23, is helping a campaign to bring back the widespread use of sign language in schools, which mostly provide only oral teaching and lip-reading tuition.

"It is vitally important that hearing people find out what deaf children are suffering", she said yesterday through an interpreter, at a lobby by the National Union of the Deaf at the Department of Education and Science.

"I learnt sign language at school from other children who had learnt it from their deaf parents. But I was always punished if I was caught using it."

Miss Tumim is one of an estimated 60,000 profoundly deaf people in Britain who have struggled through school.

She was lucky. She gained two O levels and starts a diploma course this year.

The NUD claims that profoundly deaf school leavers have an average reading age of 8½, can barely lip-read and are unintelligible. Yesterday's lobby launched a campaign for courses which insist that teachers of the deaf are skilled in sign language.

Mr Raymond Lee, secretary of the union, said: "We have up to now been attacking individual schools for banning sign language but now we are putting the blame where it belongs, with the DES".

Miss Emma Tumim signals a message yesterday at a lobby campaigning for a return to sign language teaching in schools for the deaf (Photograph: Peter Trievnor)

'RIGGED AGENDA' CHARGE AS CONGRESS DEBATES EAR OPERATIONS

Newspaper cuttings from the Press

Preface

The main argument of this paper was to point out the lies of the oralists and match their lies with the truths. Deaf people have never understood why their sign language, culture and community are not respected; neither do they understand why they were hindered from trying to get involved in all levels of Deaf education. Integration is meant to split up the roots of the Deaf community by closing down Deaf schools. Currently, the future is not looking bright for Deaf children with cochlea implants looming up on the horizon. The medical and teaching profession, as well as one organisation for the Deaf, have said they would not use cochlea implants on Deaf children at a very young age. How can one believe this when the experience of the past 100 years has shown the Deaf time and again that they are being told lies and nothing but damned lies?

Deaf people will need to work doubly hard to ensure that Deaf children's future is improved and, given the present situation, it is going to be one hell of a task ahead.

On Integration and the Lies of the Oralists

London March 1986. Raymond Lee

When I was invited to give a Deaf person's viewpoint on integration. I decided that it would be pointless attempting to answer the oralists' approach on a point for point basis as such people completely misunderstood, and are not capable of understanding, the experience of being a member of the Deaf community. The oralists could only see the problem in terms of somehow making Deaf people as much like the hearing as possible.

Here, I am going to tackle the issue by presenting three of the most important aspects concerned with the background to Deaf education and after that, I shall conclude with an analysis of their relationship to the current idea of integration.

1. HISTORICAL FACTS CONCERNING DEAF EDUCATION IN BRITAIN

What is the history of Deaf education in Britain and what kind of picture does it paint? Since the late 1880s the historical picture of educational provisions for the Deaf has been one of consistent failure in achieving its educational purpose.

The people responsible for this provision have been and are aware of that failure but for several reasons continue the attempt to make Deaf children hearing without giving them the corresponding education. These people are known in the Deaf language as the Oralists. The educational tool these people use is that of oralism; the grinding obsession with speech and audiological training that overrides all other aspects of a well rounded educational experience.

Oralism, through the ban of sign language, produces the Deaf 'dummy' living in fear, isolation and oblivion. Fear, because Deaf people do not wish to be mocked and exploited because of their communicative and educational inadequacies. Isolation, because they are unable to communicate with hearing people outside of their schools, Deaf community and families. Oblivion, because society ignores them and they have no status.

Strange as it may appear, there is not a single book in existence in Britain which chronicles the history of the British Deaf community. There is no history of the Deaf in Britain written by the Deaf. Any person can search up and down the country, bury oneself in the RNID and BDA libraries and run amok in the British Library in search of the British histories of the Deaf written by the Deaf. But no one shall find a single book. This may appear strange to a lot of us today, but it is not so to the oralists.

All this is a result guaranteed by the oralists' continuing vigilance in preventing the Deaf from acquiring an acceptable level of literacy. The strict policy of oralism, with its paramount emphasis on speech and audiology, ensures that no Deaf person is to read and write well, for it would be too embarrassing for the oralists if Deaf people were to end up with a higher and acceptable level of education, even to the extent of being better educated than the hearing. The reasons for that are:

a) Hearing people are the dominant and superior race - so keep the Deaf people down.
b) The oralists need this state of affairs to continue their exalted expert role in the educational domination of Deaf children.
c) If Deaf people were to achieve literacy, just imagine all the terrible things they could write about the cruelties and failures of the oralists and their system of education. This, for the oralists, must not happen - so literacy levels were kept to the absolute acceptable minimum. This is the dirty trick of oralism.

Some six years ago, Dr Reuben Conrad conducted research into the reading and writing abilities of Deaf children. He found that Deaf school leavers have a reading age equal to hearing children at the age of 8.75 years. If this is that bad at the present, just imagine how bad it must have been for Deaf children in the past all the way back to 1880 when hearing people started to take over Deaf education.

The same Dr Conrad also discovered that Deaf children do not lipread any better than their hearing counterparts who were put to the test a few hours after they were introduced to lipreading for the first time in their lives.

The terrible picture of oralism begins to build up.

2. HEARING PEOPLE'S MONOPOLY ON DEAF EDUCATION

Throughout history, hearing people have had the absolute monopoly in the education of the Deaf. Deaf people are not even considered capable of sharing decision making and are deliberately shunned. This monopolisation of Deaf education is in keeping in line with hearing people's inbuilt desire to control everything under the sun.

Whatever a hearing person's view on deafness, it can only be just that - a view, not a philosophy derived from experience. The common view held by nearly all hearing people involved in education is that deafness causes language and communication difficulties and thus created a limited capacity for intellectual and imaginative development. This notion, foisted on many hearing people by the oralists, prompted the change in educational provisions that occurred at the infamous 1880 Milan Congress that resulted in the banning of Deaf adults and sign language from all aspects of school life. The oralists judged Deaf people incapable of making decisions on the future of every Deaf child at school. By removing Deaf adults' involvement in Deaf education, the oralists have ensured that sign language went out of the window too for they have claimed, very wrongly, that it interfered with speech development.

One hundred and five years after this infamous Congress, there are only three Deaf and perhaps five hard of hearing teachers of the Deaf in Britain. The Deaf adult, having come through the mill himself, knows precisely what is missing in the education of the profoundly Deaf child. Whilst the Deaf person is seen as a second class citizen, the oralists will never share the power arising from their monopoly and their lies and treacheries will never be revealed and challenged.

3. BRITISH SIGN LANGUAGE

Having lived through history with the label of gesture and animalistic arm-waving, British Sign Language (BSL) has over the past few years achieved recognition as a true language. BSL is the natural and official language of the British Deaf Community; it has been proved by linguists to be an intelligent language, with its own features, structures and grammar. Like the Deaf people themselves, it has a history of suppression, abuse and mockery. The oralists preached, and still preach, that BSL is a mere animal-like arm-waving assortment of unintelligible gestures known only to those who use it. They reported that this sign language destroys Deaf children's abilities to speak and learn and blamed it for the educational failures of Deaf children. In the late 1960s and early 1970s some educators, worried about the poor educational achievements of Deaf children under oral-onlyism, began to introduce signing into the classrooms as a part of the Total Communication (TC) package. TC had been imported from the USA where it enjoyed success wherever it was used. And what happened? Many educators and teachers were shocked when Deaf children began to develop an interest in learning and produced higher levels of attainments in most areas of the curriculum including, of all things, speech! This gainsaid the oralist dogma that a child who learns sign language will never use their voice. Now many Deaf schools use total communication, television programmes have appeared with Deaf presenters and guests, BSL classes are springing up all over the country and Deaf children no longer dread going to school. It appears that BSL is springing back with a vengeance. Things are beginning to look bright for the Deaf. But....all this is much to the dismay of the oralists. And they sounded their alarm bells.

4. INTEGRATION - THE LAST BASTION OF ORALISM

With the increasing public interest in BSL, educational authorities began to consider and adopting the use of TC in Deaf schools. Whilst this was going on, the oralists were hard at work to halt the march of TC. What could they do? How could they prevent the spread of both BSL and TC? The situation appeared to be desperate for the oralists. Impending defeat did not seem far off........ until the Warnock Report. The Warnock Report, among other things, recommended that the disabled be integrated with the able bodied into local mainstream schools. It did not specify that the Deaf should be integrated but left this idea open. This alone turned out to be the lifeline for the oralists. In a desperate attempt to bolster their crumbling credibility they clung onto the Warnock Report. Although the Report did not specify that Deaf children should be integrated into local hearing mainstream schools, its terms were sufficiently ambiguous to enable the oralists to stretch the definition of disablement to include the Deaf. No time was wasted in accomplishing such inclusion to uninformed and ill-prepared local education authorities who subsequently colluded in a programme of Deaf school closures on the rationale that both humane interests and economic viability were provided by the wonderful innovation of an integrationalist policy. Before we discuss any further, I'd like to point out that there is nothing innovative about the oralists' underlying arguments. This turned out to be the same old formula that was long familiar with the Deaf community and which every Deaf person knows by heart.

1. The world is hearing. Therefore the Deaf must learn to speak and hear in order to live in this world. Deaf children must be separated from each other at all costs Integration must be separate - individualised.

2. If the education authorities are to accept this tenet, they must be persuaded of and to accept certain 'facts':

a) The numbers of Deaf children are falling due to vastly improved medical resources which eliminate the risk of Deafness.

b) The education authorities are required by the 1981 Education Act to implement integration of the disabled.

c) The Deaf are disabled and therefore must be integrated under that stipulation.

d) The education authorities were encouraged to believe that there are financial benefits to be gained in such integrationalist policies.

e) Parents were made to understand how cruel it was to deprive their children of parental and family love by sending them away to special schools for the Deaf. Also Deaf children will end up hearing if they attend hearing schools locally.

Such are the lies of the oralists. And the treacheries too. The members of the Deaf community hold different views and in reply:

1. The world is not hearing - Deaf people do exist in the world, even though the oralists do not like the idea.

2 (a). The numbers of Deaf children are not falling and there is no official evidence to support this wild claim by the oralists. On the contrary, it has been shown that more and more Deaf children are coming into the world. It must be made clear here how the oralists fiddle with the figures. What it appears so in official statistics is the reclassification of different forms of hearing impairment as non-deaf. Deaf without speech coupled with a degree of educational retardation, Deaf with speech, Deaf with-out speech, hearing without speech (!), hard of hearing and so on. Through this reclassification method, kids coming under the "severely Deaf with severe speech impairment" category are the ones usually counted as the "only" Deaf children and the rest counted as hard of hearing. With this method and fiddling about, the oralists present their own figures of the availability of Deaf children for Deaf schools and through these figures Deaf schools saw their annual intake roll of new Deaf pupils drop at an alarming rate - usually no more than 7 pupils per year. Cunningly, the oralists then persuade the

local education authorities that it is not financially viable to maintain large Deaf schools with so few pupils. While all this is going on, vast numbers of Deaf children are being herded like cattle into hearing schools.

2 (b) & 2 (c). It is interesting to note the oralists' (and society's) views and concept on what a Deaf person is. To them, a Deaf person is disabled because he is unable to hear and is therefore not normal. So Deaf children as well as Deaf adults are grouped as 'disabled' like those of the mongols, the mentally retarded or similar. This attitude is of course wrong and serves to show how heartless hearing people - especially the oralists - are, and it is also a measure of society's ignorance towards the Deaf. The NUD regard Deaf people as members of a linguistic minority group because sign language is Deaf people's official and natural language. Hearing people, however, are in the main only interested in making their lives and work easier by simply putting the Deaf under the 'disabled' category. When the Warnock Report recommended integration of the disabled into local mainstream schools, the oralists went to great lengths to ensure that Deaf children are being treated as disabled and are therefore not excluded from integration.

2 (d). Integration is a money-saving venture for many local authorities. One local education officer has said that his authority is making a minimum saving of £9,000 per annum per child sent to ordinary school instead of a special school for the Deaf. This goes a long way to show how much the authorities care for the education and future of Deaf children. Integration may be cheap but the money saved does not find its way back to Deaf education and the long term effect of this is that specialist Deaf education will suffer and eventually disappear altogether.

2 (e). To ensure that the policy of integration is to work well, it is important for the oralists to get in touch with as many parents of Deaf children as possible. To do this, they created a system whereby parents are always being directed to the oralists. This was, and still is, done in two different ways:

i) Through the local clinics and health visitors.

ii) Through the peripatetic services, whose workers very often falsely encourage parents that their Deaf children can be made to be like any hearing child and offer information on the education available - oralist education.

Local education authorities do not give parents comprehensive information on the various systems of education available for Deaf children. While we know that some authorities do, most only offer oralist education in local mainstream schools. In that way, parents have been denied the right of choice and of access to full information. What has been said so far represents Deaf people's knowledge, experiences and observations of the lies used by the oralists to gain their own ends. And furthermore, Deaf people say that:

A. Current integration is not true integration. It is one way integration, forcing Deaf children to integrate with hearing children on hearing people's terms. What is called integration is essentially assimilation; forcing Deaf children to look, talk, act and behave like hearing children.

B. The education of the Deaf based on pure oralism has been a proven failure and some schools have admitted to this fact. The oralists, fearing that their dismal track record might be revealed to the public, have put Deaf children into hearing schools to cover up and hide this terrible fact. As one can see, Deaf children in units or individualised integration surroundings become only tiny dots among the vast numbers of hearing children; meaningless numbers and well tucked away. It reasons therefore that the success or failure of the education of these Deaf children in hearing schools becomes a small and negligible part of the whole school.

C. The very existence of specialist Deaf schools, whether residential or day schools, is a thorn in the oralists' backsides; they are a lasting testimony to the cruelties and failures of oralism. The oralists are perfectly well aware that these specialist Deaf schools are the cornerstones of the Deaf communities; closing the schools down and dispersing the Deaf children results in the destruction of the roots of the Deaf communities. Doing this can only mean committing GENOCIDE. And genocide against the roots of the British Deaf community is an on-going fact; Deaf children as members of one linguistic minority group are being forcibly transferred to another group that is hearing people. The United Nation's Convention on the Prevention and Punishment of the Crime of Genocide clearly states the following:

1. Under Article 2(5) forcibly transferring children of one group to another is an act of genocide.

2. Article 3 defines five punishable acts which are:

a) genocide itself.

b) conspiracy to commit genocide.

c) direct and public incitement to commit genocide.

d) attempt to commit genocide.

e) complicity in genocide.

The NUD contends that the oralists, their supporters and the education authorities are guilty of the above charges when they set about to close down Deaf schools and put Deaf children into hearing schools - thus breaking up the roots of the Deaf communities. The NUD has met a large number of Deaf school leavers who went to mainstream hearing schools and its members have been appalled these school leavers' limited educational achievements and communicative skills. Not only that, but they seem lacking in self-worth, self-confidence and self-identity, as well as being devoid of character. On the other hand, Deaf schools tend to turn out better school leavers, not only in terms of the ability to communicate, understand and express oneself but in terms of character and self identity. Deaf children from Deaf schools are more accepting of their condition of Deafness and do not hide from this fact and they do not try to pretend they are hearing. They are more honest with themselves and live and work accordingly.

D. The oralists' policy of playing on the heartstrings of parents of Deaf children contributes to the highly successful persuasion of parents to send their Deaf children into local units in hearing schools. Saying things like: "Would it not be terrible to send your poor Deaf child away far from home just to get an education whilst other hearing children attend local schools and stay close to home and family? Is it not awful to deprive your lovely little child of family love, home and friends? But fear not, for we have schools that can cater for his special needs locally and what's more, we can make him be like any other hearing child." Parents are very often won over to the side of integration by things like that. But parents who send their Deaf children away from home to specialist Deaf schools are the ones who are expressing greater love for their child than those who keep their Deaf children on local mainstream schools. Where the love of mainstreamed Deaf children's parents is seen as narrow, selfish and obsessive, the love of parents who sent their children away from home for specialist education is seen in glowing light. I am bold enough to say that no greater love have the parents than that; that they give their Deaf child senses of freedom, independence, confidence and brotherhood. These four qualities are provided for by residential schools for the Deaf - and I speak with pride and affection when I say I have experienced and inherited these qualities and lived around them. With these four qualities bestowed on them by their parents and school, Deaf children grow up and leave their schools as individuals with self-confidence, with a character of their own and with the ability to decide their own destinies. More than that, they belong to a brotherhood of friends whose community knows no bounds; their community is nationwide as opposed to the community of integrated Deaf children which is limited to a certain local area of their hometown. These Deaf children from Deaf schools are a disappointment to the oralists for they do not conform to the normal structures and patterns of hearing society. As I said before, oralism is one long history of failures and lies. Integration has not been successful and the oralists know that. A new idea, "Individualised Integration", instigated by the oralists is being tried out. This idea will of course fail. Anything connected with the oralists and oralism is a certified failure. The greatest concern Deaf adults have is for those Deaf children who are the victims of the integrationalist policies. Their lives, futures and education will be destroyed. These children must be saved. For the present Deaf adults, this is going to be one hell of an uphill battle for their paths are riddled with one barrier after another on an endless road. History is telling us that the oralists have arrived at the last desperate stage of their quest to fulfil the "Great Oralist Dream", which is to turn every Deaf person into hearing person. So great is their desperation that they have resorted to commiting genocide against the Deaf community by attacking its roots. And at this last stage, they are at their most dangerous - like a frightened rat trapped in a dark corner, preparing to fight for its survival. Should they succeed in surviving and achieving their dream, then the

British Deaf community as we know it is doomed within a few generations. Deaf people and their friends are beginning to fight against the oralists and integration. And it will be a fight to the bitter end, for we Deaf people are keen to win this one. And we know deep in our hearts that integration is the last bastion of oralism - and crack it we will! However, the Deaf community is not narrow minded. Doors are open for discussion of new ideas. A kind of integration based on equal participation and functioning as a two-way process would be considered. But whilst the oralists remain entrenched, refusing to meet and discuss, what is to be done? Between the oralists in one trench and the Deaf in another lies a no man's land. This is a good half-way ground where both sides can meet, and why cannot they?

The Deaf have tried to and the oralists have refused to meet each other. It is probably because the oralists feel it beneath themselves as members of the superior and dominant 'race' to make concessions to Deaf members of a minority 'race'. On the other hand, Deaf people have grown to distrust the oralists and have learned not to come begging to them. I am myself at a loss at present as to how to remedy the situation but I have every confidence that time will eventually present us with a solution. I once remembered a poem when I was young. I cannot remember its title or author. But two lines remained imprinted on my memory:

"A taste of honey must be there,
"To keep the bitter from the sweet."

I get the feeling that we can get an inspiration for the solution from the two lines but I don't quite know what it is yet.

PART FIVE

Towards a Future

Preface

The NUD was asked by a member of staff of Doncaster College of Further Education if it could send someone over to give a talk and persuade students to form their own students' union. The students of the college were at that time hesitant in forming their own union; this, the NUD felt may be due to their lack of condfidence within themselves to take such a course of action. Most of the students were between 16 and 18 years old and needed encouragement and reassurances. Hence the following paper.

Pride and Confidence.

Doncaster. May 1986. Raymond Lee.

There is some twenty years difference between your ages and mine. Every one of you here today are young and vigorous and it has suddenly hit me how old I am. You are all here in Doncaster College of Further Education to improve your education and gain experiences and skills for your future jobs when you leave. You are all fortunate to have such an excellent college and facilities. You are all lucky too in that signing is used in your education here. But did you know that only twenty years ago Deaf people were not as lucky as you all are now? There were no col-leges of further education for the Deaf, with the exception of very few schools which offered additional year further education. Deaf people had great difficulties in finding and getting re-spectable and better paid jobs - because of both discrimination against the Deaf in employment and the Deaf did not have very good educational qualifications, though it was no fault of their own.

Let me tell you something else as well. You all learn about history, ranging from the cavemen to present day events. Did your teachers tell you about the history of the Deaf people? Did they tell you about deaf people's oppression and about society's awful treatment and attitude towards them? You are all correct. The answer is no! Why didn't the schools or anyone else tell us about our own people and our own history? In many of the books written on the history of the Deaf in Britain, we read about hearing people who work hard trying to help the Deaf to hear and talk, but rarely about Deaf people themselves. Why? We can't blame the teachers here today for not telling us about our own history because they do not know much about it. It is not their fault because they have not been taught or given any facts about it. Would it not be interesting and wonderful for us to learn and get to know how Deaf people in the past lived and worked, what they did for leisure and hobbies and what did they fight for or struggled for, and their achievements? We may never know a very large part of it because there are no books written by Deaf people about Deaf people at different eras in the past.

To answer the question, the truth is that Deaf people received very poor education in the past 100 years - so poor that many cannot read or write. The hearing teachers spent a lot of time trying to make Deaf people speak and speak, talk and talk. As a result, Deaf people left schools illiterate. And because many are illiterate, our history cannot be written down on paper. Deaf people in the past did have sign language but this may not have been fully developed; or if it was fully developed, it was not like spoken English or written English. Sign language had (and still has) no written form. Without history Deaf people have no pride. And without pride they have no confidence.

In 1976 a group of Deaf people met in London and formed the National Union of the Deaf (NUD) because Deaf people were fed up of having things being done for them. They wanted to do their own work themselves. They did not want their views, grievances and needs to be presented to the authorities and society on their behalf by hearing people. So this group of Deaf people went about on its own way and worked hard to show the hearing world what Deaf people can do and are capable of. The other organisations for the Deaf like the BDA and the RNID were against the NUD because they were jealous that Deaf people have proved they can run their own organisation and make decisions without hearing people's help. With the NUD Deaf people have, for the first time in their lives, taken command of their own affairs and destinies. The NUD did a lot of things that only Deaf people can do. In 1976 the NUD campaigned for total communication and signing to be allowed in Deaf schools. Now almost more than half of the present Deaf schools in this country use signing. In 1977 and 1978 the NUD fought for Deaf people to keep their jobs driving HGV lorries when the medical profession tried to ban Deaf people from driving or getting HGV licences. In 1979 the NUD scripted and produced the first ever television pilot programme for the Deaf, *"Signs of Life"*, on BBC access slot. This programme was the forerunner of many programmes for the Deaf you all now see on TV. We will now show you the original programme, *"Signs of Life"*.

In 1982 the NUD recognised Deaf people as members of a linguistic minority group; Deaf people have their own language (BSL), cul-ture and community. Along with this, the NUD published *"The Rights of the Deaf Child"* which was presented to the United Nations Human Rights Commission. This "Rights" listed the cruel-ties of oralism forced on Deaf children and proposed a list of ten rights to be adopted.

In 1985 last year, the NUD campaigned at Manchester to fight against cochlea implants and oralism, as well as the integratio-nalist policies, at the International Congress on the Education of the Deaf. There were many things the NUD did since 1976 which include helping Deaf people to obtain employment or sort out their problems at work. When I say the NUD did this and that, what I really mean is that Deaf people did this and that. Hearing people did give NUD help in some ways, like assisting with the telephone or giving expert advice on complex matters, but theirs was a very small part in comparison with the part Deaf people played. What the NUD had really done in its works since 1976 was that it created history. Remember what I said earlier: without history Deaf people have no pride and without pride Deaf people have no confidence. The NUD gave Deaf people confidence and through confidence Deaf people became proud of their achievements and of what they can do. This is pride. And this pride gave Deaf people history, for they are proud to record their works, achie-vements, failures and hopes.

You are all now living in a more enlightened era. In Britain today more and more hearing people are more understanding of the Deaf, their language, their community, their views and their needs. Hearing people are attending classes to learn sign lan-guage so that they can communicate with the Deaf. Local councils and authorities are beginning to provide interpreters at their meetings so that you all can understand and follow what is going on and take active part in the discussions. Deafness is now no longer a stigma - it is no longer something to be ashamed of. I must say that there are lots of areas at different levels of society where discrimination against the Deaf is prevalent but in a few years' time this too may be overcome if we, the Deaf people, fight and campaign against it. You are all lucky to be in a wonderful college with superb tutors. I was told that you all were encouraged to form a students' union and participate in the affairs and running of this college. I see that you have done nothing about it so far.

What the college is trying to do is to give you all a say in the running of this college and also to give you all a share of authority. You all have nothing to lose! Come on and start to do something about it! Do you know what you can do and learn by starting a students' union? You can set up a meeting among yourselves and from there elect a number of people to form a committee to represent your views and decisions. As an union, you can hold meetings and discuss ways in which improvements and changes on the day to day running of your college can be made. You can also discuss your objections to some of the present rules or whatever and put forward proposals for change. You can meet the members of the college staff and discuss your proposals, views and feelings. The college staff want you to do this. They are giving you all an opportunity to show them what you all can do, what you all can tell them and prove to them that you all can wisely, and collectively, manage your own affairs. Twenty years ago Deaf people were not given this chance. Please see the importance of this.

While you are all studying, it is worth learning how to make collective decisions and thus actions. This will build your confidence in decision-making. This will also build your confi-dence in dealing with the college authorities on an equal basis. When you all, as an union, have made a decision and presented it to the college, and if the college accepts your decision, you will have the satisfaction of seeing your views being accepted. This will give you all pride. And pride makes you all remember what you have contributed and achieved - this is history. You will always tell your friends about it and it will not be forgot-ten. I will be more than happy to talk to you about forming the union afterwards.

When you go out to work and live in the world after you have completed your courses, remember that every hearing person is your equal; no hearing person is "higher" than you. Deafness is nothing to be ashamed of. There may be problems out there in the world which may intimidate most of you. Do not run away from it; running away does not solve anything. Face it! Deal with it! Every one of you are capable of overcoming any problem you may face. Get together with your friends and work together to over-come any obstacles which come in your way. This was how members of the NUD faced the obstacles - they took it on and dealt with it. And more than that, they attacked it. You can all do the same and this is the best way to go about it and make Deaf people's lives better.

As Deaf people of ten years ago fought to make Britain a better place for Deaf people to live in, so must you continue that fight. You are all young and every one of you has a duty to create better conditions and better lives for Deaf people of the future. It will soon be your responsibility to take up the works of the Deaf in the past and continue to create a better future. A responsibility will fall on you all to see that the sign lan-guage, culture and history of the British Deaf community is

preserved. You can do that because you have the self-confidence. Take pride in your own selves and in that of many of your Deaf friends. Be proud of your sign language and culture. Do your duty; get together, work together and take action together, with confidence and pride. And the rest will be history.

1976 – 1986: 'Ten Years Burning Down the Road'

Report to the 5th Convention. London. August 1986. Paddy Ladd.

When I was asked to write this piece about the NUD, I had hopes of putting together a calm and collected series of facts and achievements and building that into a review of changes in the Deaf world in general that have occurred in that time.

But now after reading through the 44 Newsletters, the Convention Reports and the seminal "Blueprint for the Future", not to mention the "Charter of Rights", I find myself far too overwhelmed with 10 years worth of emotion to be able to do justice to that kind of Deaf history. It seems to be that the best way to achieve that is for the NUD to publish a rather large collection of "The Best of......" and to sell this as widely as possible.

In fact, an emotional summary of 10 years is altogether more appropriate to the NUD spirit. This is partly because of what we did right from the start, which was to introduce emotion back into Deaf affairs. In 1976 our world was moribund, dull and grey, reeking of Victorian institutionalism and the whole thing was dominated by 'professionals' who insisted on seeing only the 'problems of the Deaf'. The spirit of the 1960s had still not broken into those enclaves.

If one read those early NUD pamphlets, emotion and naivete is so strong it is hard now not to feel embarrassed. But as I recall, we were aware at the time that this was the only right and proper way for the Deaf people to express themselves in English. To hell with sophistication and with words! As Dr Johnson said, "Words were invented to hide men's thoughts." One could not say that about sign language! For when one has a just cause, emotion comes to represent honesty, the most crucial way to fight oralism, which has one of the longest records of dishonesty humankind has ever witnessed. And sure enough, ten years later we can record that this honesty of emotion has worked. Our very first action, at a teachers conference in Harrogate 1976, was a turning point - the first conference for decades where Deaf people picketed and leafletted. Some of the young teachers we met on that day are still with us now, and it was with delight that I read the comments of one of them, Harry Cayton, now Director of the National Deaf Children's Society, in the *British Deaf News* earlier this year when he looked back at his influences. The leaflet we gave out that day has a legend of its own, composed as it was on a typewriter with jumping 'i's. That rough and ready approach let us down a few times over the last few years and meant that people were put off initially. But often, oh so often, their views changed when their emotions calmed.

And thus as it started so it has gone on, campaign after campaign right up to Manchester 1985. But there is another reason why emotion is implicitly accepted as the NUD way. It has to do with the whole status of Deaf people at that time, deprived for decades of an education with their language sneered at by most people, and regarded a little more than mentally retarded by many others. The sheer pressure of people's attitudes to us, from hostility to patronage, makes it hard to avoid feeling small. The first task is therefore to take pride in oneself; that though one is small, one is of equal worth. It is the task of people in the next ten years to take that sense of full worth and grow to equal size, without losing that gut feeling of the small and stocky fighter.

When our beloved President Stan Woodhouse died, Raymond Lee wrote an obituary in which he put his finger on this whole argument. Stan was small in stature and very humble. A gentle man, he was nevertheless an inspirer, a fighter and builder in his own time, in his own Deaf campaign and in his work in creating Slough Deaf Club, the first Deaf club in Britain built by Deaf people themselves. Stan had the habit of referring to Deaf people as the 'little people'. But this did not entail any loss of pride, or imply inferior status. Rather it was his way of affirming his belief in what one might call the Common (Deaf) Man and Woman. When I read this phrase it resonated for me and the image that came to my head was of the Hobbits in *"The Lord of the Rings"*. They had the same status as small people but their warmth, honesty and integrity as well as their fighting skill, was the equal of any. And just now when I re-read all the NUD Newsletters, what did I find in the very first issue but an eight line declaration of the NUD's aims, taken from..... *The Lord of the Rings,* and spoken by the hobbit, Bilbo Baggins!

This may be in danger of sounding very trivial. But be careful, because the point is still emerging. For when I look at the last ten years, all the names of Deaf and hearing people who contributed to the NUD's work, who were honoured or went unthanked, I am overwhelmed by the sense of the enormity of the odds against us. Most of us, in poor jobs, unable to write English, with vague snatches of information as to how the world worked, or how to harness its power, unable to communicate by the telephone, with very little money, an annual turnover less than one-third of what one single RNID switchboard person takes home every week and frowned on by all other Deaf organisations, social workers and teachers; with all this stacked against us, humble ordinary Deaf people tried to put together something that would make a better world for their Deaf children. Not to become Grand Councillors or Vice-Presidents, for to be associated with the NUD was, and is, to ensure that those kind of doors would be shut in one's face. But just out of love for our people and our anger at what is being done to our children.

That is what the little people were all about and that too is where the choice of using emotional approaches come from. To use complex English is to betray that sense of common loyalty and unashamedness of our roots. And so we blundered on, from one crazy dream to the next, struggling to find the time to meet, to travel to the other parts of the UK to talk with other Deaf folk there, to reopen long lost contact with Deaf people in Northern Ireland even and attempting everything from assaults on the United Nations to finding jobs for young Deaf school-leavers. And, in looking back over the ten years, I want to thank every single one of those people, Deaf and hearing, who were involved with us, no matter in how small a way or for how short a time. You all gave us something valuable and contributed to where we stand today. Those of us who are still going are in many cases tired, ill, temporarily burnt out or completely worn out. Whatever form we continue in, we have an obvious priority now - to get ourselves well and strong. And we have the consolation of knowing that there are now new waves of Deaf people, confident and active, who were not there ten years ago; who will carry on the struggle in new forms, working themselves to the ground for our people until they too become worn out in ten years time. By that time the snowball effect will be in full stride and there will be many more to take us into the 21st Century, who will see the real harvest of the years 1976 - 1986.

Well, Mr Ladd; that is all very well to try to dig out the roots of emotional politics. But if that were all there was to the NUD, it would have collapsed years ago. For we now come to the intellectual content of the NUD's policies and try to assess what they themselves achieved. In *"Blueprint for the Future"*, published in 1977, we find over 100 aims and there is no way short of re-publishing that booklet that can do justice to the scope of those visions. But before we concentrate on specific areas, it is worth remarking that each of those aims was the tip of an iceberg of a set of points that, if presented by university professors, would each take an hour's lecture to do justice to the depth of thought that they contained. Many of them still remain as radical, stimulating and useful, nay necessary, to a world of Deaf equality as they did ten years ago. I will pick out a few that we failed to achieve to give you the flavour:-

1. MEMBERSHIP OF TUC

The original aim of affiliating to the TUC was not achieved. But in recognising that the only way for Deaf people to achieve change was through political channels and that to remedy the job situation needed allies whose speciality was the politics of employment, is an even more crying need now than ever. There are ten other aims in this field - almost all of them remain untouched by anyone.

2. DEAF PRIDE COURSES FOR DEAF CHILDREN

This area, about courses run by Deaf adults for Deaf children, has still not been thought about in the UK, but we are pleased to note that in France and Sweden such ideas are well into practice.

3. DEAF CULTURE AND DEAF THEATRE

This area too remains untouched but there are signs that this will start to take off in the next couple of years. We are proud, however, to be the first in Britain to promote the artistic genius of Dorothy Miles.

4. DEAF TELEPHONE NETWORK

Although this has started to develop in theory, the actuality is that the Vistel machines on the market are so poor in quality that they are virtually unusable and if they had been made for hearing people, they would have been taken to court long ago. Deaf bodies still seem to be tragically unaware that if the Deaf world is to become active, it must have good rapid contact to be able to call up numbers of activists at short notice.

And so the list goes on. In addition we find in the Blueprint many ideas which the NUD was unable to implement but which have been taken up by the BDA when it changed for the better in 1981. These include Sign Marathons, Deaf Foster Parents, Junior NUD, Interpreters, Active Grass Roots Branches, Discrimination in Employment, a National Deaf Newspaper, Deaf Full-Time Workers and many more. Some of these have been started, some may emerge in the next few years. Whatever watered down form they take, they are nonetheless very warmly welcomed.

Let us now look at what has been achieved by the NUD since 1976. Perhaps the most important single thing is :-

1. DEAF TELEVISION PROGRAMMES

Quote from the 1976 original:

"We need to be seen. We must reach TV (Open Door, Nationwide, etc), and put Deaf people in places they have never been seen before."

As you know, the NUD made it to Open Door in 1979 with the first programme in sign language, *"Signs of Life"*, which resulted then in the DBC and in "See Hear" and thus every single sign you now see on television. Deaf Pride, employment opportunities, political leverage and respect from society as a whole have resulted from all this. But perhaps the most crucial area, that of using television programmes to nurture, control and carefully shape the growth of a national Deaf community, has not really occurred. For the most part, this is because TV refuses to bend itself to accept the fact that Deaf TV programming is completely different from the way in which hearing people need and use TV, and also because all the programmes are scared of controversy. Nevertheless, by achieving this aim the NUD were able to raise the whole Deaf struggle into a completely new dimension. It now remains for future Deaf people to make proper programmes - perhaps in video form - to build on this base.

2. DEAF EDUCATION

In 1976, there were virtually no deaf children taught in sign language. Now it is estimated that over half the children are taught through some variant of this method. Behind those sober words lie a decade of fighting and anger, of love and tears, of new allies found among teachers and of new friends made among Deaf children's parents. This achievement is not the NUD's alone. The BDA, sometimes following up behind and sometimes in tandem, provided the sober details, negotiated the reasonable compromises that made the whole operation seem an excellent match although, of course, if they had actually worked consciously with the NUD, much more would have been achieved. Research into BSL also came along at the perfect time to outflank the oralists.

Nevertheless, if the NUD were able to eavesdrop on oralists dreams and nightmares, we would find the spectre of NUD, together with Dr Conrad's report, as the single largest factors in that change. The reasons for these seem to be twofold: one, that because the NUD is exclusively Deaf-run, it does not in any way conform to hearing people's negotiating structures - it cannot be bought off or watered down and two, that the passion and anger with which the NUD conducted its own campaigns has a deeper impact on more people. To this we can add: three, that the type of campaigns, of picketing, of leaflets, banners and slogans brought the issue home to more people than before. No doubt there are other reasons too.

And yet there is still so, so much further to go. Integration has become a new threat; Deaf teachers are still nowhere in sight and proper teaching via sign language is barely begun. It has become clear that Deaf people and their allies must step up the quality of their fight in the decade ahead. Harlan Lane was one of the few people brave enough to realise this when he concluded his paper at the Alternative Congress in Manchester 1985 by saying: "Put the education of the Deaf back into the hands of Deaf people themselves." We would not have dared to be so outspoken but in fact he is right because the whole drive Deaf people possess in this field is of a different quality. This, allied to the many excellent young hearing teachers who have now emerged, is a recipe for success.

Two events deserve to be highlighted from the last decade. The first was the NUD *"CHARTER OF RIGHTS OF THE DEAF CHILD."* This 70-plus page booklet is by far the most radical and comprehensive document on this subject in the world. Marred by some over-aggressive language, it nevertheless raised the whole level of debate to one of human rights, of Deaf people as a linguistic minority and by pursuing the United Nation's own logic to its own conclusions proved that oralism is in fact genocidal. We achieved little success in persuading the UN of this, due to our own political naivete and also over hastiness to publish, but there is no doubt that in the next decade the concepts expressed in this book will prove to be the only way forward on a world-wide basis. Indeed, the BDA has taken the initiative in pulling Deaf organisations in Europe together, and persuading the EEC to recognise all the community's sign languages. This is but the first step, but one of incalculable eventual value.

The other event was the mass assault with the NWRC of the BDA on the infamous EDUCATION CONGRESS, held in Manchester 1985. The main reason for its being worthy of mention is that the methods here were largely new. Aiming for maximum impact on the hearing world via the time honoured method of being controversial got us all the radio and TV coverage and a spot on the national Six o'clock news, and the tactics of street theatre, badges, banners and so on, paved the way for the future. Deaf people in the UK, unlike those in Spain, France, Italy, America, Scandinavia, etc., have not yet been willing to actually march. But that day is significantly nearer. We are all beginning to grow up in political terms and to do what hearing folks have been doing for hundreds of years.

3. DEAF SELF HELP

In 1976 the idea of Deaf people running their own affairs was quite inconceivable. If there has been one achievement by the NUD, it has been to make this not only a possibility, but a necessity. The BDA's positive new administration took its first steps on that path in 1981; the RNID set up a puppet consumer committee and throughout the land this pattern developed from the Deaf club level outwards. There is still a long way to go however, and the problem is different now. It is now more a question of having good Deaf people able to take on the highest jobs of administration and fulfil them in a steady, responsible way with no favouritism or blind prejudice. This task is not easy to pull off. If some hearing people wonder why, it means we have not yet succeeded in spelling out the utter decimation of Deaf talent in the last 100 years and the channelling off of our natural leaders by infamous places like Mary Hare Grammar School. Nevertheless, things are now on the right path; everyone has to pay lip service to this concept and the NUD can feel proud that it managed to light this fire which will never be put out again.

4. ACCEPTANCE AND RECOGNITION OF BSL

This first crops up in NUD literature in 1977, pre-dating the American acceptance of ASL (by Deafpride Inc.) by one year and the NAD by eight years! Nevertheless, the main credit in this field is due to the two research projects at Edinburgh and Bristol whose work, together with NUD associate member Margaret Deuchar's book on BSL, took the whole subject and its implications into a new dimension. Likewise, the BDA following Allan B. Hayhurst's vision, have done a tremendous amount to develop and formalise this work, which we hope will see fruition when the BSLTA gets off the ground. Nevertheless, if we are to make further strides, we will have to follow Sweden and be prepared to march for the recognition of our own language and the BDA will have to accept that this is their responsibility - the NUD being too small for that kind of action.

There is much we could say on other issues, but those details await the historian's hard labour. It is only right now that after all this trumpet blowing, we look back at what has not worked out in the last ten years.

The main area is the lack of growth in terms of membership numbers and in the lack of sufficient people coming forward to take office. There are several reasons to hand. One is simply personality clashes which can be put down to having strong personalities together. Although this is unfortunate, if we take a longer distance view of it, we can see that it is perhaps inevitable for such a body as the NUD to start and survive it would have to be kept going by strong personalities. It is crucial in the next ten years that not only the NUD but the Deaf community as a whole rises above this, for there are too few of us to repair the damage of 100 years as it is.

The issue of too few Deaf survivors of the oral holocaust is a very major reason. Once the BDA began to revive in 1981, it made such more sense for newly emerging Deaf people to join a structure that was already there, with national scope and money and influence, and then try to change it even further for the better. After a short time of that, people found themselves deeply committed to work on all levels as the demand for Deaf participation all across the nation exploded. Soon there were many harassed people giving 150%, 7 days a week, just as the NUD personnel had done. There was simply no chance of them being able to give any more time to anyone else.

On a local level, the idea of branches did not survive with the same reasons applying. On top of that was the problem of time and energy, for the NUD Steering Committee simply could not have given them the support they needed, and so with communication mainly reduced to the written form of Deaf people's second language, enthusiasm was hard to maintain. The same was true when it came to keeping the membership numbers going. Thus the NUD came to save its energy for short bursts and effective sallies, though helping membership with problems and running the Newsletter have always remained a constant. If we look back, we could have done better to have become registered as a charity, eaten a bit of humble pie to do so and thus obtained full time salaries. But such is history.

In summary, we can look back and see that the NUD ushered in an age of Deaf revolution as much as Mao did the Chinese one. It remains to be seen whether the Deaf one will go as wrong as that one has. As for the future, the NUD needs to stand back and look at the 1980s and see what is still needed before deciding upon its new role. The other organisations are still too wishy-washy for the NUD to pack up and consider that its job of stretching awareness to the limits is finished. The BDA broke new ground with their mass lobby of the Houses of Parliament, an absolutely superb move - but on educational issues its refusal to co-operate with the NUD and the suppressing of Deaf grass roots anger could yet lose the Deaf world some of its residential schools.

A new problem awaits us. Up to now the new wave of Deaf people have been wonderful in their unselfishness, not wishing to hold power at the expense of others. Yet we must face the fact that the Old Guard still control vast areas of the North, Scotland and Wales and their mealy-mouthed rejection not only of the NUD, but of other grass roots Deaf groups like the Tribune Group, means that the kind of honesty and commitment that the Deaf world needs in this new age could be blocked for as long as the hearing Old Guard managed. We have seen too the selfishness and complacency of Deaf professionals at Gallaudet start to happen here, especially in the south where people who have never fought for Deaf persons in their lives are given jobs by the hearing people who we have persuaded to change their views on Deaf employment. Perhaps it is inevitable. Yet nonetheless it needs new thinking from the NUD as to how best to operate in the future. Grass roots Deaf people are still barely benefiting from this first stage of the revolution. This was our struggle in the beginning and it still holds true today. All of which brings us back to where we started. It is hard to get through to the people the astonishing fact that the NUD is simply there for anyone to work under its heading to get change in any field, rather than to have to work alone. Yet this is how history gets made.

Mention of history brings us to a consideration of our final achievement. We have always been fortunate in having Arthur Dimmock close by our side and the Ancient Warrior, as he has been called, is world renowned for collecting stories of Deaf history and Deaf pride. If you read through the 'British Deaf Mute' of the last century, you will find two things. One is that he is the sole inheritor of the proud tradition of the Golden Age. The second is that the style of these magazines resembles nothing so much as ...... yes, the NUD Newsletters and pamphlets. This I found out by chance and it points to a deeper meaning. What is it? It seems that it is once again the emotional tone of expression, the little people - proud and irreverent. But that is only part of it. The second factor that comes with true Deaf pride is a sense of history.

Oralism so insists that each child is an individual medical problem that it has obliterated the fact that we have a history. And a people without a history are a lost race indeed. What comes through so much of NUD's writings is the concept of a Deaf race, still a phrase which many people still cannot accept, and to me it felt like the final broken link of Deaf history was put back together when that great man Harlan Lane was invited by the NUD to address its 4th Convention. Harlan's achievement has been to give Deaf people back their history and in the last two years that has immensely strengthened our pride and our resolve.

Thus it may be true that when we look back and try to sum up the NUD's historical achievements, this may in turn be done by deciding that the most crucial achievement of all was to re-awaken the pride and the sense of history of the "Little People" and to prepare us for a new age when little people no longer, we oust the tyrant from his Dark Tower for the last time.

Let us end on the same rough and ready way we have begun, with another cry from the heart. On the back of "Blueprint for the Future" it says: "THIS PAMPHLET IS FOR ALL DEAF PEOPLE. PLEASE INTERPRET WHERE NECESSARY."

It has been the constant tragedy for the NUD that many of our members cannot read what we print without laborious help from colleagues. Let us fight to ensure that in two years' time they can watch these words in their own language on video and that in ten years' time our new generation of Deaf schoolchildren will be able to do the same IN BOTH OUR LANGUAGES.

Postscript

Since the last paper, NUD activities have been greatly scaled down. It is no longer a membership-based organisation; instead it regroups whenever a campaign is most needed and the energy is available. There has indeed been both an explosion of opening doors and a lack of readily qualified Deaf people to get through them. There are 101 demands on Deaf activists' time now, and there are simply not enough minutes in the hour to expend on building one single unified voice of the Deaf.

This is a great pity, for although the British Deaf Association (BDA) has stepped up its active role in the 1980s, there is still a crying need for radical, vocal and media-visible Deaf campaigns, especially in education. Despite all the gains of the 1980s, Deaf children are still suffering in almost as large numbers as before - languishing in hearing schools, beyond our reach and our help.

In other fields, there have been tremendous changes. The Royal National Institute for the Deaf (RNID) brought in Deaf people and modified its policies. The interpreting profession began and multiplied. British Sign Language (BSL) teaching mushroomed. Cochlea Implants finally took off, with the seal of approval from organisations "for the Deaf", of course. New problems present themselves. New hierarchies and power blocs form. Yet still we lack a Deaf media to act as watchdogs over them. Soon there will be a pressing need for another "State of the Nation" pamphlet like the *"NUD 1976"* one at the start of this book.

The NUD's next step, however, is to first of all finish off bringing the past into view. Although there is no money available for video translations, alas, there remains to be published "The Best of NUD Newsletter" and other works, with its diverse and entertaining pieces and cartoons by a wider range of NUD membership. And there are many other pieces that deserve attention that will hopefully inspire younger Deaf people and perhaps incite another generation of Deaf and hearing people to carry on the struggle. Perhaps you who are reading this are one of those people...?

Acknowledgements

The Editor and the NUD would like to thank the following persons for their valuable assistance in the preparation of this publication:

Patrick O'Toole (London) for transferring all written papers onto computer disks and proofreading. All this was done in his spare time and the NUD is indebted to his unyielding determination in completing the task at the expense of his free time.

Alain Holcroft (Portsmouth) for his help in the design of the front cover and all the illustrated artwork in this book.

Maggie Woolley of SHAPE (London) for her kind permission to allow the NUD the use of her company's photocopy and printing facilities during the course of creating draft copies.

Ian Clear (Portsmouth) for his expert assistance and advice on the cost-saving layout and style of the book. This book would not materialise in its present form but for Mr Clear's selfless help and generosity.

Paddy Ladd (London), Brian Davies (London) and Arthur Dimmock (Portsmouth) have given valued assistance and suggestions in developing and shaping the contents of the book. Their constructive criticisms during draft stages have been most helpful.

Sincere thanks are extended to Harlan Lane (Boston, USA) and G.W.G. Montgomery (Edinburgh) for their kind permission to allow their papers to be included in this publication - and also for their introductory articles.

Finally, the NUD wishes to thank Dr Reuben Conrad for generously donating the NUD a copy of his paper at the Harrogate RNID Conference in 1976. Thanks are extended to Mike Whitlam and the RNID for their kind permission allowing the NUD to use Conrad's paper in this book. And gratitute is expressed towards Austin Reeves of Deaf Broadcasting Campaigin (DBC) for his blessing for the use of DBC paper in the book.